DYING
FOR THE
GODS

For Stephen, Elisabeth, Antigone,
Oedipus, Poseidon & Apollo

DYING
FOR THE
GODS

Human Sacrifice in Iron Age & Roman Europe

Miranda Aldhouse Green

TEMPUS

First published 2001

PUBLISHED IN THE UNITED KINGDOM BY:

Tempus Publishing Ltd
The Mill, Brimscombe Port
Stroud, Gloucestershire GL5 2QG
www.tempus-publishing.com

PUBLISHED IN THE UNITED STATES OF AMERICA BY:

Tempus Publishing Inc.
2 Cumberland Street
Charleston, SC 29401
1-888-313-2665
www.arcadiapublishing.com

Tempus books are available in France and Germany
from the following addresses:

Tempus Publishing Group   Tempus Publishing Group
21 Avenue de la République   Gustav-Adolf-Straße 3
37300 Joué-lès-Tours   99084 Erfurt
FRANCE   GERMANY

British Library Cataloguing in Publication Data.
A catalogue record for this book is available from the British Library.

ISBN 0 7524 1940 4

Typesetting and origination by Tempus Publishing.
PRINTED AND BOUND IN GREAT BRITAIN

Contents

List of illustrations

Text figures

Colour plates

Acknowledgements

I would like to thank a number of institutions and individuals who have supported the work for this book in various ways. The following have displayed considerable generosity in supplying illustrations free of charge or at reduced cost: British Museum Press; Centre archéologique européen du Mont Beuvray; Danebury Trust; English Heritage; London Underground; National Museums & Galleries of Wales, Cardiff; National Museums of Scotland; Nationalmuseet København; Oxford Archaeological Unit; Thames & Hudson; U.G.C. Films at Pinewood Studios; University of Edinburgh; Worthing Museum & Art Gallery; Württem-bergisches Landesmuseum, Stuttgart; Professors Mick Aston, Barry Cunliffe and Alfredo Jimeno and Elias Teres Navarro, Museo Numantino, Soria; Dr Lynn Foulston; Vincent Guichard; Philip Macdonald; Betty Naggar; Niall Sharples.

I am very grateful also to University of Wales College, Newport and, in particular, its Principal, Professor Ken Overshott, for unwavering support and financial help; *Time Team* and Electric Sky TV (particularly Sally Jenkins and Natasha Khidhayir) for enabling access to unpublished material (Alveston and Haraldskaer respectively); Rosalind Niblett; Dr Lone Hvass and Dr Alison Sheridan; Vincent Guichard has been tremendously helpful in providing access to material from the temporary exhibition *Les Druides Gaulois* at the Musée de Bibracte; Paul Jenkins and Anne Leaver provided several excellent line-drawings. Professors John Collis and Francisco Marco Simón drew my attention to some recently-discovered material, and Jenny Cann provided generous help with Spanish translation. Other people who have helped me greatly include Dr Christine Morris (information on Crete), George Findlater (Ballachulish) and Dr Marilynne Raybould (Latin translations). Finally, my sincere thanks go to Drs Stephen Aldhouse-Green and Mike Parker Pearson for reading and commenting on the text in draft, and I would like to express my appreciation to the staff at Tempus, especially Anne Phipps and Tim Clarke.

Prologue

The evidence for ritual murder: challenges and opportunities

Their oblations and sacrifices in these dayes of blindnesse, were performed with such inhumane and ungodly fashions, with the effusion and shedding of human blood in that lamentable and cruel manner, as is too straunge to be reported.
(Richard Lynche Travels of Noah into Europe, *1601)*

This book explores the evidence for human sacrifice in the ancient European Iron Age and Roman period. The specific focus lies in the north and west of Europe, including Britain, though forays outside this region are made where appropriate. In terms of chronology, the nucleus of study covers the period from around 600 BC to AD 400; but here, again, relevant material pertaining to earlier or later periods may be considered.

Testimony to the practice of human sacrifice in later European antiquity is derived from both archaeology and from the records of Classical writers on their northern neighbours. The archaeological evidence consists, for the most part, of the remains of human beings, generally the skeleton or part of it, the exception being the bodies preserved in peat-bogs, where soft tissue also may be well-preserved, with even skin, stomach-contents, fingernails and eyelashes surviving. Whilst the material remains of people suspected as being sacrificial victims range widely over the millennium, the comments of authors from the Mediterranean world contain far more temporal bias, for they belong, almost entirely, to a narrow band of time between the first century BC and the third century AD. The danger of relying on such material arises from the tendency for scholars to indulge in academic 'backstitch' or retrospective inference, wherein a Classical text describing a particular cult-practice in the late first century BC is assumed not only to be an accurate record for that time (itself a highly questionable presumption) but also valid for much earlier (or, indeed, later) periods.

Interpretational problems exist with respect to both the archaeology and literature of human sacrifice. The documentary evidence is useful in so far as it can provide identities for the very late Iron Age of Gaul and Britain — names of communities and individuals — and descriptions of ritual processes, including sacred murder, the reasons and methods associated with such practice, and even the nature of the divine recipients. However, these sources suffer from the flaw of being products of alien observations which, at best, contain elements of ignorance and misunderstanding and, at worst, are guilty of unashamed 'barbaric' stereotyping akin to the worst kind of today's 'tabloid' journalism; it is clear that, on occasions, stock literary motifs, including human sacrifice, cannibalism and other habits outrageous to the 'civilised' Classical world, were used to describe peoples living 'beyond the pale' of the Mediterranean. Writers like Julius Caesar, Strabo and Tacitus were undoubtedly constructing texts that, perhaps, set out to be 'objective' histories, geographies or ethnologies, but fell foul of their own literary conventions and embedded social prejudices, which included romanticism and 'noble savage' models as well as images of barbarism. What is interesting about Graeco-Roman literary references to human sacrifice is that they are not confined to descriptions of the foreign lands beyond the margins of the Mediterranean littoral: in Roman literature, for instance, ritual murder is mentioned in connection with prominent Roman republicans of the first century BC, even with Julius Caesar himself (chapter 8). Significantly, too, the motif of human sacrifice crops up in the context of early Christianity: in certain texts of the later imperial period, the charge of ritual killing (and cannibalism) is laid against both Christians by pagans and pagans by Christians.

1 *Ceremonial bronze, enamel-inlaid shield-cover, cast into the River Thames at Battersea, London, as an offering to the spirit world; second/first century BC. © The British Museum*

While archaeological evidence does not present a deliberately distorted image of the past, it nonetheless suffers from a variety of problems and ambiguities based, in part, upon degrees of preservation and, in no small measure, upon our interpretational models. One of the difficulties in the necessary reliance on the text-free archaeology of Iron Age Europe relates to the absence of a clear context in which to situate human sacrifice. We can have little clue as to the cosmologies perceived by the communities enacting sacred murder, although such habitual behaviour as the deposition of precious objects in water (**1**) or the deliberate orientation of graves, house and shrine entrances, in certain regions and time-frames, may allow us tentatively to associate religious foci with natural phenomena. The paucity of iconic representation means that we are unable archaeologically to identify perceptions relating to the divinities that may have been venerated when human sacrifice was perpetrated, with any certainty: indeed, the small number of surviving images from Iron Age contexts (Bonenfant & Guillaumet 1998; Roper 2001) may depict heroes or ancestors rather than gods *per se* (**2**).

In considering candidates for victims of ritual human killing, a fundamental issue concerns whether evidence for physical injury occurred pre- or post-mortem; in other words, whether trauma identified on a body was the cause of death or took place — whether by human action or natural taphonomic processes — after death as a result of accident, warfare or disease. In the case of the latter, ritual activity may still have been involved but it is necessary to draw a distinction between post-mortem ceremonial behaviour and human sacrifice, where a religious reason for the killing is strongly suggested. This is often extremely difficult to ascertain, especially where only skeletal material survives. Almost all the archaeological evidence suggestive of ritual murder is capable of alternative interpretation: thus, for instance, the young male bodies found in the cleared-out grain silos at Iron Age Danebury (and elsewhere) (**colour plate 1**) might have been present in the pits as the result of sacrificial activity *or* they could have received ritualised treatment after death in battle; the same is true of the human remains at the 'war-sanctuaries' of Gaul, such as Gournay-sur-Aronde in northern France. The bog-bodies from northern Europe, some with ropes around their necks and with evidence of bondage, may be interpreted as ritual killings, but they could equally have been executed because they were malefactors, foreign hostages or social deviants. Even retributive slaughter would probably have been hedged about with formulaic ritual, not least for fear of pollution or of releasing malignant spirit-force into the community.

Despite the problems, ambiguities and distortions presented by both literary and archaeological testimony, the pages that follow argue with conviction for the existence of human sacrifice in later prehistoric Europe and even in the Roman period. Close scrutiny of the available evidence indicates the unlikelihood that such practice occurred in other than exceptional circumstances and, in assessing the reliability of the written and material data, it is always necessary to be aware that it may allow for alternative models of interpretation. But in seeking to evaluate the enactment of ritual murder in antiquity, it is necessary to confront our present-day distaste for admittance of such practice, a viewpoint which — though entirely understandable — is in danger of blinding us to what may, in fact, have been going on. Denial of ritual killing in the face

2   *Facsimiles of stone images from a late Iron Age high-status site at Saint-Symphorien à Paule
(Côtes-d'Armor); second century BC. Antoine Maillier © Centre archéologique européen du
Mont Beuvray*

of evidence is probably as injurious to the truth as over-credulous acceptance of its
occurrence. While it is never possible totally to discard our own embedded social
sensibilities, it is advantageous to bear in mind that one society's 'murder most horrid'
is another's most holy act.

1
The nature of
sacrifice in antiquity

Sacrifice, like death, is one of the great taboo subjects of the late twentieth century.
(Bradley 1995, 4)

At first glance the concept of sacrifice appears easily comprehended. In modern western parlance, a sacrifice involves giving up something important to an individual or community for a reason perceived to be of greater importance in some manner than what is to be sacrificed. Sacrifice has connotations of altruism and deprivation. But closer scrutiny of sacrifice as a theoretical issue reveals complexities, nuances and potential paradoxes that are elusive and demand analysis. This introductory chapter has two main objectives: first, to discuss the broad concern of sacrifice, particularly as is pertinent to European antiquity; second, to define the nature and function of human sacrifice and its place within the general spectrum of sacrificial activity. Both issues are revisited within the chapters that follow.

Definitions of sacrifice

The word 'sacrifice' comes from the Latin, meaning 'to make holy' (Beattie 1980, 29) and, in origin, therefore, has no specific association with either giving or loss. Ian Bradley (1995, 9-10) suggests that sacrifice may have had its genesis in the sacramental: in other words, sacrificial activity may originally have been linked with communal feasting, involving both humans and the gods in a sacred partnership, rather than being contingent upon the giving and receiving of gifts. The function of such commensality (collective ritual feasting) (**3**) was probably associated with the creation of a bond between people and the supernatural world, between the sacrificers and the divine recipient (**4**), through the slaughter and consumption of animal victims. If sacrifice, in origin, is not necessarily connected with giving, then it follows that negative connotations of loss are inappropriate. Indeed, the point has been made by a number of scholars that it is mistaken to view sacrifice in other than positive, celebratory terms. In the context of ancient meanings of sacrifice, there seem to have been few undertones of doom, sorrow or renunciation. Sacrificial ceremonies were, on the contrary, associated with rejoicing, with festivities and thanksgiving; they were perceived to facilitate communication with the divine world and therefore to be a cause for elation (Yerkes 1953, 4-6; I. Bradley 1995, 10). Indeed, the very word 'holiday' (holy day) specifically links sacral activity with celebration. This essentially positive attitude to sacrifice in antiquity may explain why, for the ancient Greeks, it was important for the animal victims of sacrificial rites to consent — at least in symbolic terms — to their deaths (van Straten 1995, 45-6). Where it seems to me that the positive, celebratory perception of sacrifice works less well is where human sacrifice is involved. Here, as we shall see later in the book, somewhat different rules and attitudes may have prevailed. It is significant that where Greek playwrights, such as Euripides (in, for example, *Iphigeneia in Aulis*), allude to ritual murder, it is hedged about with doom-laden anxiety. The same is true of reference to Gaulish and British human sacrifice by such Graeco-Roman chroniclers as Tacitus (*Annales* XIV, 30-1) and Lucan (*Pharsalia* I, 422-65). Both writers deliberately emphasise the gloomy and frightening circumstances under which such rites took place, presumably in order to enhance the drama of their descriptions of foreign barbarity.

3 *Gilded silver cauldron, dismantled and placed as a votive object in a dry place within the Raevemose peat-bog at Gundestrup, Jutland; first century BC.* © *Nationalmuseet, København*

Sacrifice is a means to an end rather than an end in itself: it is carried out in order to acquire benefits for an individual or a community. Such reciprocal expectation may be associated with the earthworld or the Otherworld: sacrifice might be intended to generate tangible benefits, such as victory in battle, aversion of famine, a good harvest, the birth of a healthy child, recovery from illness, wealth or some other change in the circumstance of a person or group, or to ensure the maintenance of existing good fortune. Sacrifice may also serve to acknowledge human rites of passage: birth, puberty, marriage or death; or natural change: the diurnal, lunar or seasonal cycle or elemental phenomena, such as storms, drought or flood. Even in these contexts, benefits are expected. In the case of celestial or seasonal rituals, for instance, sacrifice may be carried out in order to ensure the return of the sun after winter, the continuing reappearance of the moon each month, the occurrence of rain following periods of drought, the cessation of rain after flooding. Sacrifice may serve to bless the lives of newborn children, or a marriage with offspring. The death of a person might necessitate the initiation of sacrificial ritual in order to cleanse the community of pollution whilst, at the same time, serving to ensure the peaceful transference of the dead person's spirit to the next world. So benefit and reciprocity lie at the very roots of sacrificial ritual, whatever the precise nature of the sacrifice may be.

4   *Stone image of a deity seated cross-legged, from Entremont (Bouches du Rhône); third-second century BC.* © *author*

In any consideration of sacrifice as a concept, the issue of the recipient is crucial. Dennis Hughes (1991, 3) is of the view that what distinguishes sacrifice from any other kind of ritual destruction or slaughter is the perception of a supernatural recipient of the sacrificial offering, or of at least a portion of the sacrificial meal. But others, such as Girard (1977, 90), question the essentiality of the supernatural in sacrifice, emphasising instead that the rite is centred on humankind and that it has, therefore, to be approached — and attempts made to understand it — in essentially anthropocentric terms. If I read this argument correctly, the centrality of humans in no way obviates the perception of a supernatural presence, the target of the ritual, but what it serves to do is to remind us that sacrifice, at least in antiquity, was a response to human needs and circumstances and that it has therefore to be interpreted according to human criteria; in other words, the sacrificial process is human-driven rather than divine-driven.

A legitimate question concerning definitions of sacrifice relates to the nature of the 'gift' itself. In antiquity, did the sacred offering of an inanimate object — a torc, a sword, money, figurine or altar — possess the same function as a slaughtered ox, pig or sheep? In discussing the deliberate and ritual deposition of a large wooden boat, heaped with military hardware, in a Danish peat-bog at Hjortspring in the third century BC, Randsborg (1995, 74-89) is adamant that the ritual perceptions resulting in such an act enjoy precisely the same sacrificial status or currency as the killing of a domestic animal as a sacred act. In the same way, Chris Lynn argues (1992, 33-57) that the deliberate firing of the great wooden structure at Navan in Co. Armagh, immediately after it was built in the early first century BC, was an act of sacrifice. Richard Bradley (1990, 37), however, takes the view that a distinction should be made between live sacrifice and the offering of things: for him, true sacrifice involves the killing of a live being; the ritual deposition of inanimate material constitutes votive offerings. My own inclination is towards Randsborg's viewpoint, not least because of the ancient European (and wider) practice of ritual destruction of inanimate offerings. In studying Late Bronze Age weapon-deposition in the Netherlands, Harry Fokkens (2001) has proposed that destruction and placement of spears and swords in the landscape might be associated with male rites of passage and the symbolic relinquishment of warriorhood when mature men entered a new state as 'elders' or wise men (**5**). If this were so, the consignment of martial items may be interpreted as acts of sacrifice. Here, we may refer to two examples of numerous instances of such occurrences in the Iron Age of temperate Europe: the deliberately damaged sacred assemblages of prestigious, mainly martial, equipment deposited both in the sacred lake at Llyn Cerrig Bach, on the island of Anglesey between the second century BC and the first century AD (Fox 1946; Lynch 1991, 285-315) (**colour plate 16**), and in the shrine at Gournay-sur-Aronde (Oise) during the fourth-third centuries BC (Brunaux 1988) (**6**). Such damage within a ritual context, frequently demanding the expenditure of considerable force in snapping or bending bronze or iron objects, would seem to reflect violence of a kind, akin to the sacrificial act of killing.

Two essential, and related, elements involved in the sacrificial act — be it animal, human or inanimate object — are giving and separation. Giving may be underlain by several perceptions at least one of which involves reciprocity: in other words, something is given to the gods in order to elicit benefits to the donor and thus to engender feelings

5 *Stone image of a ?deity wearing a torc (neckring), a symbol of prestige, from Alesia, Burgundy.*
   © *author*

6   *Ritually-damaged iron sword from the sanctuary of Gournay-sur-Aronde (Oise); third/second century BC. Antoine Maillier © Centre archéologique européen du Mont Beuvray*

of obligation between deity and human. But a gift to the gods must also be predicated on its successful transformation from earthworld to the realm of the spirits, by an act of sacralisation, of transference involving separation from the profane to the sacred. A holy gift, designed for the supernatural powers, must be physically or metaphorically removed from the human world to that of the divine. One way of doing this is to defunctionalise something by destroying it: in the case of a sword or spear (**6 & 7**), this may be achieved by damaging it to make it useless as a practical object; in the case of living beings — animals or humans — the process of destruction means slaughter. Removing sacrificial gifts from earthworld may also involve their physical inaccessibility and invisibility by means of burial, immersion or other means of concealment. This may explain why assemblages of material were recurrently buried in disused grain storage pits at Iron Age Danebury (Cunliffe 1993a) or cast into the waters of the fen edge at Flag Fen (Cambs) during the later Bronze and Iron Ages (Pryor 1991). Transference of holy offerings might, alternatively, be achieved by their emplacement in sanctified space: a temple, sacred enclosure or some other demarcated area. Such separated space acted as a sacred link (and barrier) between worlds and served to create on earth what was, in effect, a divine 'embassy', a terrestrial manifestation of the supernatural world. Separation could be achieved in other ways, too. The Old Testament makes a number of references to the consecration of beings by particular symbolic acts: the Book of *Leviticus* (8, vv 23-4), for instance, describes the consecration of God's servant Aaron and his sons by means of certain rituals, including the marking of their right ears, thumbs and big toes with blood (Rogerson 1980, 55). Both giving and separation are, I would argue, crucial ingredients to enable the essential alchemy of the sacrifice, its successful

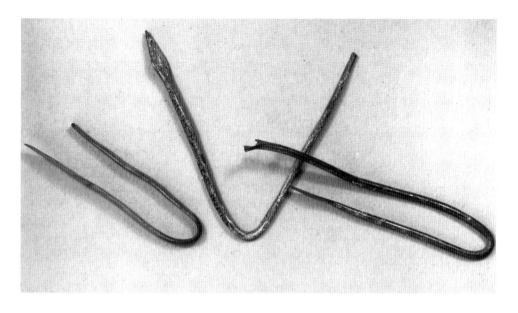

7   *Set of miniature, ritually-bent spears, from the Romano-British shrine at Woodeaton (Oxon).*
   © *Betty Naggar*

transference from profane to sacred, to take place with its consequent acceptance as a a legitimate and efficacious offering.

Sacrifice and value

In considering the nature of sacrificial gifts, the issue of value is important, particularly in the assessment of animateness and of human relative to animal. In dealing with perceptions possibly obtaining in antiquity, modern western attitudes to value are at best irrelevant and, at worst, a hindrance to understanding since unquestioning anthropocentric rules may cloud our judgement concerning past hierarchies of worth. Two questions are relevant to the argument: we need, on the one hand, to ask whether life, the presence of *anima* (breath) in a potential sacrificial offering was considered to be of greater intrinsic value than inert inanimateness; and, on the other, whether humans necessarily possessed a more valuable currency than animals. The answer to these questions is neither straightforward nor unequivocal. Even in our present-day systems of relative value there is ambiguity in the ratings of animals as compared to expensive or luxury items, such as cars, electronic goods, jewellery or paintings: an animal *per se* is not automatically near the apex of value simply because it shares *anima* with humans. In the past, then, it is reasonable to suppose that animals and inanimate possessions assumed relative denominational value, for sacrificial purposes, according to rules or formulae associated with the particular benefit desired, the nature of the divine recipient or some other religious circumstance; sacred value may not have been identical to economic or practical worth. Judgement of sacral value would presumably have been predicated upon criteria different from those associated with secular worth. Furthermore, different animals might have been endowed with sacrificial status that may or may not have been associated with economic factors but, rather, other socio-religious criteria related to context would undoubtedly be relevant to the choice of a particular species for centre-stage in a sacrificial ceremony. It is clear from anthropological and archaeological examples of animal sacrifice that it is the domestic animals — those in closest association with human communities — that are accorded primacy in ritual terms (**8**). Indeed, the choice of domestic animals may be associated with principles of surrogacy, wherein a cow or sheep was deemed an appropriate substitute for a human life. Whilst economics or cost can be a factor in selection of a sacrificial offering, 'questions of cost and gain can be completely overshadowed by cosmological meanings of corporate ritual symbolism' (Bourdillon 1980, 12).

When we come to consider human sacrifice in European antiquity, it is necessary to ask the fundamental question as to whether — for spiritual purposes — human beings were at the pinnacle of value. Such a question may be resolved by observation of the secular value of humans. Here, it is of the utmost importance that we avoid imposing our own values upon the world of antiquity. In seeking to acknowledge the possibility of human sacrificial practice in ancient Europe during the last few centuries BC and even later, we need to overcome our quite natural but arguably inappropriate repugnance to the notion of ritual murder, given fundamentally different past attitudes to the status of human life. As a first step, it is essential to examine the nature of societies of Classical and temperate Europe at this period, and the status of various categories of person within them. It is clear from the copious contemporary documentary sources that the Classical world was organised according to strict social hierarchies, although levels within these ranked structures could be transgressed (unlike the rigid social divisions in, for instance, Victorian England). In the ancient Mediterranean world of Greece and Rome social inequality, inclusion or exclusion from full or partial citizenhood was embedded in the fabric of society. Additional to the ranking imposed by birth and — to an extent — also wealth, such social imbalances were also associated with gender, on the one hand, and slavery, on the other. In Greek and Roman society, women possessed only limited franchise. Fantham (1994, 74) makes the point that women were excluded from the 'men's club' of the Athenian democracy from the time of its establishment in the fifth century BC. In the Greek world generally, the lives of free women were circumscribed by their virtual confinement to the *oikos* (the household), and they had an extremely limited public profile, almost entirely associated with participation in religious ceremonies and in funerals. In the Roman Republic, the male head of the family, the *paterfamilias*, had technical powers of life and death (*patria potestas*) over his entire household, from the lowest of his slaves to his wife and children.

The greatest social inequality in the Classical world lay in the endemic presence of slavery as a key element in social organisation. It has been estimated that there may have been three million slaves in Italy at any one time (Brunt 1971, 121). By the mid-second century BC, persons of servile status may have accounted for more than 20% of the Roman population, making Rome a truly slave-dependent society (Brunt 1971, 212;

8   Stone carved with a frieze of horse-heads, from the cliff-top sanctuary at Roquepertuse (Bouches-du-Rhône); fourth/third century BC. © author

Bradley 1989, 19-20; Taylor 2001a; 2001b). The Greek geographer Strabo, writing in the late first century BC, maintained (*Geographia* XIV, 5, 2) that, on the Greek island of Delos, 10,000 slaves could change hands in the market during a single day. There is, furthermore, both documentary and archaeological evidence to indicate the presence of slaves in western Europe, including Britain, in the late Iron Age: Strabo speaks specifically of goods exported from Britain to the Mediterranean world, including grain, hunting-dogs and slaves (*Geographia* IV, 5, 2); Diodorus Siculus, a near-contemporary of Strabo, records the information that a Gaulish slave was worth one amphora of Italian wine (*Library of History* V, 26, 3). Archaeological evidence attests the presence of iron slave-gang chains in late Iron Age contexts at, for instance, the sacred lake of Llyn Cerrig Bach on Anglesey (Fox 1946), an indication of slave-ownership in British society on the eve of the Roman conquest, although Vincent Guichard (pers. comm.) has raised the possibility that such objects might have possessed ritual significance.

In a system of entrenched and formalised social inequality, slavery is at one extreme of the spectrum (Wiedemann 1992, 1). In a slave-owning society, one human being is — because of birth, the fortunes of war or other circumstance — the property of another; where there was a formalised legal system, as in ancient Rome, slave-ownership was enshrined in law. In Classical antiquity, as in nineteenth-century Europe, slaves were possessions 'denied any moral worth of their own' (Wiedemann 1992, 5). Slaves were without rights and although, in the Mediterranean world, acknowledgement of the humanity of slaves imposed certain limits on the level of brutality that could be meted out to them, care was taken that no constraints should challenge the basic rights concomitant with absolute ownership (*ibid.*, 9). The point about slavery, in the present context, is that given a situation in which certain persons were denied most, if not all, human rights, and were thus not protected from inhuman treatment by their humanity alone, the practice of human sacrifice should not appear unduly shocking. Furthermore, we should not forget that hundreds of thousands of men, women and children were 'sacrificed' for sport in the gladiatorial combat of the Roman arena, in a custom whose genesis lay in funerary rituals.

Human sacrifice and substitution

> A woman is dying in this house.
> She is giving up her life
> So that her husband can live.
> And this is the day of her death.
> (Euripides *Alcestis*: Hughes 1999, 1)

Thus, at the beginning of a Greek drama written in 438 BC, the god Apollo introduces the play's central theme, the substitution of Alcestis's life in exchange for that of her husband, Admetus, who was restored to health by the healer-god after a dangerous sickness, on the understanding that another human life was given up. Alcestis volunteered as Admetus's surrogate within a context wherein — although the marriage was loving and harmonious — it was deemed 'right' for the man's life to come first.

In any sacrificial act, there is an underlying expectation of reciprocal benefit associated with self-interest on the part of the sacrificer. Technically, the most valuable gift to the gods was self-sacrifice but, if that meant self-destruction, it would of course prevent the sacrificer from deriving personal benefit from the offering. (Indeed, auto-sacrifice by starvation used to be a regular part of Indian Jain devotional activity, and is still very occasionally practised even today (Kamdar 1993).) This being so, the concept of sacrifice was underpinned by the nodal issue of substitution, the exchange of one type of sacrificial gift for another. Since pragmatism underlies sacrifice itself, inasmuch as it occurs for gain (or aversion), practicalities also obtain in the choice of gift. The sacrifice of self is untenable, so something must be substituted for the sacrificer. This may, in certain circumstances, involve animals as surrogate victims but, as argued in a later chapter, this may not always be the case. What is interesting in the present context is that the closest form of substitution is another human being.

In considering surrogacy, reference to an idiosyncratic Roman custom is perhaps illuminating. Several Classical authors, including Ovid (*Fasti* V, 621-34), Varro (*de Lingua Latina* VII, 44), Dionysius of Halicarnassus (*Roman Antiquities* I, 38) and Plutarch (*Quaestiones Romanae* 272B) make reference to a rite involving the casting of puppets, known as *Argei*, into the Tiber from the Pons Sublicius in the city of Rome. The occasion of such a bizarre custom was an annual religious ceremony, the *Argei* acting as substitutes for human sacrificial victims. Dionysius explains the origin of the ritual in terms of an episode in early Roman history in which captured Greeks (Argives, hence *Argei*) were ritually murdered. According to him, 30 puppet-substitutes were thrown into the river during the ceremony.

The Roman festival of the *Argei* illustrates substitution at its most benign, here perhaps treated as no more than a folk-tradition but with a serious core of meaning associated with attitudes to foreigners as lesser beings. We can see a variation on this kind of 'inanimate' substitution being acted out in, for instance, Gallo-Roman healing ritual which took place at such therapeutic spring-sanctuaries as *Fontes Sequanae* in Burgundy (**9**) and Chamalières near Clermont-Ferrand, in the Auvergne. At these sacred places pilgrim-visitors, in search of a cure for physical maladies, placed in the spring or elsewhere in the holy precinct stone or wooden images of themselves as offerings to the presiding deity, in hope and expectation of a reciprocal exchange, whereby the diseased organ would be replaced by one that was whole (Green 1999). A more sinister form of substitution may, however, involve the choice of a live human surrogate as a vicarious sacrificial victim (Bourdillon 1980, 30). The kernel of human substitution is the notion that the surrogate is of less value, of lesser importance, and thus more dispensable than the person on behalf

9   *Bronze figurine of the Gallo-Roman goddess Sequana, from a healing spring-sanctuary at Fontes Sequanae, near Dijon, Burgundy.*
© *Paul Jenkins*

of whom the sacrifice is enacted. As Shelby Brown argues, in the context of Carthaginian child-sacrifice (1991, 147-9), the victim's death is a form of 'life-insurance' for the survivor. If the surrogate consists of a lesser human life, it may explain why, as discussed later, the Classical writers on Gaulish human sacrifice make repeated reference to ritual murder-victims of low or marginal social status: criminals, poor people, slaves, foreigners (often prisoners-of-war), or children. The nature of the relationship between sacrificer and sacrificial victim is, in most instances, one of superior and inferior being (Wenham 1995, 75-87). This relative status is frequently determined by subjective perception which may relate to exclusion (as in the case of aliens) or to social rank but may simply be associated with 'otherness' of some kind. In his bloody tragedy, *Titus Andronicus*, Shakespeare provides us with a splendid example of surrogacy in human sacrifice, presenting a circumstance in which Titus's surviving sons ensure that the spirits of their brothers, slain in battle, pass without mishap across the Styx to the Otherworld, by the sacrifice of the foreign enemy Alarbus, eldest son of Tamora, queen of the Goths (Barker 1993, 143) 'that we may hew his limbs, and on a pile . . . sacrifice his flesh' (Act I, scene 1, lines 97-8). However elevated Alarbus' rank among his own people, to the Romans his foreignness, together with the desire for bloody vengeance, makes him a suitable surrogate victim: Alarbus is sacrificed in order to free the spirits of Titus's dead sons from eternal wandering in limbo, a state imposed by the lack of proper burial-rites following death on the battlefield. If we apply the Alarbus situation to European antiquity, it may be possible to interpret the young male bog-victim, Lindow Man, in a similar manner: he was a man of reasonably high rank (Stead 1986; Green 1998a), yet he was subjected to systematic physical abuse as part of sacrificial ritual, as if to degrade him: perhaps he, too, was a foreigner (**colour plate 12**).

To make substitution work efficiently, the choice of victim is important. The surrogate must be separate, in some sense, from the mainstream of the community engaged in the sacrifice — criminals, strangers, foreigners, slaves or other marginal individuals occupying the fringes of society — but not too far removed, otherwise the substitution is based on insufficient equality. This may explain why, for certain ancient communities, animals were sometimes unacceptable surrogates. It may also be that an essential difference between fellow humans and animals as substitutes was that only beasts could legitimately figure on the sacrificial feasting menu in instances where commensality followed the slaughter of the victim: ritual cannibalism does not appear to have been habitual practice in later European prehistory (although it was sometimes the subject of Greek myth). So I would disagree with René Girard (1977, 10) in his contention that there may be little difference in perceptions of sacrificial efficacy between humans and animals; to my mind, the issue of consumption creates a huge gulf between people and beasts as ritual victims. The need to identify formal categories of persons as potential sacrificial material, and to separate them from the general community, may derive, in origin at least, from the desirability of avoiding killing adult kin. This leads to a further issue concerning substitution: the choice of 'lesser' victims — children, slaves or foreigners — makes violence the more acceptable, thus reinforcing the beneficial effects of surrogacy. Substitution is also relevant to the concept of the scapegoat (examined in detail later) which acts as a legitimate agent of deferred responsibility.

A final introductory issue relating to substitution concerns the mythologising of human sacrifice: the ancient Greeks, for example, kept ritual murder to the realm of myth, thus Euripides explores the issue of mythic human sacrifice in plays such as *Iphigeneia in Aulis* and the *Bacchae*. Things that occur in myth are acceptable, even if shunned in real society; the otherness of myth serves to separate what goes on in mythic stories from real life occurrences (**10**). The function of Greek myth may be as a form of social cleansing. Whatever the realities of human sacrificial practice, its consignment to the mythic realm obviates the need to take responsibility for what may be seen as 'uncivilised' behaviour.

Human sacrifice: function and meaning

The thought-processes lying behind ritual action are, of course, crucial to the interpretation of such behaviour. Sacrifice, particularly involving the slaughter of animals or human beings, is perhaps the most dramatic form of communication between people and the supernatural world but it is, paradoxically, the most enigmatic. The problems

10 *Mythical human sacrificial scene on a sixth-century BC Greek vase-painting. Polyxena, royal daughter of the Trojan king Priam and Hecuba, is sacrificed by Neoptolemus at the tomb of Achilles. © Anne Leaver (after Detienne & Vernant 1989)*

associated with the comprehension of human sacrifice, or any other form of cult activity in Iron Age Europe, lie in the absence of a recorded historical context. On the one hand, the documentary sources are less than reliable both because they are the observations of foreigners, of writers who belonged not to the world upon which they commented but to an alien Classical world, and because their testimony is chronologically 'bunched' towards the end of the Iron Age, the first centuries BC and AD. So, inasmuch as they do not record earlier cult practices, the texts must not be used to argue retrospectively: what may have obtained in the first century BC, when Caesar and Strabo were writing about Gaul and Britain, may not have been relevant to the fifth-second centuries. On the other hand, we are largely reliant upon the evidence of material culture for information concerning ritual action during the later first millennium BC, and the archaeological data associated with possible cultic murder, notably the survival of human bodies, is equivocal: while some skeletons or well-preserved bog-bodies may exhibit signs of violent, untimely death (**11**), it is often difficult to distinguish between murder, punitive execution and sacrifice. Indeed, the three are not necessarily mutually exclusive. So, in seeking to understand the mental attitude underlying sacrifice in Iron Age Europe, we are in a distinctly less favourable position than the student of Old Testament Judaic antiquity, where information concerning the complex rules and circumstances surrounding cult-action, including sacrifice, are explained by writers who understood what they recorded. Thus the Old Testament texts provide detailed information concerning the function and meaning of various animal sacrifices, with purification, reparation, atonement and protection stated as the main reasons for ritual slaughter. We read of grain-offerings, burnt offerings, blood offerings, all with subtly or obviously different functions, meanings and circumstances

11 Bludgeoned human skull, found in a disused grain storage pit at Danebury. © Danebury Trust

(Jenson 1995, 25-40). The predication of meaning upon context severely limits opportunities for any such interpretations of sacrificial activity in ancient Europe where the cognitive matrix is very uncertain.

An example from the text-rich societies of the Classical world serves to underpin the importance of a contextual backdrop. Greek and Roman sacrificial practices are contextualised by the presence of contemporary and indigenous literature. Human sacrifice in ancient Rome — which only became illegal in 97 BC, although it was always rare — is occasionally chronicled in Classical literature. Taking a particular episode in Roman history as an illustration, we learn from several ancient authors of an extreme response to a severe threat to Rome itself in the late third century BC, namely the sacrificial murder of gendered pairs of Greeks and Gauls who were ritually buried alive in the Forum Boarium (the central cattle-market) in the city of Rome. In his *Life of Marcellus* (III), Plutarch (who died *c*.AD 120) describes how, at the end of the first Punic War (which lasted from 265-241 BC), the Romans renewed their conflict with the Gallic tribes to the north of Italy, of whom they had been wary as adversaries ever since Rome was sacked by a Gallic army in 390 BC. He records how, while Rome was engaged in war with the Carthaginians, the Gauls bided their time, waiting to see who would emerge as the victor. The southern Gaulish tribe of the Insubres finally invaded Italy in 225 BC, but Plutarch reports that the Romans were already so alarmed by the Gallic threat that, in 228 BC, they made an 'extraordinary' (Plutarch's word) sacrifice of two Greeks and two Gauls, a male and female in each pair, in obedience to a command found in the prophetic Sibylline

Books. Plutarch comments that 'in memory of the victims, they still to this day, in the month of November, perform mysterious and secret ceremonies' (Perrin 1971a, 441-3).

The Sibylline Books were the records of utterances made by female prophets, the *Sibyllae* of whom the most famous in the ancient literature were those attached to the oracular Apolline sanctuaries at Cumae in southern Italy and Delphi in Greece, which were served by successive Sibyls. Their role was to act as intermediaries between the god and supplicants seeking to know the future and to interpret divine messages. Their prophetic sayings were allegedly collected and written down in Greek hexameter verse, originally — in the case of the Cumaean Sibyl at least — on palm-leaves. Collections of these verses were copied for consultation by the Romans from as early as the sixth century BC until the destruction of the texts in the burning of the Capitol in 83 BC. The lost documents were replaced by a new collection gathered from a range of sources. The last recorded consultation took place in AD 363 and the official collection was deliberately destroyed in the early fifth century.

The human sacrifices recorded by Plutarch and other broadly contemporary writers (see chapter 6) were clearly aversion rituals, special religious events that occurred at a time of great threat to the survival of Rome. Dio Cassius, writing much later, in the third century AD, remarks (*Roman History* XII, 50) that the rite was carried out in order to fulfil a prophecy that the Greeks and Gauls would occupy the city. Thus, in artificially causing the prediction to come true, the genuine threat of foreign occupation was thereby deflected. Interestingly, the human sacrifice enacted in 228 BC, because of the anticipated Gaulish invasion, was replicated in 216 BC *after* the severe defeat of Roman forces by the Carthaginians in the Battle of Cannae (Liebeschutz 1979, 449-50). This second episode, therefore, appears to have occurred following a catastrophe rather than to avert a future one, although it was presumably designed to reverse Roman military fortunes. It is evident from the literary sources that the Romans of the late Republic and early Empire regarded past human sacrifice as only applicable as an extreme measure in the manipulation of the supernatural powers. Livy (*Ab Urbe Condita* XXII, 57, 6) clearly viewed it as very un-Roman behaviour, and Plutarch also refers to the practice as a weird and alien rite. But the remarks of authors like Plutarch and Pliny nonetheless provide a context and setting for the enactment of ritual murder and these are lacking when we are dealing — as in the case of the European Iron Age — with archaeological evidence (**12**), supported only by a few obscure and perfunctory comments by Classical commentators on customs of 'barbarians' to the north and west of the Mediterranean world whose 'otherness' was clearly being emphasised (or in some instances perhaps invented) in the literature.

Aversion sacrifice, exemplified so graphically by the Roman ritual enacted in the Forum Boarium in the third century BC, is one of several rationales for sacrificial activity and is, perhaps, the most likely context for ritual murder. Beattie (1980, 38-9) proposes a four-fold classification of sacrifice, of which two are 'conjunctive', or associated with positive acquisition of benefit; the other two are 'disjunctive', associated with deflection or aversion. Beattie separates conjunctive and disjunctive sacrifice into ritual action that, on the one hand, is linked with acquisition and maintenance or repellence of contact with the spirits and, on the other, with gaining or avoidance of surges of sacred force, such power being perceived as either created or released by sacrificial action. To my mind, such

12 Anthropomorphic image carved in granite, from Lanneunoc, Brittany; second-first century BC.
© author

division between divine entities and unidentified supernatural force is both unnecessary and spurious. What matters is the relationship between earthworld and Otherworld, and the welcome or unwanted intervention with the former by the latter. The sacrifice of Gauls and Greeks by the Romans is a clear instance of disjunctive sacrifice. Indeed, it seems likely that disjunctive sacrifice is the more often associated with the killing of humans.

The perception of interaction between spirits and human beings lies at the very root of sacrificial function and meaning. There is a wide range of reasons for such ritual behaviour. Jaussen (1908, 342-3) describes a form of apotropaic (or protective) blood-sacrifice among certain Bedouin groups who, in their earlier nomadic lifestyle, used the blood of sacrificed animals to mark tent-poles and tent-fabric and who, in their modern, more settled state, carry on this practice by daubing blood on the walls and lintels of their houses during construction, in a kind of sacred 'good-luck' symbolism. Such action has similarities in meaning with the enactment of foundation sacrifices, animals and infants. These have been noted in antiquity, for instance in the building of temples, farms or other structures, such as the Romano-British shrine-complex at Springhead (Kent) and the farm at Winterton (Lincs) (Green 1998a, 185). It could be argued that apotropaic sacrifices like these involve both conjunctive and disjunctive symbolism: the buildings were protected from harmful spiritual intervention while, at the same time, the sacrifices invited and requested positive blessing from benign supernatural beings.

The importance of killing as an act of communion (whether or not the resultant body was consumed) brings us to two crucial and related areas of concern: performance and violence. In an act of animal or human sacrificial ritual, the process, the drama, the sequence of events all play essential roles in the communication between people and the supernatural world. The preliminaries to many ancient sacrificial ceremonies involved processions of religious officials, worshippers and, of course, the victim; this would contribute to the anticipation of the central event, the act of slaughter itself. The prayers, invocations, music, dancing (**13**), chanting or other activity, the decoration of the victim would all build up the tension which would be released only by the catharsis of death. In

Greek ceremonies involving animal sacrifice, we know from the literature that there were three stages in the ritual sequence: pre-kill, the killing and post-kill (van Straten 1995, 9). The entire event would comprise a drama, an artform, all elements serving to enrich and enhance the central rite of sacrifice (van Straten 1995, 10; Beattie 1980, 33-6).

The collective nature of sacrificial ritual is important; it is generally a group event involving part or the whole of a community. The catharsis is a shared experience, as is the sacred meal that may conclude a sacrificial rite. Girard (1977, 100-1) exemplifies this collectivity by reference to the human sacrificial rituals, involving the slaughter of slaves, followed by the Ngadju-Dayaks of Borneo, in which it is perceived as necessary for all participants to share by each striking the victim. Such assumption of joint responsibility has far-reaching resonances with other collective violence: the assassination of Julius Caesar by supporters of the Roman Republic in 44 BC was, in a sense, a group sacrifice in which all the conspirators attacked the dictator with a dagger-thrust. Archaeologically, there may be evidence for a similar group catharsis in the so-called 'ghost-killings' for which there is testimony in Iron Age Yorkshire, where certain interred human bodies were

13 Bronze figurine of a dancer, from a sacred hoard of images found at Neuvy-en-Sullias (Loiret), and originally from a sanctuary; first century BC.
© Paul Jenkins

found to have been penetrated after death by several spears (Stead 1991, 33; Giles 2001).

The role of violence in flesh-sacrifice is examined in the next chapter, but a brief mention should be made here, inasmuch as it is highly relevant both to sacrifice as performance and to collective responsibility for it. Violence is, by its nature, dramatic, tense and climactic; it is also dangerous to the community and this may, in part, account for the need for shared participation in the dispatching of victims. Girard (1977, 3) takes the view that the presence of violence in sacrificial ritual fulfils a specific social purpose, namely to neutralise, deflect and control societal aggression, to channel violence towards ritual and religion to prevent its anarchic rampancy within communities. In rather the same manner, ritual murder in ancient Greece is confined to myth (see above). According to Hélène Foley (1985, 38), 'sacrifice denies by its procedures its own violence'. In other words, the ritualisation of sacrifice may so separate it from its social context that its intrinsic violence might be deemed as irrelevant, and thus unthreatening, to the community within which it takes place. I am uncertain as to whether this argument is always valid: it is possible to invert it and suggest that violence, even within the sacral context, may so inure people to bloody slaughter that secular violence may be encouraged rather than controlled by its practice. In a recent book on cannibalism in the prehistory of the American South-West (Turner & Turner 1999, 1-10), the authors make the point that violence in society and the practice of human sacrifice sometimes go together. Girard argues for the presence of dualism or ambiguity in sacrificial violence, in that — like the spilling of blood in hunting — it is both harmful and beneficial. As explored in the next chapter, it seems to be the case that unnecessary 'overkill' violence was the hallmark of many sacrificial killings in European antiquity (**colour plate 2**). Whatever the reality behind the evidence for ritual murder in ancient literature and material culture, we should not lose sight of its embeddedness within the mindsets and cosmologies of the particular communities who followed such cult practice. The chapters that follow examine the evidence for human sacrifice within the specific context of the European Iron Age and the western Roman provinces.

2
Flesh for the Gods

Sacrificial killing is the basic experience of the 'sacred': homo religiosus acts and attains self-awareness as homo necans [killer].
(Burkert 1983, 3, speaking of Greek animal sacrifice)

The dedication of flesh-offerings, whether animal or human, to the supernatural powers is clearly distinct from the donation of inanimate gifts, such as coins, weapons or images. The distinction is based upon the presence of breath, or *anima*, and upon the visibly abrupt transition from living being to corpse or carcass. Further linkages between human and beast include recognition of shared somatic structure: bones, flesh, blood, movement, the five senses, voice and the ingestion of sustenance by mouth. The perception of strong similarities between the behaviour of animals and people may be relevant to sacrificial practice, particularly in consideration of whether or not beasts sometimes acted as surrogate human victims of ritual killing.

Sacrificial slaughter involves violence. One of the themes of this chapter is the notion of violence, not simply in terms of its necessity in the context of killing, but as a source of energy or spiritual force. The evidence for apparently unnecessary savagery, mutilation or 'overkill' in the treatment of sacrificial victims suggests that violence possessed a symbolic function similar, perhaps, to the perceptions underlying the ritual destruction of weapons prior to their deposition in graves, shrines or watery places. Consideration of violence as an identifiably significant element in sacrificial practice leads to the question of ritual cannibalism. Anthropophagy is, perhaps, the ultimate violence that can be meted out to people by other people. There is a body of anthropological material relating to ritualised cannibalism within a range of non-western contexts — from India to Polynesia. A number of Classical texts refer to this practice in ancient Europe, even in republican Rome itself and, while it is possible to dismiss these as apocryphal, or as a means of conveying ethnic, social or political deviancy, there is nonetheless rare but plausible testimony from the archaeological record that the symbolic consumption of human sacrificial victims might occasionally have occurred.

Humans and animals

Flesh and blood

> Animals, and even humans, were not slaughtered in these rituals to be offered as a gift to the gods but rather to release the life-blood which had a unique and mysterious sacrificial efficacy.
> (I. Bradley 1995, 9-10)

The above illustrates the need to avoid applying simplistic, unifunctional interpretations to flesh-sacrifice. Although there is strong evidence that, in European antiquity, people did conduct ritual killings of beasts in order to placate the divine powers, the flesh itself may have possessed additional symbolic meaning. Given the flesh-and-blood bond between humans and animals, we should pose the question of whether the act of slaughter *per se* carried significance. Clearly, animal-sacrifice was — and is — endemic to a broad range of societies, past and present, and the worldview, the cosmologies of different communities,

14 Goat-burial in disused grain silo at Danebury. © Danebury Trust

are likely to be equally discrepant one from the other. So it is senseless to try and homogenise meaning in any specific way, without falling into the trap of essentialism. However, certain fundamental attitudes to flesh-offerings may inform our thinking, particularly with reference to possible linkages between human and animal ritual. One important element in killing is the shedding of blood which, in ancient Greek religion, carried with it a set of meanings associated with cathartic experience (in the sudden spurt of blood), together with the perception of flowing blood as a liminal connector between the living and the dead (and between earthworld and the supernatural), with the paradoxical properties of draining life but also nourishment of the ground on which the blood falls (Durand 1989, 119-28) (**14**).

Ian Bradley (1995, 9-10) argues that the death of a ritual victim created a sacred bond between the divine recipient of the sacrificial gift and the individual or community enacting the sacrifice. Such linkage is further forged — in the case of animal-victims, at least — by the consumption of the flesh within the context of sacral feasting, a ceremony in which the gods and their worshippers both participate, sharing meat, nourishment and conviviality (**15**). In ancient Greece, the only meat available for food was from sacrificial

15 Bronze 'flesh-fork', probably for spearing meat boiling in a cauldron, from Dunaverney, Co. Antrim, Northern Ireland; seventh century BC. © Paul Jenkins

animals. Flesh-offerings might be especially meaningful within belief-systems involving symbolic constructs in which the spirits were perceived as essentially composed of matter similar to that of the offerings dedicated to them, albeit in a parallel world (Green 1998a, 172-3). Ritual consumption possessed both practical and symbolic meaning, the latter associated, perhaps, with sacramental transformatory process (Hill 1995a, 103), in which human and deity came close to being one. Animals may have been 'manipulated to mediate spiritually but also spatially and socially' with the Otherworld (Hill 1995a, 103, after Gibson 1986, 182).

Thinking with animals

On the Saturday nearest 12 November, the ceremony of the 'Toro de Fuego' takes place at 11.30pm in the main square of the little town of Medinaceli, near Soria in northern Spain, as part of an annual winter festival. The central figure is a bull, its body smeared with mud, and with false horns attached which are set on fire. The bull is then released to run around a makeshift bullring and is chased towards five bonfires, one for each of the town's patrons, or *Cuerpos Santos* (Holy Bodies), as they are known; although the animal is terrified, it is unhurt, for the mud protects it from the flames. The ceremony celebrates the triumph of the sun over the moon, symbolised by the engulfing of the lunar 'feminine' horn by its solar male fellow. The festival ends with a traditional bullfight (De Gracía 1998), in a form of celebratory sacrifice..

The notion of animal sacrifices as substitutes for people is examined later in this chapter. But first, it is interesting and informative to glance briefly at the ritual treatment of animals that may reflect perceptions of close affinities between 'sharers of flesh': humans and beasts. Animals can stand as metaphors for aspects of the human condition and can be used by people both as symbolic negotiators with the spirit world and as a means of expressing the relationship between earthly and Otherworld dimensions. So, for example, the shaman, in many divergent societies — from Namibia to the Navajo, and from Australasia to circumpolar Siberia — may assume animal personae, by donning pelts, feathers or horns, in order to negotiate pathways between states of consciousness and between earth- and spirit-worlds (Vitebsky 1995; Clottes & Lewis-Williams 1998). In Iron Age and Roman Gaul and Britain, material culture occasionally provides glimpses of such religious beings: the antler headdresses from the pre-Roman shrine at Digeon (Somme) and the Romano-British site at Hook's Cross (Herts), for instance, may have been worn by such persons (Meniel 1987, 101-43; Green 1997, 58; 2001a).

41

The manner in which animals are and were treated in ritual contexts may frequently point to their function as sacred mediators or as a means of expressing human concerns and needs to the gods. A good example is provided by a rare piece of evidence for details surrounding the sacrifice of beasts, from the ancient Italic city of Iguvium in Umbria (modern Gubbio) where, in 1444, the *tabulae Iguvinae* were discovered. These artefacts consist of seven bronze tablets, ranging in date from *c.*200 to the first century BC, inscribed with sacred texts, describing cult and liturgy pertaining to a priesthood known as the Atiedian Brethren (Poultenay 1959; Devoto 1940). These important documents have preserved, in minute detail, the context within which the townsfolk of Iguvium sacrificed animals according to different rituals enacted at each of its three town gates. In selecting the victims, attention was paid to gender, age, appearance, pregnancy or lactation and number (Brunaux 1988, 116-17; Green 1992a, 93-4). All belonged to domestic species: cattle, pigs and sheep. Indeed, in the Classical world generally, where a rigid distinction was made between farmed and wild animals, sacrificial flesh was usually taken from the former, perhaps because they were deemed to have a greater affinity with humankind. The same was apparently true of Gallo-British cult-practice (Meniel 1987, 101-43; Green 1992a, 92-127) (**16**).

The beasts chosen for sacrifice in the Graeco-Roman world had, in most instances, to be physically perfect and free from disease. The dedication of a sick or deformed creature would constitute an insult to the gods and might bring ill-luck on the community. What is more, since — in the Greek system — only sacrificed meat was eaten, the taboo on infected animals probably had a practical aspect too. The beautification of a sacrificial beast was an integral part of the pre-slaughter ceremonial process: '*Tà hierà kalá*' ('Holy things are beautiful') (van Straten 1995, 43). It is interesting that descriptions of contemporary human scapegoat rituals (see chapter 7) include accounts of the care lavished on the victim prior to his death, and the sumptuous clothing in which he was clad before he was cursed and cast out or murdered. Although beauty and perfection were the normative criteria for the selection of sacrificial animals in the Mediterranean world, the Italian author Aelian alludes to an exception: the villagers of Amarynthus, an Eretrian settlement on the west coast of Euboea, sacrificed maimed

16 A funerary cortège of animals, found in a late Iron Age cart-grave at Soissons, France.
© Paul Jenkins
(after Meniel 1987)

animals to the hunter-goddess Artemis (*De Natura Animalium* XII, 34; Scholfield 1959, 59). Such a practice resonates with ritual behaviour associated with human sacrificial victims in north-west Europe who, according to anatomical evidence, appear often to have been especially selected because of some physical defect (chapter 7).

In the ancient world, two main categories of animal-sacrifice were enacted: holocausts, in which the entire victim was offered to the gods, and commensality, wherein beasts were slaughtered, butchered, cooked and partially eaten, in rituals of shared consumption between members of the community and spirit beings. Though the concept of 'holocaust' originally meant consumption by fire, the term may be used, in a looser sense, to describe any flesh-offering which is dedicated to the gods in its entirety. In holocausts, the victim's carcass could be burnt, its essence rising to the upper world in smoke and ash, or deposited in the ground, to decay and release its vital nutrients into the earth and underworld. Both holocausts and ritual feasting are recorded in Old Testament Judaism, Greek and Roman ritual, and cult-praxis in Gaul and Britain. One problem in interpreting remains of butchery on archaeological sites in Iron Age Europe is the difficulty in distinguishing between the remnants of ceremonial consumption and the debris of ordinary food-preparation. In many traditional societies, the slaughter of large domesticates constitutes ceremonial consumption: the meat only keeps for a short time without artificial means of preservation. However, where faunal evidence occurs on temple-sites, we are on surer ground. At the Iron Age shrine of Gournay in Picardy, sacrificial animals were subjected both to holocaust and sacred feasting: elderly cattle and horses were interred whole, while young pigs and lambs were butchered and consumed. The oxen were first placed in a central decomposition pit for about six months, the remains then being re-deposited in the enclosure ditch, by the entrance (Meniel 1992, 47-63; Brunaux 1988; Green 1992a, 109) (**17**). The same kind of thing was occurring at Danebury where animals, particularly horses and dogs, were buried in disused grain silos to rot and replenish the earth (**18**).

It is interesting to note that the ritual deposits at both Gournay and Danebury included a combination of people and animals, almost as if the two groups were — to a degree —

17 Skulls of cattle sacrificed at the Iron Age sanctuary of Gournay in Picardy. © Paul Jenkins

18 Skeletons of a horse and a dog, interred together in a grain storage pit at Danebury.
  © *Danebury Trust*

interchangeable. There is other evidence, too, for a perceived affinity between the two. So, for instance, certain pit-burials of humans at Danebury were found associated with appropriate faunal deposits: in one pit (437, Dep. 19), the body of a neonatal infant was placed with that of a newborn calf (Walker 1984, 442-63). At the same site, the skulls of both humans and horses were preferentially selected (**19**). At the Iron Age shrines of Gournay and Ribemont in northern France, again, particular portions of both men and animals (horses at Ribemont, dogs at Gournay) were retained for special deposition; the curious 'ossuaries' at Ribemont were constructed from the long-bones of horses and humans. In all these sites, the beasts singled out for repeated cult activity were among those that were closest — economically speaking — to people: horses, dogs and cattle (Green 1996, 199; Hill 1995a, 103; Brunaux 1988).

19 Horse-skull, from the base of a grain silo at Danebury. © Danebury Trust

The repeated association of human, horse and dog remains in Iron Age deposits may have significance, in terms of sacrifice. We have literary testimony to this effect from Spanish contexts: thus, Strabo comments (*Geographia* III.3.6-7) that communities living in the mountains of Iberia sacrificed both male prisoners and horses, elaborating that the entrails of prisoners were used in divination and their severed right hands dedicated to the gods (Curchin 1991, 170; Almagro-Gorbea 1995, 175-207) and Livy (*Per.* 49) speaks of similar cult-practice in Lusitania, in which men and horses were ritually slaughtered. The custom was given as the reason for the massacre of Lusitanians by the Roman governor Galba in 150 BC (Curchin, *op. cit.*). This kind of literary testimony should cause us to examine archaeological evidence for the association of humans and horses. The Iron Age site of Blewburton in Berkshire produced the bodies of a horse, a dog and a man interred together in a pit as a synchronous act of deposition (Grant 1989, 79-86). During work on the extension of the Jubilee Line in East London in the early 1990s, the skeletons of a man and his horse were discovered in a grave, where they were buried in the third century BC (Green 1992a, 99; fig. 5.5) (**20**). While such associations may be interpreted in terms of 'retainer' sacrifice, in which a person's valued possessions accompanied him or her to

20 Burial of a horse, found with its rider during work on the Jubilee Line extension to the London Underground in 1992, at Stratford, Langthorne Abbey, East London. © London Underground & Oxford Archaeological Unit

the Otherworld, it is possible to offer alternative explanations, such as sacrificial practice similar to that attested for Iberia.

> The Vaccaei . . . insult the corpses of such as die from disease as having died a cowardly and effeminate death, and dispose of them by burning; whereas those who laid down their lives in war they regard as noble, heroic and full of valour, and them they cast to the Vultures, believing this bird to be sacred.
> (Aelian *De Natura Animalium* X, 22; trans. Scholfield 1959, 315)

> The Celts who have added to their name that of the Hiberi came also. To these men death in battle is glorious; and they consider it a crime to burn the body of such a warrior; for they believe that the soul goes up to the gods in heaven, if the body is devoured on the field by the hungry vulture.
> (Silius Italicus *Punica* III, 342-348; trans. Duff 1949, 139)

This curious funerary practice among the Celtiberians was recorded by Aelian and Silius Italicus, who describe the great honour done to prestigious persons when they died. These writers allege that such people were laid out in the open air specifically for the vultures to consume, as sacrificial offerings to the celestial spirits. Interestingly, some of the Iron Age polychrome pottery from Celtiberian sites, such as Numancia and Tiermes, appears to depict scenes that could be interpreted in terms of excarnation rituals: they show stylised human figures lying supine, with large birds perched on their bodies (Martínez 1999, fig. on p.13) (**colour plate 3**). One pot depicts a scene in which an excarnation table is inspected by an animal standing on its hind legs; another scene on the same vessel shows a vulture depicted next to a human who appears to be urinating or defecating (Sopeña Genzor 2000): the attitude of the man is commensurate with his role as a victim of sacrificial ritual, in so far as extreme stress causes lack of control over bodily functions. Sepulchral evidence from Numancia and cognate sites appears to bear out excarnatory practice, for several graves have produced cremated bone which is far too light in weight to represent the bones of an entire human body; indeed, the skull and leg-bones seem to have been singled out for formal incineration within the urban complex, the rest of the body perhaps being disposed of elsewhere (Sopeña Genzor 2000). Similar selective processes have been noted in late Iron Age British funerary contexts (Brookes pers. comm.). It is of interest that, in an entirely different context from Iron Age Celtiberia — that of Peruvian Moche ritual (AD 100-800) — ceramic vessels depict the consumption of female sacrificial victims by vultures (E. Hill 2000, 317-26).

Like us but different

The similar manner in which human and animal remains were treated on certain Gallo-British Iron Age sites, like Gournay and Danebury, leads naturally to the issue of surrogacy. The evidence for sacrificial substitution of one human being for another was introduced in chapter 1 and is revisited later (chapter 7). Here, it is relevant to examine the notion that — because of the paradox of similarity and difference — animals were fitting surrogates for human sacrificial victims. For René Girard (1977, 10), there appears to be little basic difference between human and animal sacrifice (**21**), although he fails to acknowledge a fundamental problem in this approach — that of consumption. Generally-speaking, with some very rare exceptions (considered below), human sacrificial victims were not eaten. It is interesting that Porphyry, a Christian philosopher of Syrian origin, born in AD 234, condemned the Greek rite of consuming sacrificial animal-flesh, in a spirited treatise advocating vegetarianism (*De Abstinentia* II, 5-32), because of perceived analogies with cannibalism.

There is a body of Classical and other ancient literature, together with a limited amount of archaeological testimony, for the treatment of sacrificial animals as substitutes for human beings. In Greek religion it was considered important for a beast to be seen to 'consent' to its death, thereby neutralising the negative element of violence involved in its dispatch. This was effected in one of two ways: by offering the victim water, causing it to lower its head to drink, or by sprinkling it with water so that it shook its head; both actions were taken to symbolise assent (Detienne 1989, 9). The treatment of the cattle sacrificially slaughtered at Gournay (**17**) could be interpreted in terms of metaphoric consent, in so far as each beast was killed according to a precise, formulaic ritual, with a blow to the nape of the neck, an action only made possible if the creature's head was lowered (Brunaux 1988, 123; Meniel 1987, 101-43; 1989, 87-97). Of course, such a blow could also be effected by fixing a rope around the animal's head and pulling it downwards.

Certain Classical observers described sacrificial processes which make it clear that animals were sometimes treated as if they were people. In his treatise on animals (*De Natura Animalium* XII, 34), Aelian gives a graphic account of one such ritual, as enacted by the community living on the small Greek island of Tenedos, off the Ionian coast, who dressed up a calf in boots and treated its mother like a post-parturitive woman:

> The people of Tenedos keep a cow that is in calf for Dionysus the man-slayer,
> and as soon as it has calved they tend it as though it were a woman in childbed.
> But they put buskins on the newly-born calf and then sacrifice it . . .

The use of beasts as substitutes for human sacrificial victims is recorded in a range of non-western religious traditions. The most well-known, perhaps, is the episode of Abraham and Isaac in the Old Testament:

> . . . and Abraham built an altar there, and laid the wood in order, and bound
> Isaac, his son, and laid him on the altar upon the wood. And Abraham stretched
> forth his hand, and took the knife to slay his son. And the angel of the Lord
> called unto him out of heaven, and said, Abraham, Abraham: and he said, Here
> am I. And he said, Lay not thine hand upon the lad, neither do thou any thing
> unto him . . . And Abraham lifted up his eyes, and looked, and behold behind
> him a ram caught in a thicket by his horns: and Abraham went and took the
> ram, and offered him up for a burnt offering in the stead of his son.
> (*Genesis* 22, vv 10-13)

Ritual traditions occurring among two southern Sudanese peoples — the Dinka and the Nuer — involve a form of substitution, in so far as, in each instance, animals are used as scapegoats for humans. The Dinka, whose whole economy is based upon cattle, conduct a sacrificial ceremony that involves the physical and verbal abuse of a cow or calf; the creature is insulted and beaten, the curses held symbolically responsible for its death, but it is often killed by the young men of the village, who rush upon the victim, trampling it to death beneath their feet (Girard 1977, 97-100). The Nuer have a similar scapegoat ritual, in which the action of rubbing ash from the family byre on an animal's back metaphorically heaps all the evil thoughts of the community onto the beast (Beattie 1980, 42; Evans-Pritchard 1956). The Sudanese rituals have much in common with the Old Testament scapegoat, an actual goat, which was used by the Israelites to cleanse them of sin:

> And Aaron shall lay both his hands upon the head of the live goat, and confess
> over him all the iniquities of the children of Israel, and all their transgressions
> in all their sins, putting them upon the head of the goat, and shall send him
> away by the hand of a fit man into the wilderness.
> (*Leviticus* 16, 21)

It is worth anticipating later chapters in making brief reference here to the Greek custom of the *pharmakos*, a human scapegoat selected to bear away the impurities of the city, and his southern Gaulish (Massilian) counterpart who, according to literary testimony, was actually put to death after being laden with the evils of the townsfolk (chapter 7).

South India has a complex set of traditions pertaining to human/animal surrogate sacrifice. Bishop Whitehead, a missionary to the region in the early twentieth century, records two forms of this practice. He recounts that when a new ward was opened in a local dispensary attached to the mission at Kalaspad in the Cuddapah district, no patient dared to be the first across the threshold of the new building for fear of being seized as a foundation sacrifice 'because the people imagined that the first to go in would be the needful sacrifice'. The patients' fears were allayed by the conducting of a Christian opening ceremony. Whitehead commented that, had the ward been part of a Hindu hospital, a sheep or goat would have been ritually slaughtered as a substitute for a human sacrifice, to bless the building (Whitehead 1921, 60). Whitehead also recorded the custom of pig-sacrifice at the time of cattle-disease in the Telagu district of South India (**21**). The unfortunate creature was buried up to its neck, a heap of boiled rice placed nearby (perhaps to placate its spirit); then all the cattle of the village were driven over it. Quoting an earlier source, Whitehead refers to the ancestry of this ritual, enacted by the nomadic Lambadis tribe, when human children were the sacrificial victims:

> In former times, the Lambadis, before setting out on a journey, used to procure a little child and bury it in the ground up to its shoulders, and then drive their loaded bullocks over the unfortunate victim. In proportion to the bullocks thoroughly trampling the child to death, so their belief in a successful journey increased.
> (Whitehead 1921, 59, after Thurston 1907, 507)

In certain instances, then, animals could take the place of human sacrificial victims. It is clear that the rituals of South India have some features in common with those of the ancient inhabitants of Tenedos. For Iron Age Britain and Gaul, the evidence is only suggestive. It may be that, just as human victims of ritual killing in antiquity (chapter 7) may have been selected because they were categorised as social outcasts, physically abnormal, foreign or otherwise deviant from the mainstream of the community, so animals could likewise be regarded as similar but sufficiently different from people for them to be considered acceptable surrogates. But for at least one ancient religious tradition, surrogate sacrifice could backfire: in the third century BC, the Carthaginians interpreted their defeat at the hands of the Syracusans as vengeance by their god Kronos for substituting lesser offerings in place of high-born children (Diodorus Siculus XX, 14.6). There is archaeological evidence, too, that young kids or lambs were sometimes substituted for infants in Punic ritual during the first millennium BC (Brown 1991, 13-15) (chapters 3 and 7).

21 Bronze plaque depicting a slain boar, from the first century AD shrine at Muntham Court, Sussex. © Worthing Museum & Art Gallery

Sacred violence

A feature pervading much of the testimony to ritual activity in ancient Europe, associated with the treatment of humans, animals and inanimate objects, is that of extreme force, sometimes far in excess of what was necessary to achieve the desired action of defunctionalising or killing. Thus, weapons — particularly swords and spears — were habitually snapped or savagely bent out of shape, presumably as an act of sacred destruction (**22**). Aggression appears to have been a significant component in certain rites of offering to, or communicating with, the gods. Many of the penetrative weapons deposited at Gournay were tortured into shapes that would have been physically difficult to achieve (**23**) (Lejars 1994, 232-3; Rapin 1988, 47-54); the same is true of spears buried with the high-status dead at Iron Age Numancia, in northern Spain, and in other Celtiberian sites (Martínez 1999, 5-18, fig. on p.6), as if force acted as a transformatory agent in 'sending' the gift to its supernatural recipients. The work of Sue Bridgeford on Bronze Age weapons (Bridgeford 1997) has shown that it is possible to use scientific analysis to distinguish between deliberate destruction and battle-damage.

Mutilation and dismemberment
Exaggerated violence is identifiable in the treatment of animals and humans. An Iron Age cemetery at Tartigny (Oise) in northern Gaul produced a burial of a man interred with a hare, the jaw of a horse and the body of a young dog whose skeleton showed signs of skinning marks and the bones around the stomach bore scoring that suggests the unfortunate creature had been eviscerated (Meniel 1987, 25-31; Green 1992a, 113). Similar violence was used in the treatment of a dog buried in the late Roman cemetery at Lankhills, Winchester, where a decapitated human body was found accompanied by two

22 *Ritually damaged iron helmet, from the 'war-sanctuary' at Ribemont-sur-Ancre (Somme); third/second century BC. Antoine Maillier © Centre archéologique européen du Mont Beuvray*

23 *Ritually bent iron sword, from the 'war-sanctuary' at Gournay (Oise); third/second century BC. Antoine Maillier © Centre archéologique européen du Mont Beuvray*

dogs, of which one had been dismembered, with the ends of its backbone bent and the two ends tied together (Macdonald 1979, 415-24).

Many of the bog-bodies from northern Europe exhibit signs of mutilation or severe trauma before or at the time of death. One of the men deposited at Lindow Moss, the individual known as 'Lindow Man' (Lindow II), suffered three deaths: he sustained two skull-fracturing blows to his head, he was garrotted and his throat was cut; he was then apparently kneed in the back and flung face-down into a marsh-pool, as if the excessive violence was a necessary part of the ritual involved in his sacrificial killing (Stead *et al.* 1986). Similar 'overkill' injuries can be identified on many Danish Iron Age bog-victims: the Grauballe man received such a savage cut to his throat that it all but severed his gullet; the woman from Huldremose (**colour plate 2**) had her right arm cut off before she died;

51

*24 Female bog-body with mutilated face, from Borremose, Denmark;
dated to the later first millennium BC. © Nationalmuseet København*

25 Butchered human pelvis, from disused grain silo at Danebury. © Danebury Trust

another female, from Haraldskaer (Juthe Fen), had a great timber hurdle driven through her knee-cap; yet another, from Borremose, may have had her face deliberately mutilated (Green 1998a, 173) (**24**), a practice noted in the treatment of Romano-British women at Dunstable and Lowbury Hill (Matthews 1981; Philpott 1991; Keys 1992; Green 1995, 154-6). On analogy with the deliberate facial disfigurement of ancient Assyrian images, it may be that these facial mutilations were associated with degradation and denial of identity (Lange 1997, 167-73).

Apart from the bog-bodies, there is a considerable body of British evidence for 'overkill' violence. Several of those buried in the Danebury pits evinced signs of extensive injury. One man (Deposit 30) had been attacked with a blunt instrument, sustaining such a severe blow to his right eye that it must have been badly damaged, maybe even destroyed. The pelvis of another (Deposit 47) had been butchered with a thin sword-like blade; the pelvic girdle and femur-heads were cut from the torso and legs while the flesh was still intact (though whether this occurred as part of the killing-process or post-mortem cannot be ascertained) (Walker 1984, 442-63; Hooper 1984, 463-74) (**25**). Other bodies had been crushed with blocks of flint or chalk (Cunliffe 1993b, 12-13) (**26**). Another Iron Age British hillfort, at Wandlebury in Cambridgeshire, was the scene of some violent behaviour, arguably within a ritualised context, which has certain similarities to Danebury. Once again, pits were the focus of human deposition: one contained the dismembered torso of a six-year-old boy, placed there after his legs had been hacked off; in another pit, dug especially for her, were the remains of an adult female, whose body had

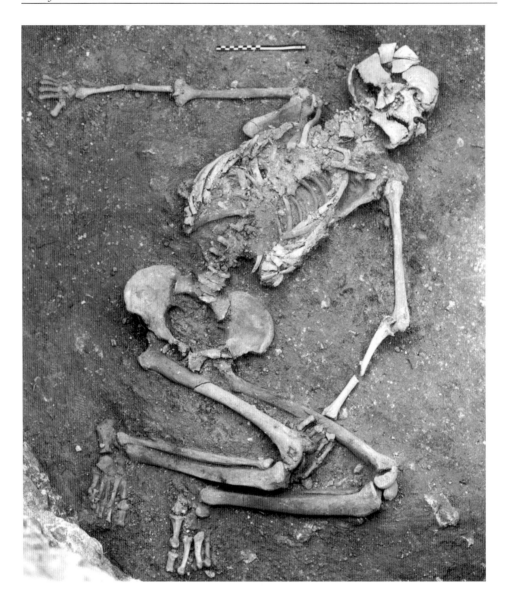

26 Crushed human body, interred in grain silo at Danebury. © Danebury Trust

been (in the words of the excavator) 'drastically mutilated' (Hartley 1957, 15). She had sustained multiple fractures, which could have occurred naturally or have been intentionally inflicted, but her head lay apart from her trunk and both femurs had been deliberately broken off a few centimetres below the pelvis; the pelvic girdle itself had been crushed by a huge block of flint (Hartley 1957, 1-26; Longton 1957, 27). The attention paid to this part of the body both here and at Danebury suggests an association with fertility and reproduction. That ritual disfigurement was not confined to north-west

Europe is demonstrated by its occurrence in the Aegean world: an example comes from the Archaic-Geometric period site of Eleutherna in Crete, where a warrior was cremated in company with a decapitated man of similar age, whose limbs had been mutilated (Stampholidis 1996, 164-73).

A rather different form of ritual violence has been identified in some of the Arras Culture graves of Iron Age Yorkshire (Stead 1991, 33; Brookes 1997, 10; Giles 2001), this time relating to the treatment of the dead. In several tombs, a large number of spears were placed not simply with the body but actually piercing it. In one grave (GS10) 14 spears accompanied the corpse: six had been plunged into the body and the others scattered around it; in another (GS7), four spears had been driven into the waist, one into the chest and three more were found near the skeleton. Similar 'ghost-killing' has been noted at Kirkburn and Rudston, in the same region. The reason for such an idiosyncratic gesture of symbolic violence is not easy to grasp, but it might be associated with a desire for the individual's spirit to stay put and not wander back to disrupt its earthly community, and may present a version of violent treatment similar to the hurdling of bog-victims or the crushing of pit-bodies. But there are alternative explanations for the Arras ritual; collectivism may be involved with, perhaps, a perception that several mourners — kin or comrades-in-arms — had to be metaphorically linked with the deceased's passing, maybe in a ceremony of honour for a valiant warrior, in order to demonstrate his fighting-prowess, in an act of shared remembrance: the spear-shafts would have been clearly visible in the landscape for a time, sticking up from the graves, reminding the community of the dead (Giles 2001). The notion of communal responsibility is sometimes attested within the context of a ritual killing: among some Borneo Dayak groups, everyone has to participate in the sacrificial killing of slaves (Girard 1977, 93). The same kind of perception may explain the curious activity at Folly Lane, St Albans, in the second century AD, when the head of a teenage boy was deliberately defleshed before its deposition in a pit outside a temple (Niblett 1999, 83-8; pers. comm.) The skinning process involved far more cutmarks than would have been necessary to achieve the desired result, perhaps because of the need for several participants to join in the ritual (**27**).

The sanctity of violence

> . . . society is seeking to deflect upon a relatively indifferent victim, a 'sacrificeable' victim, the violence that would otherwise be vented on its own members, the people it most desires to protect.
> (Girard 1977, 4)

In considering the recurrent use of apparently excessive violence in the treatment of sacrificial offerings — particularly of human victims — care must be taken not to impose our own twenty-first-century values and ethics on ancient societies. What seems to us as violence and extreme cruelty may have been perceived very differently in the past, perhaps being regarded within a perspective of positive and beneficial ritual action. The use of force could have been applied in order to generate spiritual energy both to the offering and its recipient. Furthermore, violence is surrounded by drama which may

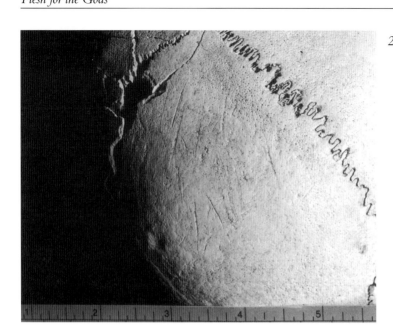

27 Close-up of defleshing-marks on the skull of a Romano-British teenage boy, found at Folly Lane, St Albans.
© English Heritage Photo Library

have been an important component in the performance element of the sacrificial process (Beattie 1980, 29-44).

The quotation above relates to another possible aspect of ritual violence, that of providing a means of controlling society and its natural tendency towards uncontrolled violent behaviour towards fellow humans. In his seminal work *Violence and the Sacred* (1977, 4-17), Girard suggests that violence played a crucial role in sacrifice, deflecting into a controlled, ritualised environment the violence that would otherwise destructively erupt into uncontrolled, chaotic killing. So he sees sacred violence as a healthy antidote to social anarchy, as a neutralising safety-valve and as a means of channelling human behaviour into positive and cathartic cult-activity which released the energy of violence in an acceptable forum and prevented indiscriminate aggression. In interpreting Greek animal-sacrifice, Hélène Foley (1985, 38) makes similar claims: according to her, the ritual surrounding the killing negated its harmful connotations. In any event, violence within ancient European sacrificial contexts appears to have possessed a function over and above the force required to overpower and destroy a sacrificial offering. It is my contention that ritual violence pervaded the gift itself, charging it with energy and enhancing its value both to giver and recipient.

The ultimate violation: ritual cannibalism

It is better to show human sacrifice in the realm of the imaginary past, just as the cannibalism so close to it is best imagined in the far away reaches of myth or in the tales of another people.
(Durand 1989, 91)

Cannibalism is one of the last great taboos.
(Cornwell 1997, 17)

In *Titus Andronicus*, Shakespeare explored the primitive, taboo-ridden and savage world of ancient Rome, where violence, human sacrifice and even cannibalism occurred; in one scene, the limbs of the Gothic prince Alarbus are hacked off during a sacrificial ceremony (Barker 1993, 143). The image presented in *Titus* has an irony in so far as it is the Romans who are depicted as uncouth barbarians, while the Goths are treated as dignified and noble, the precise reverse of the way in which the Classical world of antiquity perceived itself in relation to its 'uncivilised' neighbours.

If human sacrifice is a problematic model for the interpretation of human remains in antiquity, then admittance of cannibalism attracts even greater prejudice among scholars (Taylor 2001c). It is true that archaeological evidence for the ritual consumption of people seldom presents itself, although one or two recent discoveries may force us to rethink the unthinkable. But it is of considerable interest that mention is made of the eating of human sacrificial flesh by Romans, as described in a group of ancient texts. The status of these documents has to be questioned, however, since the descriptions of such practice invariably occur within a highly pejorative context of contempt and the image of social marginality, as if a charge of cannibalism was the greatest possible insult, one which demonstrated the extent of a deviant individual's exclusion from civilised society.

One set of texts describes ritual cannibalism as allegedly enacted in the late Roman Republic by a demagogue called Lucius Sergius Catilina who, disaffected because Cicero defeated him in the consulship elections, whipped up political unrest in Rome and Italy, leading a conspiracy of rebellion against the Roman government in 63 BC. He was ousted and killed the following year at the instigation of Cicero, who castigated him as a 'monster of depravity' (Adkins & Adkins 1994, 14; Rives 1995, 73). In his *Bellum Catilinae* (XXII, 1-2), the Roman writer Sallust recorded that, when the rebel-leader was swearing an oath of loyalty with his fellow conspirators, he passed round bowls of human blood for each of them to drink, presumably as a means of bonding them together. Plutarch and Dio Cassius each mention the episode, but allude to it in the context of human sacrifice:

Taking this man, then, as their leader, the miscreants gave various pledges to one another, one of which was the sacrifice of a man and the tasting of his flesh.
(Plutarch *Life of Cicero* X.4; trans. Perrin 1971b, 107)

For he [Catiline] sacrificed a boy, and after administering the oath over his vitals, ate these in company with the others.
(Dio Cassius *Roman History* XXXVII. 30.3; trans. Cary 1914, 149)

The interest of these texts is not so much that they give an account of ritual cannibalism but that such anecdotes were evidently meant to be believed! Catiline and all he stood for was utterly detested by Cicero, that pillar of conventional Roman political values, who attacked him so bitterly in the Senate. It is appropriate that the opprobrium which the very name of Catiline attracted included accusations of two abhorrent practices: human sacrifice and cannibalism.

Another group of ancient documents was compiled within the context of the embryonic Christian communities struggling to assert themselves in the pagan, often hostile, milieu of the second and third centuries AD. Certain early Christian authors, particularly those of North African origin, responded to charges, levelled at them by ignorant and scornful pagans, that the followers of Christ ate human flesh and drank human blood, in a wilfully manipulated travesty of the Eucharist. The Christian writers retaliated by means of 'retorsion' counter-arguments, which turned the same charge against their accusers, namely that it was the pagans themselves who indulged in such abhorrent practices as human sacrifice and ritual cannibalism. In the AD 150s, Justin Martyr (*Apologeticus* II) retorted that the Christians would not behave with such fortitude if they ate human flesh, as accused (Rives 1995, 74). Instead, affirmed Justin, it was the non-Christians who were guilty of such atrocities. Minucius Felix, who lived during the late second and early third centuries AD, wrote an anti-pagan document, called *Octavius*, a fictitious dialogue in which the eponymous Christian Octavius presents the case for the faith to the pagan Caecilius, who responds in kind. In denouncing the Roman gods Octavius, like Justin, turns the charge of sacrificial cannibalism against his opponent (*Octavius* IX.5; Rives 1995, 74).

Both groups of literature — the first-century BC diatribes against Catiline and the imperial denunciations of paganism — have in common their treatment of human sacrifice, and particularly ritual consumption of human flesh, with horror: such practices were beyond the pale, inhuman and utterly barbaric. None of the texts necessarily has any truth in it whatsoever. But what of the ancient world outside the Mediterranean littoral? It is interesting that virtually none of the many literary references, by Greek and Roman authors, to human sacrifice in Gaul make any mention of cannibalistic behaviour. One exception is Pliny the Elder (*Natural History* XXX, 3), who spoke of the Gaulish belief that killing men for religious purposes and consuming their flesh was regarded as beneficial. He comments that this uncivilised practice was prohibited by Rome from the reign of the emperor Tiberius (Simón 1999, 2). In a casual statement, Strabo alludes to anthropophagy as occurrent in Ireland, in a — perhaps — invented narrative designed to illustrate the extreme barbarism of people on the very edge of the world:

> Besides some small islands round about Britain, there is also a large island, Ierne, which stretches parallel to Britain on the north, its breadth being greater than its length. Concerning this island I have nothing to tell, except that its inhabitants are more savage than the Britons since they are man-eaters as well as herb-eaters.
> (*Geographia* IV, 5, 4; trans. Jones 1923, 259)

There is very little archaeological testimony to the consumption of human flesh in the European Iron Age. However, investigations in the grounds of Eton College during construction of a new rowing-lake in early 2000 revealed traces of ritual activity dating to the first millennium BC, which *may* have included cannibalism. There is evidence that the bodies of the dead were interred in water following their excarnation. The remains of about 20 individuals have been discovered, some apparently deposited, with complete pots, on sandbanks in the ancient course of the Thames; timber uprights had been erected near these banks, as if, perhaps, for mooring funerary boats. On examining the Iron Age skeletal material, Prof. Margaret Cox of the University of Bournemouth, a human-bone expert, identified cutmarks on some of the limb-bones commensurate with butchery and the smashing of the bone-ends to extract the nutritious marrow (Charter 2000, 19). The site has not yet been published but Prof. Cox (pers. comm.) is fairly certain that something odd was happening to the Iron Age dead of Eton.

A second, even more recent, British discovery suggests that human bones were occasionally exploited within the context of disposal. In September 2000, the author was invited to join a *Time Team* investigation of a 'swallet' (a sink-hole cave) called Fishmonger's Hole, at Alveston near Bristol. Human remains from many periods have repeatedly found their way into these swallets, but the Alveston assemblage may be special: the bones of at least eight adults, together with about the same number of dogs and a small quantity of other animal remains, have been recovered by cavers working in chambers more than 20m below ground, beneath a twisting vertical shaft. Three bone-samples (animal and human) have given consistent radiocarbon dates centred *c.*30 BC-AD 55. The assemblage may not, of course, be the result of a single episode of deposition; it is not possible to be certain that the dogs and people were interred in association, and indeed some of the humans and animals might have fallen down the hole by accident and died there, but the number of both people and dogs at least raises the question of deliberate disposal. There is abundant evidence, in later prehistoric and Roman south-west Britain, for cult-activity associated with dogs: in the Roman town of Caerwent, the skulls of five dogs were found placed at the bottom of a deep well (Green 1976, Ross 1968, 262); not far away at Lydney is the great sanctuary to the Romano-British god Nodens, to whom worshippers dedicated several images of dogs (Wheeler & Wheeler 1932, pl. XXVI). The curious treatment of two of the human bones from Alveston deserves close attention: the cranium of a girl (**28**), about 16-18 years old, shows signs of injury, there being a central hole with radiating cracks, as if she had been poleaxed; and a human femur had apparently been cracked open in antiquity, signifying an intention to extract the marrow (**colour plate 4**). Is it possible that — as may have occurred at Eton — people in Gloucestershire during the late Iron Age (or even in the early Roman period) were occasionally killing and consuming ritual victims? There is other evidence for the 'modification' of human bones on British Iron Age sites that might reflect anthropophagy: for instance, a site at Warly Hill, Coveney, in the Cambridgeshire Fens produced 17 fragments of human bone including two bearing butchery marks; the epiphyses of one femur had been sawn off, leaving the shaft intact (Luff 1996, 5).

If practised in European antiquity, the reasons for sacrificial cannibalism may be very varied, ranging from insult to honour, from expressions of contempt to the desire to retain and recycle the essence of kin or hero. There is solid anthropological testimony to the notion of ritual consumption of human flesh, as a response to a variety of circumstances, in addition to archaeological evidence, notably from the American South-West. In their investigations of ancient Anasazi communities within a region encompassing Arizona, N.

28 Cranium of a young woman, who suffered a depressed skull-fracture and whose head was placed deep in a swallet-hole at Alveston, Bristol around 30 BC. © Professor Mick Aston

Mexico, parts of Colorado and Utah, the Turners (1999) have identified traces of ritual anthropophagy that allegedly occurred over four centuries, from *c.*AD 900, particularly among communities inhabiting the Chaco Canyon. Here, a distinction is recognised between endo-cannibalism (the consumption of kin-flesh) and exo-cannibalism (the eating of foreigners or outsiders) which is hostile, something enacted in the context of enmity and warfare. It is suggested that certain warrior-priests from peoples practising sacrificial anthropophagy in Mexico during the period AD 650-1200 moved northwards, when their old theocracies were collapsing, to dominate the small farming communities, including the Anasazi, using these fearsome cult-practices as a means of terror-control over the population (Turner & Turner 1999, 1-10, 459-84). Certainly, ethnohistorical documents compiled by the Conquistadores record ritual cannibalism of sacrificial victims in collective ceremonies, whose purpose was to absorb the essential elements of the dead (Parker Pearson 1999, 52). An Aztec term *tlacatlaolli* ('man corn') refers to a sacred meal of sacrificed human meat cooked with maize (Fernandéz 1992; Turner & Turner 1999, 1-10). There are some compelling, though highly controversial, archaeological indicators that the ritual consumption of human flesh did occur among these prehistoric American groups: in Arizona, for instance, sites (like Houck K) have produced not only suggestively cutmarked human bones but also the identification of human proteins as residues in cooking-vessels and in human faeces (Diamond 2000, 25-6). But we need to be cautious in our interpretations: recent claims for anthropophagy amongst seventeenth-century Hopi, in the American South-West, may be refuted; the remains of people in smashed-up bone-heaps may, instead, represent the destroying of witches (Parker Pearson pers. comm.).

Numerous ethnographic reports of ritual anthropophagy demonstrate something of the broad range of traditions in which such practice is said to have taken place. Among the Yanomami of Amazonia, endo-cannibalism occurs as part of funerary ceremonies, in which the ashes of cremated corpses are ground into powder, mixed into plantain soup and drunk by kin and friends from gourd-bowls. The ideas prompting such custom embrace both the recycling of the vital essence and remembering the dead (Chagnon 1992, cited in Parker Pearson 1999, 50). An apparently similar rite is allegedly enacted in parts of Hindu India, in the context of rituals associated with the god Shiva, in which the ground-up remains of a sacrificed pregnant Brahmin woman are said to be consumed by the presiding priest (Foulston 1999, 312). But this chapter ends with a very different account from the Pacific, a description of insult-cannibalism among the Polynesian communities of the Marquesas, recorded by Robert Louis Stevenson in the 1880s. The following is a quotation from his book *In the South Seas*:

> We had been but three days in Anaho when we received the visit of the chief of Hatiheu, a man of weight and fame, late leader of a war upon the French, late prisoner in Tahiti, and the last eater of long-pig in Nuku-Hiva. Not many years have elapsed since he was seen striding on the beach of Anaho, a dead man's arm across his shoulder. 'So does Kooamua to his enemies!' he roared to the passers by, and took a bite from the raw flesh.
> (Bell 1994, 57)

3

Rites of fire

And he shall flay the burnt offering, and cut it into his pieces. and the sons of Aaron the priest shall put fire upon the altar, and lay the wood in order upon the fire . . .
(Leviticus 1. 5-7)

Fire and blood, the themes of this and the following chapter, share certain features: both are transformative symbols, evocative both of destruction and of the life-force. Fire transforms (**colour plate 5**) and consumes by turning matter into ash; blood itself alters at death (or exposure to the air) and is changed from a flowing liquid to a viscous and finally a dried substance after death (or in the healing process). Fire and blood are both red and, in many religious traditions, both blood and fire are related to purification, fertility, the vibrancy of being, ambiguities of life and death, and solar symbolism (Berlin & Kay 1969; Aldhouse-Green 2000, 235; Jones 2000, 257-9; Trevarthen 2000, 295-315). The cosmologies of Baktaman communities in New Guinea place red at the apex of sacral significance, making a symbolic association between fire, red and masculinity (Tilley 1999, 30). Both blood and fire are linked with violence and the inspiration of fear; warfare often involves both mass bloodletting and destruction of settlements and property by burning.

By its very nature, the sacrifice of human beings by fire is seldom recognisable in the archaeological record. The whole point of fire-sacrifice is its utter consumption, leaving nothing but ash or small pieces of calcined bone, sufficient (in the words of the late Professor Richard Atkinson) 'to fill a bowler hat'. However, the ritual killing of people by fire in antiquity is well-documented in contemporary literature, and it is to literary sources that we must turn for evidence of holocaust (from the Greek term *holokauston*, meaning the complete burning of a sacrifice) in ancient Europe. It is also possible to learn something of the perceptions underpinning such ritual activity from analogous practice elsewhere in antiquity and from specific anthropological comparanda.

The basic difference between fire-sacrifice and any other form of ritual killing, including penetrative death, concerns the 'biography' of the body at and after death. Fire causes the virtually-complete disappearance of the victim, whose vaporised remains rise in the smoke to the upper air (where the divine recipients of the sacrifice might be perceived to dwell); rites not involving fire preserve the body — in some form — to be disposed of by means of further ritual: burial, exposure or consignment to watery places. These fundamental differences in treatment of victims probably relate, in part, to specific perceptions about cosmologies and beliefs concerning the supernatural and in part, perhaps, to ideas about the spirit powers for whom the sacrificial gift is offered. It may even be that rank is sometimes associated with methods of body-disposal, whether or not a sacrifice is intended. Excavators of the Catuvellaunian nobleman, whose remains were cremated in about AD 55 at Folly Lane, St Albans (Herts) argue that the contemporary inhumation of three women in the ditch of the surrounding enclosure might be evocative of their comparatively lowly status, in contrast to the rich cremation inside the enclosure. The inference is that the women were attendant sacrifices, slaughtered in order to accompany their lord to the Otherworld (Niblett 1999, 17-21). Catuvellaunian ritual tradition of the mid-first century AD may have involved belief that high-ranking deceased individuals were deemed worthy of being transported skywards, whilst lesser people were consigned to the chthonic regions. Similar perceptions and patterns of behaviour may possibly be identified in Iron Age Gaul, for instance at Acy-Romance (Ardennes), where rich cremations form a marked contrast to the 'boxed' inhumations of young men without grave-goods (Lambot 1998; 2000) (chapter 6), or the two discrepant burials at the Archaic site of Eleutherna in Crete (Stampholidis 1996, 164-73) (chapter 7). In certain traditions, there is a perception that reduction to smoke is the most efficacious way of transmitting an object to the deity (Bourdillon 1980, 17).

Sacred fire

> . . . and the priest shall burn it upon the altar, upon the wood that is upon the
> fire: it is a burnt sacrifice, an offering made by fire . . .
> (*Leviticus* 1.17)

In the Madurai district of Tamilnadu in south India, a village goddess, Mariyamman, is venerated; every year, her worshippers celebrate the *pookooli* or fire-walk festival (**colour plate 6**) in which young and old, women and men, walk on a bed of hot coals, prepared outside her temple, as a mark of devotion. In a state of rapturous stupor, many participants feel no pain; in fact they liken the experience to that of walking on flowers: hence the word *pookooli*, a Tamil word meaning 'pit of flowers'. The fire-walk is regarded as an act of self-sacrifice (Foulston 1999, 285-90) and is practised elsewhere in India, for instance at Khurdapur in Orissa.

On the final Sunday of winter, the inhabitants of Minsk, capital city of Belarus, celebrate the festival of the 'seeing off of the Maslenitsa'. A female scarecrow is dressed in black garments and paraded around the city before being burnt in a huge ceremonial bonfire, while celebrants feast and make merry. The festival embraces a blend of pagan and Christian traditions, but behind the custom is the symbolic need to banish the cold weather and usher in the warm, fertile springtime (Bridgewater 2000). Cold is perceived as an enemy and is combated with its antithesis, fire; the Maslenitsa is a substitute human victim, a scapegoat blamed for winter's grip and annihilated by all-consuming fire. The black clothes signify the absence of the sun's light, and the entire ceremony represents the catharsis engendered by the end of hardship and want.

The tradition described above has resonances with what is probably a very ancient magical rite that finds parallels in many circumpolar societies whose main concern is the return of warmth and sunlight after the deprivations of dark winter. For northern peoples, fire was the terrestrial representative of the sun. In ancient Greek religion, too, fire created a link between heaven and earth: indeed, in a myth explaining the origin of fire as a human tool, the Titan demi-god Prometheus (half-mortal, half-divine) stole solar fire from the sky-god Zeus in order to foster the development of the human race (Servius on Virgil *Eclogues* VI, 42; Vellacott 1961, 9). Hesiod (*Theogony* lines 540-69) explains the original cheating of Zeus by Prometheus, who sacrificed a great ox, distributed the meat to mortals while wrapping the bones in fat and offering it as meat to the gods. In vengeance for Prometheus's insult and trickery, Zeus withheld fire from humans (Vernant 1989, 21-3). In *Prometheus Bound*, the Greek playwright Aeschylus gives these words to Strength, addressed to Hephaestus, the Greek god of fire and smithing:

Hephaestus, do your duty . . .
It was your treasure that he stole, the flowery splendour
Of all-fashioning fire, and gave to men — an offence
Intolerable to the gods, for which he now must suffer,
Till he be taught to accept the sovereignty of Zeus
And cease acting as champion of the human race.
(Aeschylus *Prometheus Bound*, trans. Vellacott 1961, 20)·ᵛ

Prometheus explains how he stole Zeus's celestial fire:

For I am he
Who hunted out the source of fire, and stole it, packed
In pith of a dry fennel-stalk.
(*Ibid.*, 24)

The fire-festivals of pre-Christian Europe, of which the Belarussian custom is one example, recurrently exhibit this close linkage between fire and the sun; such ceremonies magically induced the energisation of the sun by reproducing it on earth. A summer solstice bonfire festival still takes place in Finland according to an ancient, later Christianised tradition which evolved because of a perception of the sun to be at its weakest at the turn of the seasons (Green 1993, pl. 415). Saami tradition in northern Scandinavia includes purificatory rites associated with bear ceremonies that involve celebrants leaping over bonfires (Bäckman 1981, 50). The ninth-century AD Irish commentator Cormac records an Insular transhumant ceremony at the festival of Beltane, on 1 May, where druids drove herds of cattle in between two bonfires in a purificatory rite prior to the movement of the animals to summer pastures (Green 1992a, 15; 1997, 35) (**colour plate 7**). Indeed, the Irish mythic texts make several allusions to Beltane bonfires. Pagan midsummer sun/fire festivals gradually gave place to Christian celebrations associated with St John the Baptist, who was born at the summer solstice and whose birth was commemorated with bonfires until the beginning of the nineteenth century (Green 1991, 108; Hole 1950, 78).

Bonfire rites combined religion with pragmatism: they celebrated the sun on earth by means of its replication by fire, but the rich ash created by such conflagrations improved the fertility of the nearby fields. The Irish goddess Brigit, transmuted into a saint in the early Christian period, was closely linked with fire-symbolism: the flames, sparks, ash and smoke of her sacred fires all had significance; the hearth symbolised domesticity; the embers and ash spread on the fields were claimed as fertilising trophies from her midsummer bonfires (Ó Catháin 1992, 12, 24). The perceived relationship between fire and life is witnessed in other religions, too. In Greek religion, the word for sacrificial fire — *thusia* — conjures images of raging, violent, life-imbued fire (Yerkes 1953, 92-3). In modern Hindu funerary practice, the ritual of cremation on the banks of the sacred Ganges river, followed by the scattering of the ashes on the water, is viewed as a self-sacrifice to Agni, the god of sacred fire, to enable the fires of creation to be rekindled and transformative rebirth to take place in the next world (Parker Pearson 1999, 50, 144); other

Vedic Hindu recreation-ritual also involves fire-sacrifice to Agni, a rite supervised by the Brahmins (Klostermaier 1998, 43; Staal 1983) (**colour plate 8**).

Of mounds and wicker men

A holocaust is above all an act of homage.
(de Vaux 1964, 37)

The Gauls believe the power of the immortal gods can be appeased only if one human life is exchanged for another, and they have sacrifices of this kind regularly established by the community. Some of them have enormous images made of wickerwork the limbs of which they fill with living men; these are set on fire and the men perish, enveloped in the flames.
(Caesar *de Bello Gallico* VI, 16)

We are told of still other kinds of sacrifices . . . having built a *colossus* of straw and wood, they throw into the *colossus* cattle and animals of all sorts and human beings, and then make a burnt offering of the whole thing.
(Strabo *Geographia* IV, 4, 5; trans. Chadwick 1966, 92-93) (**colour plate 9**)

It is almost certain that both Julius Caesar and Strabo (who were near-contemporaries), in reporting on Gallic ritual practices, trawled the writings of the earlier Syrian Greek philosopher Poseidonios (*c.*135-50 BC) who travelled widely in Gaul (Chadwick 1966, 6; Tierney 1959-60, 189-275). Nora Chadwick suggests that Strabo's victims did not necessarily perish in the flames (1966, 21), arguing that the text is ambiguous and that the bodies were torched post-mortem. But Caesar's account is unequivocal in its description of slaughter by burning. Indeed, Caesar's testimony is far more informative, in many respects, than Strabo's, raising some complex issues. His comment that the practice of human sacrifice *regularly* occurred in Gaul in the mid-first century BC is interesting: it contradicts Diodorus Siculus's remark that it was only on very special occasions that people were sacrificed in Gaul, for divinatory purposes (V, 31). Caesar also appears to allude to the practice of substitution, the exchange of one human life for another and the need to ransom certain individuals by selecting others to take their place as gifts to the supernatural powers.

The consumption of victims by fire is different from any other kind of sacrificial rite in so far as fire leaves little trace of the offering, thus effecting almost total separation from the earthly world. Furthermore, the flames, smoke and ashes rise towards the sky. It might, therefore, be that burnt offerings were aimed primarily at celestial divinities. Indeed, an early medieval glossator on Lucan's epic civil war poem *The Pharsalia*, writing in Bern in the ninth century AD, makes a connection between the fire-sacrifice of people in Gaul and the thunder-god Taranis: 'Taranis Dis Pater is appeased in this way among the Gauls: some men are cremated in a wooden trough' (Zwicker 1934, 49-50; trans. M.E. Raybould), Taranis being a deity of whom mention is made in Lucan's original text (I, 422-65). There is epigraphic evidence for the veneration of a god named Taranis in Roman Gaul, the Rhineland and Britain (**29**) (Green 1982, 37-44); the etymology of his name links him firmly with thunder and — by implication — lightning, and thus fire-sacrifice would be an entirely appropriate offering to a divinity whose power was manifested in noise, light and heat.

A neglected aspect of the wicker man sacrifice is the anthropomorphic form of the cage. This clearly carries meaning in relation to the human sacrificial rite itself, perhaps serving to reinforce and emphasise the nature of the sacrifice: the victims perished in the flames, as did the wicker image itself: the image was a human being writ large perhaps, as Tilley suggests (1999, 38), acting as a metaphor for society itself. In this context it is interesting to note that a custom of building and burning straw men has been recorded as taking place in modern Christian Europe at spring festivals associated with welcoming the returning sun after winter and the celebration of Easter (rather in the manner of the Belarus festival of the Maslenitsa). In Germany, such images were constructed and burnt at Easter-time; they were called 'Judas Men' (Frazer 1922, 614-15), and were clearly associated with the perception of Jesus's fallen disciple as a scapegoat for sin, winter, darkness and the sterility of cold.

The totality of a fire-sacrifice, like the gigantic wicker image recorded by Caesar and Strabo, has further aspects, in terms of experience of those witnessing the rite. The spectacle and sound of such a conflagration, the roar and crackle of the flames, the screams of the victims, the crash of the falling edifice, the leaping tongues of fire, sparks, smoke, the smell of burning flesh, smoke-inhalation, the mirage effect of heated air and the images created by the flames themselves, would all contribute to the endowment of the image with a spurious life of its own. The spectators would, perhaps, undergo a transcendental catharsis followed by a sense of euphoria engendered by the stimulation of all the senses, together with a collective, shared experience in which societal stress was channelled and relieved (Hamilton 1995, 130). The memory of such an event would remain in people's consciousness, and the very absence of material remains — apart from a blackened area for a while — might contribute to the power of remembrance and to the crucial role of memory that the community's bards (or druids) would possess. Incidentally, people may well have linked the increased fertility of the ash-covered fire-site with the power of the sacrifice and its divine recipient.

Although there can be no unequivocal archaeological evidence for the immolation of human victims in burning wicker men, there is some sign of large-scale ritual use of fire, which may share some elements with such practice. In October 1997, archaeologists working at the Austrian town of Leonding excavated a deep pit, dating to *c*.200 BC, containing the remains of humans and animals, all apparently subjected to burning. Skeletal analysis revealed that all 12 people had suffered from the same hereditary deformity of their jawbones, causing severe speech impediments. The site has been interpreted as the focus of a grisly sacrificial ritual, repeated three times every two or three years, in which humans and beasts were tethered to a wooden device suspended above the pit, which was then set on fire so that the entire edifice, with its hapless victims, collapsed into the hole (Simón 1999, 10; Pertlwieser 1998, 3-4).

29 *Altar dedicated to the Gallo-Roman thunder-god Taranucnus, from Böckingen (Germany).*
© *Württembergisches Landesmuseum, Stuttgart*

Certain monuments belonging to Iron Age Britain and Ireland appear to have been subjected to deliberate, probably symbolic, firing. This is what seems to have happened at Navan Fort in Co. Armagh in the early first century BC. Navan is almost certainly to be identified with the royal Ulster site of Emhain Macha, recorded in early Irish historical and mythic texts, such as the Ulster Cycle of prose tales, dating to the twelfth century AD in written form, though retaining resonances of earlier, pre-Christian material. Archaeological investigations at Navan during the 1970s revealed a curious sequence of events associated with the construction and almost immediate destruction by fire of a great monument (Lynn 1992, 33-57). A multi-ring oaken structure, with a colossal central timber upright, 40m in diameter — too large for a permanent roof — was erected soon after 95/94 BC (dendrochronological date), when the trees were felled. A carefully built cairn of limestone blocks was then packed inside the wooden structure, forming a radial pattern that respected the timber alignments of the building itself. The stones of the cairn showed some signs of weathering, as though they had, perhaps, been removed from existing monuments rather than freshly quarried for use at Navan. A few human bones, including a clavicle, had been deposited among the cairn stones. The building of the wooden structure and the cairn took a considerable amount of time, effort and person-power, so the next episode in the site's history is, on the face of it, inexplicable: the entire edifice, wooden uprights, the cairn and a layer of red clay placed over the surrounding ditch was apparently deliberately set alight and razed to the ground. Dudley Waterman, the principal excavator of Navan, found charred twigs and straw which he interpreted as the remnants of heaps of kindling piled up against the outer timber wall to get the fire going. These finds, together with the thoroughness of the destruction, argue for intent. The final incident in this strange sequence of events was the careful construction of an earthen mound, made of soils and turves of varied types, probably derived from several different locations and environments.

'Deliberate burning brings us into the realms of transformation, purification and sacrifice' (Lynn 1992, 40). Scrutiny of the building's 'biography' may give clues as to its purpose, from its inception, as a sacrificial offering. It appears that the floor of the wooden structure was never finished, as though it was not intended for use; neither was there any other sign that the building had ever hosted any activity. However, the multi-ring pattern of uprights had been planned to a specific formula, evidently involving some form of processional way (although this may have been intended for use by the gods rather than by human worshippers). Taken as a whole, the cumulative evidence points to a high degree of symbolic behaviour involving the entire sequence of events and the environs of the 'sanctuary'. A great deal of human investment was dedicated to the construction and destruction of the Navan monument. Chris Lynn's idea that the building was sacrificed 'as an investment in the sacredness of the place' (1992, 40) has some credibility. Ideologies of place, memory, the ancestors and collective endeavour may have all been involved. The reuse of cairn stones from earlier monuments, and the purposeful variety of mound material, together with the human bones, all argue for specialness, highly formalised and well-orchestrated ritual action. It may even be that the fragments of human body represent a token human sacrifice, perhaps that of the community's ancestors, in order to give greater currency to the offering and a more empowered sense of linkage between the community and the spirit-world. There appear to be elements in common with Caesar's wicker man.

Navan is unique in the Iron Age of the British Isles. However, it is possible to point to some analogous events in later British prehistory. In the far west of Wales, a small but well-defended hillfort was built at Castell Henllys in North Pembrokeshire, the first major stone phase of which dates to the fifth century BC. There is evidence that the gateway, consisting of massive stone walls, a large timber tower and great wooden gates equipped with two pairs of guard-chambers, was — after a period of disuse — deliberately destroyed by an intense fire, possibly in some kind of ritual event (Mytum 1999, 166).

At first glance, it is difficult to justify making connections between Classical literary accounts of burning wicker men filled with human victims in Gaul, the destruction by fire of Navan Fort in Northern Ireland (both during the first century BC) and the deliberate firing of parts of highly visible monuments in the fifth century. But without seeking to establish direct linkages, in each instance the purposeful use of fire for controlled, public and arguably ritual transformation and reduction of these landmarks was involved, all conforming — loosely, at any rate — to the notion of holocaust, where the nature of the offering and, possibly, its recipient, dictated the use of fire and the combination of spectacle and rapid destruction. Susanne Küchler (1997, 39-60) reminds us that symbolic concepts involving 'riddance' may be highly meaningful in particular traditional cosmologies, whether such discard is associated with decomposition, burial or violent fire-damage. Such destruction may be related to non-reciprocity, non-exchange. Küchler argues that once something charged with metaphoric meaning is removed from the 'exchange reservoir', it may become significant in new ways. Riddance may be 'central to sacrifice'. In such a framework of symbolism, consumption by fire may be perceived as a powerful act of sacrificial ritual, a public, collective display of riddance, transformation and sacred memory (Küchler 1997, 39-60; R. Bradley 2000, 37). In this respect, it is noteworthy that some Late Bronze Age weapons from British sites were ritually destroyed by being incinerated (Bridgeford 1997).

An evocative act of riddance by fire is chronicled by Pausanias (*Description of Greece* IX, 3-4), who provides an account of a holocaust, which took place in the Boeotian town of Plataia. Here, a local festival was associated with a particular stretch of oak woodland, where especially large trees grew. The celebrations commenced with the boiling of joints of meat which were then hung in the branches; the tree in which crows first alighted to feed on the meat was felled and an image carved from the timber; it was then decorated, set on a cart and drawn to the summit of Mount Cithaeron, where an altar was built of wooden blocks, piled with brushwood and cattle sacrificed to the celestial deities Zeus and Hera. At the climax of the festival, the altar, wagon, image and animal victims were utterly consumed in a great conflagration (Jones trans. 1965, 183-7; R. Bradley 2000, 24) (**30**).

30 Sacrificial scene depicting 'shamanistic' beings attacking a central human figure, perhaps associated with worship of the sun-god, from Camonica Valley, North Italy. © Paul Jenkins

Fire sacrifice in the ancient Near East

> And they have built the high places of Baal, which are in the Valley of the son
> of Hinnom, to cause their sons and their daughters to pass through the fire
> unto Molech; which I commanded them not, neither came it into my mind,
> they they should do this abomination, to cause Judah to sin.
> (*Jeremiah* 32, v. 35)

Although, in the absence of contemporary literature (apart from that written by Classical writers late in the period), we possess only very limited evidence for fire-ritual in the European Iron Age, other traditions of antiquity do provide much clearer information concerning human sacrifice by fire, namely those of the ancient Near East: Palestine,

Phoenicia and Mesopotamia, though even testimony from these places is by no means unequivocal. The first two regions had close links with each other, as we shall see.

Various episodes in the Old Testament present human sacrifice as shocking, exceptional and associated with extreme crisis, frequently involving the son or daughter of the supplicant, and thus presumably related to substitution for self-sacrifice (see chapter 1). Two examples serve to illustrate this pattern of 'ransom', each involving holocaust. The first incident concerns a battle between the Moabites and the Israelites: Moab was under siege and, in desperation, the Moabite king Mesha offered his son as a burnt offering, setting fire to him on the city-ramparts, in full view of the besieging army; the Israelite forces were so horrified by the spectacle that they abandoned the blockade and fled in terror (de Vaux 1964, 62; 2 *Kings* 3, 27), presumably partly because of fear of ritual pollution. The second episode involving the sacrificer's offspring is the account of Jephthah, narrated in *Judges* (11, 38-40), and is again associated with battle, but this time linked to a vow. Jephthah promised Yahweh that he would offer as a holocaust the first person he encountered should he return home victorious: his beloved daughter ran to meet him, but Jephthah kept his pledge. This tale has strong resonances with several incidents recorded in Classical literature, in which children are recorded as falling victim to fulfil their fathers' sacred vows (chapter 7). Of course, the most famous incident in the Old Testament involving human sacrifice is the account of Abraham and Isaac (*Genesis* 22.2), once again concerning a child. God commanded Abraham to sacrifice his only son Isaac as a burnt offering upon a sacred mountain, as a test of Abraham's obedience. As the father lifted the knife against his son, God stayed his hand, and a ram caught by his horns in a nearby thicket was sacrificed in the boy's place.

A common thread running through Old Testament sacrificial ritual is the significance of fire, which was laden with religious symbolism: 'to burn something was to return it to God' (I. Bradley 1995, 9-10). Fire was associated with atonement for sin and purification. In the Levitical religious system, a burnt animal-sacrifice was a substitute for human lives forfeit through sin, and thus effectively ransomed those on whose behalf the sacrifice was made (Jenson 1995, 25-40). In the case of Jephthah's daughter (which was, incidentally, contrary to the Levitical law whereby only male creatures could be burnt as offerings), the girl was a votive gift; the Moabite king's son seems, by contrast, to have acted — perhaps unwittingly — as an aversion sacrifice. Fire could also — as illustrated in the Biblical story of Moses and the Burning Bush that was not consumed (*Exodus* 3.2) — represent theophany, the visible manifestation of God himself (Day 1989, 82-5).

The Old Testament contains repeated references to a divinity named Molech, one of which associates him with Sheol, the Judaic underworld (*Isaiah* 57.9; Day 1989, 82-5). Molech (or Moloch) was a Syro-Palestinian deity, one of a series of Baals, who demanded of his worshippers the burnt offering of humans, mainly infants or children. References in *Jeremiah* (32.35; 7,. 31), *Leviticus* (for instance 18.21) and *Kings* (2 *Kings* 23.10) represent the veneration of Molech as an unofficial, irregular and subversive popular cult which found a place in Jerusalem through influence deriving from Canaanite religion during the eighth-seventh centuries BC (de Vaux 1964, 73-5;

Selman 1995, 88-104), and that was denounced by both religious law and the Old Testament prophets. Fire-sacrifices to Molech occurred at Gehenna, in the Valley of Hinnom, at the 'tophet' immediately to the south of the city (Day 1989, 82-5; Brown 1991, 14-15). A *tophet* is an incinerator, described in *Isaiah* (30.33).

Possibly associated with the Old Testament accounts of child-sacrifice to Molech is the epigraphic evidence from Mesopotamia, relating to the burning of the victim and mentioning the god Adad as the recipient. Two inscriptions from Upper Mesopotamia dating to the tenth century BC, found in the remains of the royal palace of Kapara at Tell Halâf, allude to the punishment meted out to anyone who defaced the name of the royal family: the burning of seven of the blasphemer's sons (de Vaux 1964, 60). Assyrian contracts dated to the seventh century BC include a curious penal clause to the effect that in addition to the usual fines of gold and silver exacted as penalties for violating such legal pledges, the malefactor 'will burn his eldest son in the sacred precinct of Adad' (*ibid.*, 59).

Both the Judaic and Assyrian evidence are probably to be linked with the sacrificial rites of another ancient culture, that of Phoenicia, with its centre at the North African city-state of Carthage. There is a mass of persuasive evidence, both in the literature and the archaeology, attesting to fire-sacrifices (either burnt alive or first stabbed to death) of children to Molech or his Punic equivalent Kronos-Saturn (these two names originally belonging to ancient Greek and Italian deities). In North Africa, Saturn was worshipped as an earth and underworld divinity. Phoenician burnt offerings of children seem to have taken place over a long period of time during the first millennium BC: at Carthage itself, it was practised from *c.*750-146 BC (when the city was destroyed by the Romans). Sacrificial cremations of infants, between six months and three years old, were interred beneath mounds in cemeteries known as *tophets* (after the fire-sacrifice site outside Jerusalem), at Carthage, Hadrumetum (Tunisia), Cirta (Algeria), Motya and Lillibeum (Sicily), Tharros (Sardinia) and elsewhere in the southern Mediterranean. Sometimes the calcined bones of children were mixed with those of young lambs, kids or birds. Archaeologists distinguish these tophets from non-sacrificial burial-grounds because cremation was always practised, whereas children in 'normal' cemeteries were inhumed and their remains were, in general, treated with less formalised ceremony than those of adults. This was not the case in the tophets where child-cremations were placed in urns, frequently surmounted by commemorative stone plaques bearing inscriptions and sometimes carved scenes (**31 & 32**) (Brown 1991, 14-55). At Hadrumetum, excavation of a sanctuary unearthed what has been identified as a fire-pit with evidence of burning, perhaps the site of a fire-sacrifice (de Vaux 1964, 81).

Cremation alone provides no evidence for child-sacrifice by fire. But epigraphy and iconography on burial monuments, together with ancient texts, present a clearer picture. The stone tablets may yield valuable chronological clues: in the late third century BC, Cirta was ruled by the Numidian king Massinissa, an enemy of Carthage: nine stelai from the tophet here bear inscriptions mentioning the king and his sons by name. But some monuments date as early as the sixth century BC and there is evidence that some Punic tophets were in operation two centuries earlier still (Brown 1991, 62). Some stone

31 Carthaginian funerary stele from child-cemetery, depicting a possible priest holding an infant sacrificial victim. © Anne Leaver (after Brown 1991)

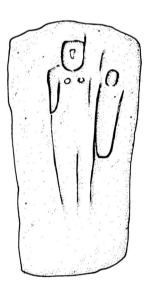

32 Punic funerary stele, from child-cemetery, depicting an adult and a child; from Sardinia. © Anne Leaver (after Brown 1991)

monuments bear representations of adults with children; one stele from Carthage depicts a man (identified as a priest) carrying a child in his arms (**31**).

The documentary sources serve to place the archaeology in context. Diodorus Siculus (*Library of History* XX, XIV, 4-6) contributes an important account of Punic child fire-sacrifice, in the circumstance of warfare between Carthage and Syracuse, whose leader, Agathocles, laid siege to the city-walls in 310 BC after inflicting a crushing defeat upon the Carthaginian army:

> They had among them a bronze statue of Kronos with outstretched hands, palms uppermost, yet inclined towards the ground, so that the child who was placed in these palms would roll off and fall into a pit filled with fire.

Diodorus's description of Kronos's image closely resembles the iconography on the stele from Carthage (above). The luckless victims may, mercifully, have been stunned, drugged or even killed before being cast into the fire-pit; the stele shows the infant lying still, not struggling or crying, though — of course — the iconography might display a somewhat sanitised scene rather different from reality. Diodorus, writing during the first century BC, may have derived his description of the Kronos statue from Cleitarchus, a somewhat sensationalist author of the third century BC, who mentions the cremation of a child while it lay in the arms of a statue (Brown 1991, 22). The Christian chroniclers Lactantius and Tertullian (naturally) make condemnatory references to Punic child-sacrifice. Lactantius (*Divinae Institutiones* I, 21) is probably drawing on Diodorus's text in his account of Agathocles's blockade of Carthage. Taken in isolation, he is an unreliable source in so far as he, like other Christian authors, was compiling polemical literature against paganism. Tertullian (*Apologeticus* IX, 2-4) makes a statement concerning priests of Kronos-Saturn who were crucified for their barbaric sacrificial practices during the early first century AD, although he comments that the rituals continued thereafter in secret (de Vaux 1964, 79-80).

Sacrifice by fire: image, myth and evidence

In any attempt to comprehend the circumstances that may have prompted human fire-sacrifice in antiquity, the descriptions of fire-sacrifice provided by Biblical and Punic texts are of particular value, for they paint a vivid picture of horror, spectacle and pitiless supernatural forces who demanded propitiation with human burnt offerings, sometimes involving children, that resonates strongly with Caesar's Wicker Man. We need to be aware that the Phoenicians and the Gauls were 'other people' in the eyes of their Graeco-Roman chroniclers and that, therefore, the tales of fire-rites may have been highly exaggerated. Nonetheless, some evidence of material culture appears to support the texts: the 'tophets' from Punic settlements and the discovery of new European Iron Age sites, like Leonding in Austria, contribute to a gradually-emerging mosaic of testimony that fire was perceived as a powerful and dramatic agent of transformation, by which human sacrificial victims could transcend to the world of the gods.

4
Rites of blood

For the life of the flesh is in the blood
And I have given it to you upon the altar
To make atonement for your souls: for it is the
blood that maketh atonement by reason of the life.
(Leviticus 17.11)

In many traditions of antiquity in which sacrifice was practised, blood was symbolically special. Indeed, sacrifice itself bears with it connotations of bloody slaughter (Jones 1991, 9-21). In common with other bodily emissions — milk, saliva, semen, for instance — blood belongs both inside and outside the body, thus engaging with metaphors of liminality and ambiguity (Hamilton 1995, 130; Tilley 1999, 38). There is a natural link between blood and violence and between blood and sexuality (Girard 1977, 35). Bloodletting is instinctively frightening, with its immediate connections with trauma and injury; its bright colour and the way it spurts from a deep wound contribute to its association with terror (**33**). Bloody destruction may be used to symbolise societal or political chaos: it is in this way that Euripides used his play *The Bacchae*, the savage dismemberment of Pentheus by the crazed Maenads serving as a metaphor to explore the dissolution of Athenian society in the civil war against Sparta in the late fifth century BC. Old Testament allusions to blood — exemplified by the quotation from *Leviticus* (above) — testify to the perception of blood as a metaphor for life itself. Blood could act as a sanctifying, consecrating agent: Aaron and his sons were marked out as chosen for the priesthood by God by anointing them with blood (*Exodus* 29.20; Rogerson 1980, 55). This ritual may also be related to symbolic protection, an apotropaic device to signal God's especial concern for particular individuals. In the ancient Greek world, the warm flowing blood of a sacrificial animal represented the catharsis engendered by sacrifice: spilt blood reflected the draining of life from the victim but also the paradox of nourishment for the earth on which it fell (Burkert 1983, 59; Durand 1989, 119-28). Blood was both pure and impure, a liminal avenue between the profanity of the victim (and its community) and the sanctity of the spirit world. The shedding of blood was pivotal to ancient Greek sacrificial ritual; the ambiguity with which it was regarded is demonstrated by the perception that spilt blood was a pollutant unless it were associated with the purification of sacrifice, a further paradox in so far as only sacrificial blood could wipe out the contamination of blood shed in battle (Girard 1977, 36). Such an emphasis on purity meant that, for the Greeks, the only meat permitted to be butchered for consumption was from sacrificial animals (Detienne 1989, 1-20).

In Greek sacrificial ritual, the *sphageion* or blood-container was centre-stage: vase-paintings from the fifth century BC depict the vessel very specifically positioned next to the altar (Durand 1989, 119-28, figs. 8, 11), so as to catch the blood as the beast's throat was cut. Other vase-paintings which depict mythic human sacrifice (as narrated, for instance, in Euripides's play *Iphigeneia in Aulis*, or the episode in Homer's *Iliad*, where the princess Polyxena is sacrificed at Achilles' tomb (van Straten 1995, 34, 113-14)) show the human victim treated in the same way. One vase-scene (Durand 1989, fig. 7) shows Polyxena held face-down over an altar while Neoptolemus plunges his sword into her throat, causing the blood to gush out in a great fountain (*see* **10**). In Greek sacrificial ritual, there seems to have been a symbolic emphasis on fluid: the flowing blood was caught in the *sphageion* and there was a second vessel holding water for the animal victim to drink before its death (Durand 1989, fig. 18). Finally, the meat was boiled in a cauldron of water over a fire (Green 1998b, 66-7).

33 Human body placed in disused grain silo at Danebury. © Danebury Trust

Rites of blood, like those involving fire, may be difficult to identify archaeologically, but the occasional preservation of the fleshy parts of human bodies in moist conditions sometimes bears witness to 'penetrative' deaths by stabbing, slashing or shooting, or some other violent injury that causes the blood to flow. Documentary testimony to human sacrifice by throat-cutting, stabbing, tearing to pieces or arrow-shot contributes information concerning the symbolic necessity of shedding blood.

Human blood-sacrifice in 'barbarian' Europe

The Classical literature

> They [the Druids] also observe a custom which is especially astonishing and incredible, in case they are taking thought with respect to matters of great concern; for in such cases they devote to death a human being and plunge a

dagger into him in the region of the diaphragm, and when the stricken victim has fallen they read the future from the manner of his fall and from the twitching of his limbs as well as from the gushing of his blood, having learned to place confidence in an ancient and long-continued practice of observing such matters.
(Diodorus Siculus V, 31. 3-4 trans. Oldfather 1939, 178-9)

They used to strike a human being, whom they had devoted to death, in the back with a sword, and then divine from his death-struggle. We are told of still other kinds of human sacrifices; for example, they would shoot victims to death with arrows, or impale them in the temples . . .
(Strabo *Geographia* IV, 4.5)

And in pursuance of their savage ways they manifest an outlandish impiety also with respect to their sacrifices; for their criminals they keep prisoner for five years and then impale them in honour of the gods, dedicating them together with many other offerings of first-fruits and constructing pyres of great size.
(Diodorus Siculus V, 32.5-6)

The Graeco-Roman commentators on Gaul and Britain emphasise the importance of bloodletting as central to sacrificial rites involving humans. Diodorus and Strabo were near-contemporaries and both derived their information from Poseidonios, Strabo overtly so. The rites they describe are all associated with 'penetrative' death: impalement, stabbing and shooting with arrows. Interestingly, Strabo diverges from Diodorus in implying that what he was recording *used* to take place, as if such practices had become obsolete by the time he was writing in the first century BC. If the two accounts constitute authentic reporting, it may be deduced that the method of death and the resulting gore were closely bound up with the function of the sacrifice and — probably — its supernatural recipient. The reference in Strabo to bows and arrows is interesting in that, according to archaeological evidence, archery seems not to have been a normal method of killing during the Iron Age.

Strabo elsewhere alludes to a blood-rite that very closely resembles the Greek animal-sacrifice so graphically recorded on vase-paintings. This practice allegedly took place among the Cimbri, a North European group of communities who inhabited what is now northern Germany and southern Denmark. According to Strabo, the practitioners of this Cimbrian ritual were women:

These women would enter the [army] camp, sword in hand, go up to the prisoners, crown them and lead them up to a bronze vessel which might hold some twenty measures. One of the women would mount a step and, leaning over the cauldron, cut the throat of a prisoner, who was held up over the vessel's rim. Others cut open the body and, after inspecting the entrails, would foretell victory for their countrymen.
(Strabo VII, 2.3)

Both authors thus make reference to the divinatory purpose of sacrificial blood-rites, the desire to consult, and to an extent control, the spirit powers by accurately foretelling the future from the dying attitudes of victims. It is clear from their accounts that this ritual behaviour was orchestrated and carried out by professional religious officials. In the case of the Cimbrian holy women, the result seems to have been a foregone conclusion! The divinatory ceremonies appear to have had a dual purpose: the victim was simultaneously a cult-offering and a means of manipulating or communicating with the spirit world. It is telling that Strabo's description of Cimbrian human sacrifice, with the study of the entrails, precisely mirrors Graeco-Roman prognosticatory practice with animal victims which, in the Roman religious system, required the offices of a *haruspex* or 'gut-gazer'. One of these *haruspices*, named Memor, was buried and remembered with a tombstone at Bath (*RIB* 155).

The centrality of blood to Gallo-British sacrificial ritual during the first centuries BC and AD is confirmed by the testimony of such authors as Lucan (commenting on southern Gaul) and Tacitus (on Britain). Both describe the physical context for human blood-rites as the sacred grove:

> The barbaric gods worshipped here had their altars heaped up with hideous offerings, and every tree was sprinkled with human blood . . .
> (Lucan *Pharsalia* III, 372-417)

Lucan was describing a holy wood near Massilia (Marseille) encountered by Julius Caesar's army on its way to confront the opposing forces of Caesar's political rival Pompey in the civil war which culminated in the Battle of Pharsalus in Thessaly in 48 BC. The grove was in the way of Caesar's planned siegeworks in his blockade of Massilia, whose townsfolk had been unwise enough to back Pompey. Caesar's soldiers, of whom some were almost certainly of Gallic origin, were superstitiously reluctant to apply the axe to these venerable trees until spurred on by Caesar, the pragmatist, who struck the first blow. Lucan may well be exaggerating (if not inventing) the encounter: by 'hideous offerings' he is presumably referring to the presence of innards, and he paints a graphic picture of trees glistening with fresh red, stale brown and black blood, altars (perhaps made of tree-stumps) festooned with steaming entrails and internal organs, the entire place reeking with the sickening stench of both freshly-killed and decaying human flesh.

In his description of the sacred grove on the holy island of Anglesey, over a hundred years later, Tacitus (*Annales* XIV, 30-1), like Lucan, is narrating an incident involving the destruction of a druidic wood by impious Roman military hands. The historical context for the episode is the campaign of the Roman governor Suetonius Paulinus in AD 60/61, who was bent on destroying what he considered to be the focus of the anti-Roman movement in Britain. Tacitus's account of the doomed trees is strongly reminiscent of Lucan:

> It was their religion to drench their altars in the blood of prisoners and consult their gods by means of human entrails.

Once again, divination is emphasised as the precise function of sacrificial ritual, but the visible (and olfactory) presence of blood seems to have been a crucially empowering and awe-inspiring element.

> Teutates who inspires terror with sacrificial blood, and whose altar bristles with weapons, is called Mercurius Teutates in the language of the Gauls. He was venerated with human blood . . . Mars Esus is appeased thus: a man is suspended in a tree until his limbs fall apart in a bloody sacrifice . . . (**34**)
> (Zwicker 1934, 50; trans. M.E. Raybould)

Lucan and Tacitus each provide accounts of human blood-sacrifice, albeit widely separated spatially and about a hundred years apart. To these narratives we can add Strabo who — following Poseidonios — chronicles a chilling and significant annual ritual apparently enacted on a small island off the mouth of the river Loire. If it took place as Strabo describes it, the sacrifice must indeed have been bloody, for it involved tearing a woman to pieces, in the manner of the rending of beasts by Dionysiac Maenads, maddened by intoxicating liquor and frenzied dancing, as described in Euripides's *The Bacchae* and visualised on Greek vase-paintings (Blundell & Williamson 1998, 130, fig. 8.1). It is significant that Strabo actually refers to the god, in whose name the island ritual was perpetrated, as Dionysus, even though the Gaulish divinity in question must, in reality, have possessed a local name. Strabo clearly regarded the whole story as quite extraordinary for he follows the account with the statement 'But the following story . . . is still more fabulous. . .'. The sacrificial scene is worth quoting in full:

> In the ocean, he [Poseidonios] says, there is a small island, not very far out to sea, situated off the outlet of the Liger river; and the island is inhabited by the women of the Samnitae, and they are possessed by Dionysus and make this god propitious by appeasing him with mystic initiations as well as other sacred performances; and no man sets foot on the island, although the women themselves, sailing from it, have intercourse with men and then return again. And, he says, it is a custom of theirs once a year to unroof the temple and roof it again on the same day before sunset, each woman bringing her load to add to the roof; but the woman whose load falls out of her arms is rent to pieces by the rest, and they carry the pieces round the temple with the cry of 'Ev-ah', and do not cease until their frenzy ceases; and it is always the case, he says, that someone jostles the woman who is to suffer this fate. (**colour plate 10**)
> (Strabo IV, 4.5-6)

The passage is interesting for a number of elements not least of which is the way the victim was selected and her status as a religious official. Furthermore, the context is illuminating: it took place every year, presumably on a day fixed — perhaps — by the season or the moon, on the occasion of the renewal of thatch on a temple-building. The sacrifice may have been carried out as a response to the perceived symbolic

34 Gallo-Roman stone relief of the Gaulish god Esus, from the Nautes Parisiacae monument, Paris; earlier first century AD. © Paul Jenkins

vulnerability of the temporarily open, roofless shrine, in order to avert its contamination by inimical or polluting spirit-presences. Strabo explains that this annual ceremony took place in honour of a god whom he calls 'Dionysus' although, if the account is authentic reporting, the divinity concerned is likely to have possessed a local name, perhaps having a persona perceived as essentially similar to that of the Greek 'flesh-eating' god of intoxication and transformation.

The archaeology of blood-sacrifice

Unless weapons, such as arrows, spears or daggers, are associated with human remains, it is generally difficult to identify a 'penetrative' death, with the exception of freak conditions of preservation, such as obtains with bog-bodies, where fleshy parts of the body may be intact. In dealing solely with skeletal material, there are still fewer circumstances in which a ritual blood-killing can be established, although the context of the death may be suggestive (**35**).

A large limestone cave at Býči Skála in Moravia appears to have been the context for what amounts to a ritualised massacre (**colour plate 11**). Vincent Megaw (1970, 58) suggests that the site was an important cult centre, established in that location because of the presence of ironworking in the vicinity. Two areas within the cave have been identified as the sites of large pyres, perhaps for funerary rituals. But as well as objects which date most of the assemblage to the sixth century BC, the remains of 40 people, mainly females, were deposited there, many dismembered, with hands, feet or heads missing. Near the human bodies were those of two horses, each chopped into four pieces. Additionally, two human skulls had been put to ceremonial use: one had been modified to form a cup; both had been placed in a bronze cauldron. There is always the possibility that the trauma to the bodies occurred post-mortem but the group appears to have met a violent end, and may have been the mass-victims of a blood sacrifice.

A great deal of controversy surrounds the discovery, over the past hundred years or so, of a number of so-called 'bog-bodies' in northern and north-western Europe. British interest in the subject surged during the early 1980s when a series of well-preserved human remains emerged from the peat-bog at Lindow Moss in Cheshire (**colour plate 12**). The anaerobic and other preservative properties of the peat have enabled the study of ancient flesh and this means that the cause and circumstances of death may sometimes be determined. The most famous body (Lindow II), a male killed in the first century AD, known to archaeologists as Lindow Man or — affectionately — as 'Pete Marsh', appears to have suffered a 'threefold' death: he was garrotted, he sustained two severe blows to the head that fractured his skull, and his throat was cut (Stead *et al.* 1986; Turner 1996, 34-5). Michael Parker Pearson has commented (1999, 68) that, were the luckless victim to have been slashed in the throat and strangled at the same time, 'a small fountain of blood' would have pumped from the gash. Indeed, under the undoubted circumstance of extreme stress, the sudden rise in the victim's blood-pressure would have increased the spurt from the wound. Apart from the three major injuries, the man's body showed signs of other trauma (Turner 1999, 227-33), as if subjected to systematic ill-treatment (see chapter 2). Far away from Cheshire, in Denmark, other bog-bodies evince signs of having met their deaths by penetrative and bloody means: the Grauballe man, who died in about 250 BC, had had his throat slit from ear to ear in a blow sufficiently savage almost to sever his gullet (**colour plate 13**). The man was found in Nebel Mose but was named after Grauballe, the home of his discoverers (Fischer 1999, 96). Like Lindow Man, this individual had sustained other injuries: a hard blow on the head and a broken leg. At the time he was found, it was reported that his face bore a look of terror (Glob 1969, 37-62; Finlay *et al.* 1997, 6), although modern pathologists discount the validity of reading

35 Human body interred in grain storage pit at Danebury. © Danebury Trust

expression on dead physiognomies. Upon investigation of the Grauballe man's innards, he was found to have ingested a substantial quantity of ergot, a fungal growth forming on decaying grain, particularly rye; this substance — lethal in such a large dose — would have caused severe burning sensations, hallucinations and convulsions. Another body from Lindow Moss (Lindow III) was probably consigned to the marsh about a hundred years later than Lindow Man. This second person was found minus his head; decapitation could have been the cause of his demise, but he may alternatively have been drowned and his head taken off after death (Turner 1996, 34-5). Another person whose head was found not far away, at Worsley near Manchester (Garland 1995; Turner 1999), had been violently beheaded, also some time in the Roman period. One bog-deposit, from Weerdinge, near Bourtangermoor in the Netherlands, resonates with Strabo's description of the Cimbrian sacrificial ritual (above, p.72), in so far as one of a pair of male bodies had his intestines protruding from his belly, as though he had been disembowelled (Van der Sanden 1996, 179, fig. 245).

It is impossible to be dogmatic about the circumstances of the bog-deaths. For some scholars, the argument for human sacrifice is very persuasive. We shall see later that other people died in different ways, such as drowning and strangulation (see chapter 6). What is certain is that many Iron Age bog-bodies met violent ends and certain features that many of them share — a special bread or gruel just before death — are suggestive of some kind of 'grammar' of treatment (Holden 1995, 76-82). Lindow Man's seeming triple-fold death may equally reflect some peculiar circumstance which is not explained by, for example, a punitive killing or straightforward murder. But other researchers (Briggs 1995, 168-82) argue with some vehemence (though, to my mind, little conviction) that there is no reason for suggesting human sacrifice, arguing that some people may have become accidentally trapped in the bog and that those who definitely met their deaths by human agency were probably executed criminals.

Postscript: ancient Oaxaca — an analogous case-study

Ancient European human blood-sacrifice can generally only be a matter for inference from extremely circumstantial and ambiguous evidence. It is, therefore, illuminating to cast envious eyes at the greater coherence of data from another ancient tradition, far away from Europe, where blood-rituals appear to have been crucial. The Zapotec culture, of Oaxaca in Mexico, flourished from *c.*1150 BC until the Spanish colonisation in the early modern period (Marcus & Flannery 1994, 55-74). The evidence for ritual murder comes from two sources: ethnohistorical documents compiled by Spaniards during the sixteenth and seventeenth centuries, and the material culture discovered by archaeologists.

The written sources, like those for Gaul and Britain in the late first millennium BC, need to be treated with reserve since they were composed by members of an alien, colonising culture, just as was the case with the Classical sources for late Iron Age Europe. Furthermore, just as we have to appreciate the anti-pagan bias of such ancient Christian authors as Tertullian and Lactantius, recording the horrors of Punic child-sacrifice, so the comments on Zapotec religion made by the Spanish chroniclers need (in the words of Marcus & Flannery: 1994, 55) to have the inherent Catholic prejudices 'factored out'. Notwithstanding these problems with the texts, the colonial observations on Oaxacan cult-practice tally remarkably with archaeological material from Zapotec sites, and literature and material culture serve here to complement each other to a high degree. Zapotec ritual is important for it demonstrates a focus on bloodletting and human sacrifice which may have features reminiscent of ancient European custom.

Like the ancient Gauls and Britons of the first millennium BC, Zapotec people revered the spirits of natural places and phenomena, including mountains and lightning, together with the ancestors whom they perceived as having undergone apotheosis. The relationship between people and the spirit forces was based on reciprocity: benefits required sacrifices in return; the divine force apparently most closely linked with human sacrifice was Lightning. The emphasis on blood-sacrifice was underpinned by perceptions involving 'pèe', the life-force, which was identifiable as present in anything capable of independent movement: people, animals, the wind, lightning, rivers, the moon and flowing blood. For the Zapotec, there were two kinds of blood, flowing and dried; the transformation of one to the other was testimony to its volatility, which reinforced its 'pèe'. The Spanish literary sources on the ancient Oaxacans specify two kinds of human blood-sacrifice: autosacrifice and ritual murder. Autosacrifice, practised by Zapotec priests, involved letting small amounts of their own blood during cult-ceremonies, using specific and elaborate instruments such as sting-ray spines, *agave* cactus spikes or obsidian blades to cut their flesh and draw blood. These clergy (called *bigaña*) generally stored their auto-sacrificial equipment in the temples. Ritual murder involved removing the still-beating heart from the designated victims, who were usually prisoners or slaves. This gruesome method of killing had a particular function: that of preserving 'pèe' in the living, pumping heart, for the spirit powers. For this operation, the priests used flint or obsidian leaf-shaped knives.

The archaeological record confirms the literature in many respects, although there is no unequivocal evidence for ritual bloodletting or human sacrifice. Obsidian blades, of a type similar to those reputedly used in sacrificial ceremonies, first appear in the twelfth century BC, and sting-ray spines by c.850 followed, a century or so later, by obsidian flakes chipped to imitate sting-ray spines. Significantly, perhaps, the early first millennium BC is the period when Lightning, as a spirit force, is first depicted in Zapotec art. The material culture of Oaxacan sacrificial ritual consists of sculpture and finds from temples. Archaeological study of the important ceremonial centre of San José Mogote, which flourished as early as 700 BC, has revealed evidence of both figure-carving and sacrificial equipment. The site was a nodal point, serving more than a thousand people living in scattered villages around it. Dating to c.500 BC is a carved stone depicting what has been interpreted as a human sacrificial victim (Marcus & Flannery 1994, fig. 7.7), a naked man with an open heart wound from which issues a flowing scroll-pattern of blood. If this sculpture has been correctly identified, it is the oldest recorded Oaxacan representation of human sacrifice.

By about 200 BC at San José Mogote (as in other Zapotec ceremonial sites), sanctuary-buildings, the abodes of the priests, conformed to a standardised architectural form, each possessing an inner and an outer room. On the floor of one temple, in c.AD 100, a priest placed a set of obsidian implements, discovered by archaeologists *in situ*; the instruments included knives of the kind associated with autosacrifice and other blades closely resembling those depicted in human sacrificial scenes. The inner sanctum of another temple was furnished with a large basin that, on analogy with ethnohistorical records, may have been used for water to wash sacrificial equipment or even to hold blood. Perhaps most interesting of all were the offerings found at some shrines, which included jade statuettes and other objects, sometimes sprinkled with red ochre. In one such assemblage was the body of an apparently sacrificed child, covered with red ochre (Marcus & Flannery 1994, 55-74). To my mind, the powdered red pigment was present to represent dried human blood and so emphasise to the gods that a blood-sacrifice had been enacted.

Zapotec ritual appears savage and barbaric to early twenty-first-century western perceptions. However, it has to be judged within the context of the cosmologies and beliefs of its perpetrators. 'Pèe' was central to the cult and to the divine powers, and the efficacy of reciprocal giving to the gods, whose power was repeatedly demonstrated in the lightning flash and thunderclap. The harness and control of these natural forces required commensurately potent sacrifices, those of people. Such ritual may have been carried out after great storms or lightning strikes in order to appease the spirits. Autosacrifice meant offering the living essence of the priests themselves, a substitute for full human sacrifice; ritual murder seems generally to have been reserved for those of lower status: foreign war-captives, children and slaves, humans on the edges of society who satisfied the requirements for the gods but who were regarded, maybe, as not quite so human as the rest of society. Central to all Zapotec ritual was blood.

5
Skulls and skullduggery

The heads of all enemies killed in battle are taken to the king; a head being a sort of ticket by which a soldier is admitted to his share of the loot — no head, no loot. He strips the skin off the head by making a circular cut round the ears and shaking out the skull; he then scrapes the flesh off the skin with the rib of an ox, and when it is clean works it in his fingers until it is supple, and fit to be used as a sort of handkerchief. He hangs these 'handkerchiefs' on the bridle of his horse, and is very proud of them. The finest fellow is the man who has the greatest number . . . They have a special way of dealing with the actual skulls — not with all of them, but only those of their worst enemies: they saw off the part below the eyebrows, and after cleaning out what remains stretch a piece of rawhide round it on the outside . . . the skull is then used to drink from.
(Herodotus *Histories* IV, 63-6; trans. De Sélincourt 1965, 262)

Herodotus, writing in the fifth century BC, was describing a Scythian battle-custom, associated with the heads of vanquished foes, that appears to relate both to honour and contempt. On the one hand, these trophies were a mark of esteem, a symbol of fighting-prowess; but, paradoxically, only the skulls of those attracting the greatest opprobrium were modified for use as drinking vessels. What is particularly interesting about Herodotus' narrative is that it bears an uncanny resemblance to descriptions of head-taking ascribed to Gaulish warriors by Classical writers of the first centuries BC/AD, such as Strabo, Diodorus and Livy. It is known that the first two mined the writings of Poseidonios, who travelled in Gaul about a century earlier, but it is always possible that Poseidonios himself used passages of Herodotus to embroider his own observations. However, there is a considerable mass of evidence, from both ancient literature and archaeology, that the human head was accorded special symbolism in later European prehistory and the western Roman provinces and, what is more, head-ritual may sometimes have been conducted within the context of ritual murder.

Gaulish head-hunting and the Classical literature

They [the Gauls] cut off the heads of enemies slain in battle and attach them to the necks of their horses. The blood-stained spoils they hand over to their attendants and carry off as booty, while striking up a paean and singing a song of victory, and they nail up these first fruits upon their houses just as do those who lay low wild animals in certain kinds of hunting. They embalm in cedar-oil the heads of the most distinguished enemies and preserve them carefully in a chest, and display them with pride to strangers, saying that for this head, one of their ancestors, or his father, or the man himself, refused the offer of a large sum of money. They say that some of them boast that they refused the weight of the head in gold; thus displaying what is only a barbarous kind of magnanimity; for it is not a sign of nobility to refrain from selling the proofs of one's valour, it is rather true that it is bestial to continue one's hostility against a slain fellow-man.
(Diodorus Siculus V, 29, 4-5; trans. Tierney 1959-60, 250)

Again, in addition to their witlessness, there is also that custom, barbarous and exotic, which attends most of the northern tribes — I mean the fact that when they depart from the battle they hang the heads of their enemies from the necks of their horses, and when they have brought them home, nail the spectacle to the entrances of their houses. At any rate, Posidonius says that he himself saw the spectacle in many places, and that, although at first he loathed it, afterwards, through his familiarity with it, he could bear it calmly. The heads of enemies of high repute, however, they used to embalm in cedar-oil and exhibit to strangers and they would not deign to give them

back even for a ransom of an equal weight of gold.
(Strabo *Geographia* IV, 4.5; trans. Jones 1923, 247)

The similarities between Strabo's account and that of Diodorus can be virtually all explained in terms of their common use of Poseidonios's testimony. Both writers are somewhat vague in attributing head-taking to specific contexts, though Diodorus (XIV, 115), in narrating the episode of Rome's attack by the Gauls, in 387 BC, does state that they 'spent the first day cutting off, according to their custom, the heads of the dead'. Livy's narrative is somewhat divergent and, furthermore, he ties his comments to particular historical events, the defeat of a Roman army by the Senonian Gauls in 295 BC at the siege of Clusium in Etruria, in which a legion had encamped, under the command of its general Scipio:

> Thus the legion was attacked in the rear and found itself surrounded, with the enemy assailing it on every quarter. Some writers say that the legion was even annihilated there, so that none survived to bear away the tidings, and that the consuls, who were not far away from Clusium, got no report of the disaster till some Gallic horsemen came in sight, with heads hanging at their horses' breasts or fixed on their lances, and singing their customary song of triumph.
> (Livy X, 26, 11; trans. Foster 1926, 459)

Later in his work, he describes the decapitation of the Roman general Postumius by the north Italian Gaulish tribe of the Boii in 216:

> The Boii stripped his [Postumius's] body, cut off the head, and carried their spoils in triumph to the most hallowed of their temples. There they cleaned out the head, as their custom is, and gilded the skull, which thereafter served them as a holy vessel to pour libations from and as a drinking-cup for the priest and the temple-attendants.
> (Livy *Ab Urbe Condita* XXIII, 24; trans. De Sélincourt 1965, 198)

It should be emphasised that none of the Graeco-Roman authors mentions the collection of trophy-heads in connection with human sacrifice, although Livy does link the fashioning of Postumius's skull into a cult-vessel with ritual activity. Diodorus hints at their cult use in the above-quoted passage, where he refers to trophy heads as 'first fruits'. Strabo's account is followed, almost in the same breath, by the statement that the Romans put a ban on head-hunting customs 'as well as to all those connected with the sacrifices and divinations that are opposed to our usages' (IV, 4.5). Taken at face-value, the Classical texts suggest that human enemy heads were taken from dead warriors and used in ritual contexts, perhaps even as sacrificial offerings, although the deaths themselves occurred in warfare.

It would be tempting to dismiss the testimony of the authors from the Mediterranean world as fictional 'purple-passage' reporting of barbarous, uncivilised and marginal peoples were it not for the eloquence of archaeological evidence which attests that, on

1   *The Iron Age hillfort at Danebury,*
    Hampshire from the air.
    © Danebury Trust

2   *Female bog-body from Huldremose,*
    Denmark. The woman had suffered
    injuries in life, including a broken leg
    (which would have left her partially
    crippled) and a nearly-severed right arm;
    the left arm was bound to the body by a
    leather strap; she was wearing two skin
    capes and a woollen skirt when she died,
    c.AD 100. © Nationalmuseet, Kobenhavn

3 Polychrome pot depicting a fallen warrior, with a vulture perched on his body, from Numancia, Spain; second century BC. © Junta de Castillo y León (Museo Numantino)

4 Human long-bone, held by palaeo-osteologist Professor Margaret Cox, apparently split open longitudinally in order to extract the marrow, and therefore providing possible evidence for cannibalism in the late Iron Age; from Alveston, Bristol. © Professor Mick Aston

5 *Modern Hindu fire-ritual. A woman possessed by the goddess Santoshi Ma (Mother of Satisfaction); while possessed, the devotee eats fire and heals people. Taken at regular Friday morning worship, in a small village near Bhubaneswar, in the State of Orissa, India in 1996.* © Dr Lynn Foulston

6 *Modern Hindu fire-ritual. A devotee walks across a fire-pit, at the annual fire festival of the goddess Mariyamman, at Natham, Tamilnadu, South India, in 1997.* © Dr Lynn Foulston

7 The ancient Irish festival of
   Beltane: according to the
   medieval commentator
   Cormac, cattle were driven
   between two bonfires lit by the
   Druids, in a purificatory cere-
   mony on 1 May.
   © Thames & Hudson/Paul
   Jenkins: by kind permission of
   Thames & Hudson

8 Modern Hindu fire-ritual: the
   Sacrificial Fire (Hom Bedi).
   Taken inside the Kalighat
   temple-complex, Calcutta, in
   1995. This form of worship is
   associated with the placement
   of clarified butter (ghee) into
   fire. 'Hom' means oblation of
   fire into which ghee is placed.
   © Dr Lynn Foulston

9 *The Wicker Man, from the film of that name. © Canal + Image, UK Ltd.: by kind permission of Thames & Hudson*

10 *Sacrificial scene described by Strabo in the first century BC: annual temple re-roofing ceremony on a holy island off the mouth of the Loire, involving the ritual murder and dismemberment of a priestess.* © *Thames & Hudson/Paul Jenkins: by kind permission of Thames & Hudson*

11 *The ritual massacre of 40 people and two horses at Býči Skála in Bohemia, in the sixth century BC.* © *Thames & Hudson/Paul Jenkins: by kind permission of Thames & Hudson*

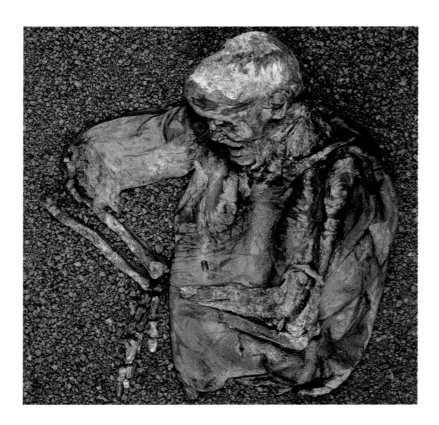

12 *Lindow Man: a young man, ritually killed by blows to the head, strangling and throat-cutting before being kneed in the back and thrust face-down in a peat-bog at Lindow Moss, Cheshire, in the first century AD. © The British Museum*

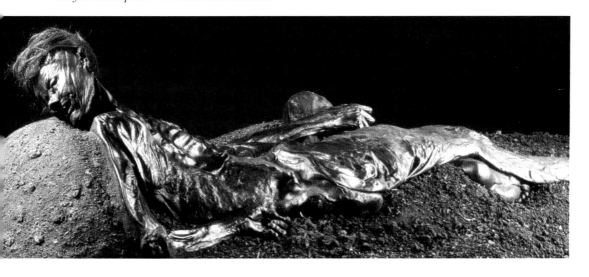

13 *The Grauballe man, whose throat was slit so savagely that it nearly severed his gullet, before he was deposited in the Nebel Mose, Denmark, in about 250 BC. © Moesgård Museum*

14 Bronze 'sceptre-terminal' depicting a rider seated between two back-to-back horses; there are severed human heads under the animals' front hooves and beneath their bodies; one of eight examples from high-status tombs at Numancia; second century BC.
© and with kind permission from Professor Alfredo Jimeno

15 Front of human skull, modified for attachment to a wall or door, from a high-status Gaulish residence at Montmaurin 'La Fosse Muette'; second century BC. Antoine Maillier © Centre archéologique européen du Mont Beuvray

16 The pool at Llyn Cerrig Bach, Anglesey, where deposits of human and animal remains and high prestige metalwork were made episodically during the Iron Age. © Philip Macdonald

17 The body of a middle-aged man, strangled and placed naked in a peat-bog at Tollund, Denmark, in the last few centuries BC. © Silkeborg Museum

18 Reconstruction of one of the 'seated' burials of young men
at Acy-Romance (Ardennes); second century BC. Antoine
Maillier © Centre archéologique européen du Mont
Beuvray

19 (left) Head of a wooden female figurine found pinned down
in a marsh, as if used as a surrogate human sacrificial victim,
at Ballachulish (Argyll) at the beginning of the Iron Age.
© National Museums of Scotland
(above) The site of Ballachulish. © University of Edinburgh

20 Romano-British bronze amulet in
the form of a bound captive, a
rope around his neck and wrists;
Brough-under-Stainmore
(Cumbria). © The British
Museum

21 The iron slave-gang chain from Llyn Cerrig Bach, Anglesey, worn by Cardiff University
archaeology students. © National Museums & Galleries of Wales, Cardiff

22 The quartered remains of
a 12-year-old boy interred
in four pits at Hornish
Point on South Uist,
during the early Iron Age.
© National Museums of
Scotland

23 Infant-burial from the
later phases of the Iron
Age hillfort at Maiden
Castle, Dorset. © Niall
Sharples

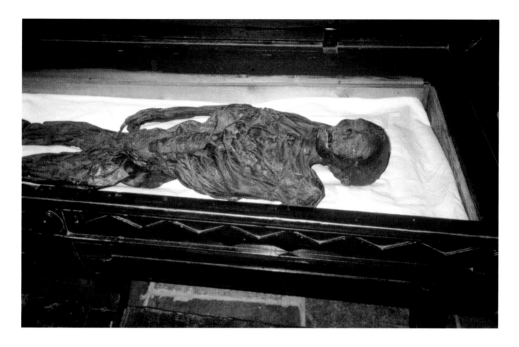

24 *The body of a peri-menopausal woman from the Haraldskaer peat-bog, Jutland, who died in the early fifth century BC; she lies in an oak coffin in the medieval Church of Saint Nicolai at Vejle.* © *author*

25 *The peat-bog at Haraldskaer, Jutland, taken in December 2000.* © *author*

26 Set of bronze razors and a knife from a rich inhumation grave at Saint-Georges-lès-Baillargeaux (Vienne), found in 1998; late second century BC. It is thought that the tools were sacrificial equipment belonging to an Iron Age priest. Antoine Maillier © Centre archéologique européen du Mont Beuvray

27 Bronze bowl and one of a pair of spoons (the other lost), perhaps used in sacrificial rituals, from a rich female inhumation grave in the cemetery of La Chaussée-sur-Marne; third-second century BC. The bowl resembles the paterae used in Roman devotional ceremonies; the spoons, engraved with crosses dividing them into quadrants, may have been used in divinatory rituals. The surviving spoon bears traces of textile, suggesting it had been wrapped in a bag before being interred with its owner. Antoine Maillier © Centre archéologique européen du Mont Beuvray

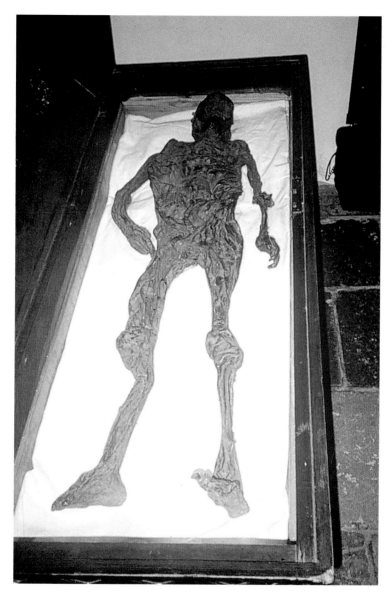

28 The lady from the Haraldskaer peat-bog, Jutland. © author

29 *The oak coffin commissioned for the Haraldskaer body by the king of Denmark in 1835, when she was thought to be an early Christian princess. © author*

30 *The interior of the Church of Saint Nicolai, Vejle, central Jutland, where the Haraldskaer woman lies today. © author*

repeated occasions, something odd happened to human heads. The problem with the texts of such as Strabo and Diodorus, which are not specific as to time or place, is the tendency to interpret their observations as if head-collection were a commonplace practice throughout Iron Age Europe, from 600 BC until the Roman occupation. What archaeology contributes to the issue is evidence for the recurrent ritual treatment of human heads in particular contexts; widespread maybe but certainly not necessarily a frequent practice.

The archaeology of head-ritual

Archaeological testimony from Iron Age southern Gaul appears to endorse the comments of Graeco-Roman writers, in so far as it offers evidence for the special and ritualised treatment of human heads. It should be acknowledged that none of the evidence of material culture points directly at human sacrifice, though it is possible to infer that — on occasions — such a practice did occur. Two sacred sites belonging to the tribe of the Saluvii, the cliff-top sanctuary at Roquepertuse and a shrine in the tribal *oppidum* at Entremont, consisted of stone temples whose architecture included upright stones and lintels in which niches were sunk for the purpose of displaying human heads, some of them still in place (Benoit 1969). These were the skulls of young men, in the prime of their fighting lives, whose injuries proclaim them to have been victims of battle.

As well as the actual remains of war-dead, these two sites, together with others in the vicinity, possess a wealth of iconography focusing on the human head. Entremont (**36**) has produced sculptures of groups of severed heads, with closed or half-closed eyes, perhaps to signify death (Benoit 1969, pl. XXII), and one relief-carving from the site depicts a warrior on horseback, with a severed head suspended from his mount's bridle (*op. cit.*, pl. XXXIII, left). This image is highly reminiscent of a painted Iron Age pot from Aulnat in the Auvergne, which depicts a warrior, with a severed human head dangling from his belt (**37a & b**) (Collis 2000; Musée de Bibracte). The site has produced other signs of head-ritual, including the burial of infants' heads without the rest of their bodies. Gaulish and British Iron Age coins, too, sometimes show people associated with severed heads: one issue depicts a standing figure — perhaps a priest or warrior — holding a decapitated head in his hand (Allen 1980, 135-6, no. 317). Also, some Gallic coins present images of horses accompanied by heads (*op. cit.* 59); and an Alesia series depicts a man with boar-standard, *carnyx* (war-trumpet) and severed head (*op. cit.* 92) (**38**), thus making a firm link between the head-motif and war. Cognate imagery comes from Iron Age sites in Celtiberia, notably at Numancia, where high-status cremation-graves have recently produced a series of curious 'sceptre-terminals' in the form of double horses, with a single central rider, with a severed head beneath each animal's front hooves and another pair below the horse (Martínez 1999, 7 [lower plate]) (**colour plate 14**). Celtiberian sites have also produced an idiosyncratic group of horseman-brooches, again with severed heads beneath the mount's hooves (Green 1992a, 74; Lorrio 1997, láminas 3, 4) (**39**).

A tall pillar, erected at Entremont, was incised with 12 severed heads all, perhaps significantly, without mouths as if, once again, to portray death (**40**): indeed, the lowest

36 Facsimile of janiform
stone head, from the
cliff-top sanctuary of
Roquepertuse
(Bouches du Rhône);
fourth/third century
BC. Antoine Maillier
© Centre
archéologique européen
du Mont Beuvray

38 Reverse of Iron Age
silver coin, depicting
warrior or priest
holding severed human
head, from Alesia,
Burgundy; the legend
reads Dubnocou-
Dubnorix, and was
struck by the tribal
leader of the Aedui,
probably Caesar's
opponent Dumnorix,
brother of Diviciacus,
in the mid-first century
BC. © Anne Leaver
(after Allen 1980)

37 *Late Iron Age pot decorated with the image of a warrior brandishing a severed human head/close-up of sherd; Aulnat, Auvergne, France. Antoine Maillier © Centre archéologique européen du Mont Beuvray*

39 Bronze fibula in the form of a horseman, with a severed human head beneath the front hooves of his mount, from Numancia; second century BC. © Paul Jenkins

head on the Entremont pillar has been carved upside down, almost as if it is leading the way to the Otherworld (*op. cit.*, pl. XXVI, 2). Interestingly, stones carved with heads in niches, in apparent imitation of the genuine skulls from Roquepertuse and Entremont, come from the Gallo-Greek town of Glanum nearby (*op. cit.*, pl. XXV). All three sites produced stone images of seated individuals, variously interpreted as deities or heroes, who are depicted holding severed heads, with closed eyes, in their hands (**41**) (Benoit 1981, 54); it has been suggested that some of the clustered head-carvings at Entremont may originally have rested between the knees of such figures (Birkhan 1999, 296). Similar imagery is associated with the carved monster, nicknamed the 'Tarasque of Noves' (**42**), a fantastic ravening half-lion, half-wolf creature from the environs of Avignon nearby: a human arm dangles from his mouth and his great claws grasp severed human heads (*op. cit.*, XVIII, XIX). The *oppidum* of Nages, in the same region, possessed a shrine, the lintel of which was carved with alternating severed human heads and galloping horses (**43**) (Benoit 1969, pl. XII). One of the most interesting of all southern Gaulish 'head' monuments dates from the Roman period, and comes from Saint-Michel-de-Valbonne (Hyères): it consists of a stone pillar incised with heads and a horseman, found in a sanctuary which, according to epigraphic evidence from the site, was dedicated to Mars

Rudianus (*op. cit.*, pl. XXVI, 3). This is particularly interesting, partly because of its Roman date and the linkage of head-ritual to a specific divinity, but also because of another find, not all that far away, at Apt (Vaucluse) where an altar to Mars was dedicated by a group of local people and erected on top of a deposit of human heads (*CIL* XII, 1077).

The grouping of heads at Apt and the images of superimposed clusters of carved heads on the iconography of, for instance, Entremont seem visually cognate with ritual practice in a number of ancient societies, perhaps the most evocative being the collection of so-called 'trophy-heads' among the Nasca of Peru. Here, a tradition spanning the period from *c.*100 BC to AD 700 included the deposition of heads and their depiction on ceramics (Browne, Silverman & García 1993, 274-94). The imagery and the skeletal evidence both point to a specific rite involving the joining of the heads by cords attached to perforations drilled into the frontal bone; sometimes the lips and eyes were sealed with cactus-spines. One cache of 48 heads has been excavated at Cerro Carapo in the Palpa Valley: although the heads are often interpreted as battle-trophies, the skulls of women and children are present as well as those of robust males, which formed the great majority of the heads. It may be that some form of ancestor-cult is represented, though it is perhaps necessary to avoid thinking in terms of a uni-interpretational framework. Although not for one moment suggesting any kind of genuine conceptual linkage between South American and western European religious practice, it is of interest that certain Breton Iron Age coin-issues minted by the Osismii depict groups of severed human heads attached to each other with chains or cords (Allen 1980, fig. 23). John Creighton (2000, 45) has recently reinterpreted this imagery from a shamanic perspective as, perhaps, a representation of an individual undergoing an out-of-body experience, leaving his earthly self for the spirit world.

There is evidence for the treatment of human heads, in ways closely resembling descriptions in the Classical commentaries, in Iron Age and Roman contexts outside the Lower Rhône Valley. Livy's account of Postumius's skull being modified to form a sacred drinking-cup in the late third century BC resonates with material culture from a ritual deposit at the cave of Býči Skála in Bohemia, the site of a massacre involving the slaughter and dismemberment of people and horses. Inside a cauldron archaeologists found

40 *'Head pillar' from Entremont (Bouches du Rhône); fourth/third century BC. © author*

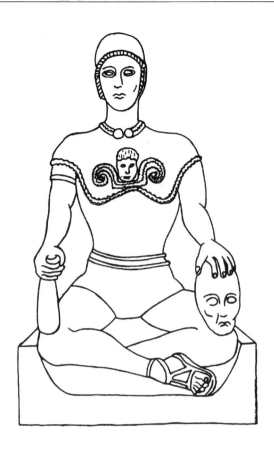

41 *Seated god, holding severed human head, from Entremont; fourth/third century BC. © author*

42 *The 'Tarasque of Noves', a carved statue of a monster, half-lion, half-wolf, in the act of devouring a human limb, and with severed human heads beneath its front paws, from Noves, near Avignon; fourth/third century BC. © Paul Jenkins*

43 *Relief carving, on the lintel of a shrine, of alternating horses and human heads, from the Iron Age oppidum of Nages, southern France. © Paul Jenkins*

44 *Fragments of perforated human cranium, drilled for suspension, from Roissy-en-France (Val d'Oise); fourth century BC. Antoine Maillier © Centre archéologique européen du Mont Beuvray*

two human skulls, of which one seems to have been made into a cup (Megaw 1970, no. 35; Green 1997, 84). Other ritual modifications were sometimes made to human heads: the front part of a skull, fashioned into a mask, adorned a cult-building within a high-status Iron Age residence at Montmartin (Oise) in the third or second century BC (**colour plate 15**) (Boulestin & Séguier 2000, 38). Sometimes multiple holes were drilled into fragments of cranium (probably for suspension rather than trepanation): this happened to part of a skull from Roissy-en-France (**44**) in the fourth century BC (*op. cit.*), and to a cranial bone of Iron Age date, pierced by three holes, found at Hillhead (**45**) on the far north-east tip of Scotland (Royal Museum of Scotland). A late Iron Age head from the river Saône bears signs of sword-cuts and a square nail-hole, as if for attachment to a building (Bonnamour 2000, No. 74). The human heads found in the enclosure ditch at the entrance to the sacred site of Gournay-sur-Aronde (Brunaux 1988) are interpreted as having once been suspended from the temple gateway; the same may have been true of a skull and the cut fragment of another from a fortified pre-Roman site at Rispain in southern Scotland (Museum of Scotland). Conversely, the conspicuous absence of skulls in the human bone-assemblages at the shrine of Ribemont may be equally significant (Smith 2000, 152-63). The entrances to hillforts, such as Bredon Hill (Worcs) and Stanwick (Yorks) in Britain and Celtiberian strongholds such as Puig Castelar and Puig de Sant Andreu were once seemingly hung about with human heads, which subsequently fell into the ditch beneath (Lorrio 1997, 336).

A recurrent pattern of head-ritual can be discerned in the material culture of Iron Age and Roman Britain. The skull of an adult male with a sword-cut, dating to the fifth/fourth centuries BC, comes from a votive deposit with early La Tène weapons from Fiskerton (Lincs) (Parker Pearson pers. comm.; Field & Parker Pearson in press). Some of the human remains consigned to the disused corn-storage pits at Danebury consisted solely of heads, those of people or horses (*see* **11, 19**): thus, eight pits contained complete or partial human skulls, of which six were those of adult males, one female and one child (Walker 1984, 442-63). What is more, some pit-bodies showed signs that their heads were treated specially: a female found lying on a bed of charcoal had had her head removed; the same was true of an adolescent boy, and the arms were also absent from both bodies. At the Roman military site of Newstead in southern Scotland, a well was found to contain a human skull, together with those of horses and cattle (Royal Museum of Scotland), as though the heads of all three species had been subjected to a chthonic rite similar to that recorded at Danebury. Simon Clarke (1999, 40; 2000, 25) has suggested that this evidence from Newstead, together with the discovery of three Roman parade helmets deposited in a pit, is highly suggestive of some form of 'head-cult'. There is, indeed, a mass of material from Roman Britain arguing for the retention of head-related ceremonial action, despite the 'civilising' influences of Mediterranean tradition. Thus a rural shrine of Roman date at Cosgrove appears to have been the scene of a cult highly reminiscent of Iron Age southern Gaul, in so far as a human skull was found embedded in a wall; the temple remained in use until the fifth century AD (Miles 1970, 9).

Many of the adult men interred in the Danebury pits had suffered from head-wounds (Hooper 1984, 463-74), though this may signify no more than the cause of death in battle (*see* **11**). But head-injuries are also a feature of a group of unstratified human skulls from

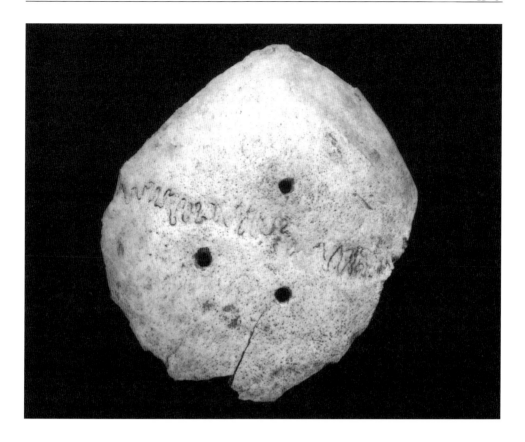

45 Part of a human skull, drilled with three suspension-holes, from an Iron Age broch at Hillhead, Caithness. © National Museums of Scotland

the rivers Thames and Walbrook in London. As at Danebury, the Walbrook heads belonged to young men, their heads cast into the water after losing their flesh, perhaps following exposure for a time before their final deposition: two have been dated by radiocarbon to the late Iron Age or early Roman period (Bradley 1990, 180-1; Marsh & West 1981; Maloney 1990; West 1996, 190-1; Isserlin 1997, 91-100). Heads were even apparently subjected to special treatment in the context of Roman army installations in Britain: outside the Balkerne Gate at the legionary fortress of Colchester the remains of six individuals were interred, consisting mainly of limbs and heads (Isserlin 1997, 91-100).

In late Roman Britain, the bodies of certain middle-aged or elderly females were accorded special post-mortem treatment that involved the removal of their heads. The cemetery at Lankhills, Winchester contained graves of elderly females who died in the fourth century AD; their heads were severed and placed by their legs (Macdonald 1979, 415-24). This happened to a woman who suffered from crippling arthritis at Guilden Morden in Cambridgeshire (Lethbridge 1936, 109-20). A similar, but very specific rite, occurring in Dorset in the late third century AD, is exhibited by the graves of elderly women around Kimmeridge, who were decapitated, their lower jaws removed and the

105

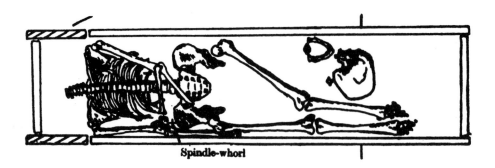

Spindle-whorl

*46 Body of an elderly Romano-British woman, decapitated and buried in a stone cist with a
spindle-whorl at Kimmeridge, Dorset in the late third century AD. The head, minus its lower
jaw, was placed near her ankles; above the cist a second woman had been interred, perhaps as
part of the same funerary ceremony. © Dorset Archaeology & Natural History Society: by kind
permission of British Museum Press*

remaining part of their heads placed by their feet; each woman was accompanied by a
spindle-whorl (Merrifield 1987, 159-63; Philpott 1991, 77-89; Green 1995, 154) (**46**).
None of these bodies need have belonged to sacrificial victims, but the arthritic condition
of the Guilden Morden woman resonates with the evidence for physical defects,
particularly those affecting mobility, that has been noted in deaths that are identified as
probable victims of ritual murder (chapter 7). It may be that we should also consider
whether these women might have been branded as witches: the removal of the lower jaws,
symbolically taking away the power of speech, might relate to a desire to stop these
women from mouthing spells and imprecations at their neighbours. The Cambridgeshire
woman must have been in extreme pain, and perhaps her snappishness and general ill-
temper might have contributed to her being regarded as a force inimical to her
community, whose spirit had to be disempowered.

Scalping, defleshing and mutilation of heads

A noticeable feature of some Danish bog-bodies (and the British ones from Lindow Moss)
is the special attention paid to their heads: Lindow II (**colour plate 12**) received savage
blows; Lindow III's head was removed; the Grauballe victim (**colour plate 13**) was also
hit hard on the head. All sustained injuries to their skulls that contributed to, if they did
not cause, their deaths. But there is further evidence for a deliberate focus on the heads of
these marsh-victims: two individuals from the Borremose bog, a man and a woman, had
sustained terrible head-injuries that may have had ritual significance. The back of the
man's skull had been smashed; the woman had been scalped and, what is more, her face
had been crushed by a heavy blow (Parker Pearson 1999, 68), as if to shame or humiliate

the victim by obliterating her identity (*see* **24**). The face of a woman buried in the sacred precinct of a Romano-British temple at Lowbury Hill in Oxfordshire was similarly disfigured; indeed, her face was mutilated by the removal of her facial bones (Green 1995, 146; Keys 1992); her deposition in this sacred spot may reflect her identity as a sacrificed priestess. A woman from a cemetery at Dunstable in Bedfordshire suffered a similar fate; her head was severed and her face obliterated (Matthews 1981).

It is interesting to note that other human deposits of Iron Age and Roman date seem to have been similarly treated. A human skull from the lake-deposit at La Tène, on the shore of Lake Neuchâtel in Switzerland, bore knife-marks as if it had been deliberately defleshed (that the person did not die by mishap is implied by the apparently ritual character of the artefacts, animal and other human remains, many of which bear signs of trauma including blows to the head, at the site) (Dunning 1991, 366-8; Bradley 1990, 164). Parker Pearson has commented on the broadly synchronous scalping of one of the Pazyryk burials from far away in Central Asia: in one barrow, the frozen body of an elderly man was found to have been injured by three battle-axe blows to his head and to have been scalped. Furthermore, the skin had been 'methodically sliced open across his body' (Parker Pearson 1999, 87). The Auvergnian site of Aulnat contained a well, of second-century BC date, in the bottom of which was a skull with clearly visible knife-cuts on its surface (Collis 2000). It may be significant that the same site produced the painted pot depicting a warrior with a human head at his belt (above).

Defleshing of heads occurred in Britain too. Folly Lane, St Albans (Verlamion) in Hertfordshire was the site of a ritual complex, in the early phase of which a deceased Catuvellaunian chieftain was laid in state inside an enclosure before being cremated in a great funeral pyre in *c*.AD 55. Later in the Roman period, during the second century AD, a series of ritual shafts was dug in the vicinity of the ceremonial enclosure and a Romano-Celtic temple. Several of the pits contained pots in the form of human heads but, at the base of one, the actual head of an adolescent youth had been deposited; he had been killed by a head injury caused by a savage blow; the skull showed clear signs of having been first stripped of its flesh with a knife: more than 90 cut-marks have been identified (**27**, **47**). The fact that the number of knife-marks is far in excess of what was necessary to do the job argues for the presence of some supra-functional, symbolic — perhaps collective — activity. The 'biography' of the skull was complex and bizarre: damage to its base suggests that it had been displayed on a pole but the absence of weathering implies that, if the head were exhibited in the open air, it was only exposed for a short time. Alternatively, it might have been on display inside the nearby temple-building before its interment in the pit as a final ritual act (Niblett 1992, 917-29; 1999, 83-8, 319-20, 414; Mays & Steele 1996, 155-61). Similar practices appear to have been followed in late Roman Britain, at Wroxeter, the *civitas* capital of the Cornovii (Shropshire). Here, fragments of human skull were found in destruction layers in the vicinity of a large Roman sanctuary; they had been deliberately stripped of their flesh and then treated with vegetable oils. One skull showed specific signs of scalping; another had green staining on its base, as though it had reposed on a bronze platter for a time (White & Barker 1998, 96-8).

Defleshing is not necessarily an indication of ritual murder: such behaviour may be associated with a variety of cult-activities, including preparation for burial, as is the case

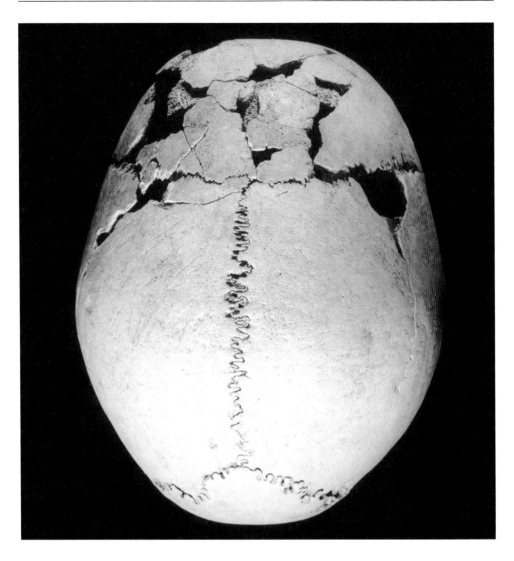

47 *The defleshed skull of a teenage boy, which had been displayed on a pole and then interred in a pit, in the vicinity of a Romano-British temple in the second century AD at Folly Lane, St Albans. © English Heritage Photo Library*

with excarnation (the exposure of a body until after the flesh has decomposed), in order to facilitate entry into the spirit world (Carr & Knüsel 1997, 167-73). This could explain why children's bones were apparently defleshed at Knossos in Crete in around 1450 BC (Hughes 1991, 18-24, 195). The defleshing of human heads at Verulamium and Wroxeter took place in the Roman period, at a time when human sacrifice had long been forbidden by Roman law. If ritual murder was still occurring (Isserlin 1997, 91-100), then it must have done so within the context of illegitimate, subversive and clandestine religious practices. White and Barker (1998, 96-8) suggest that the Wroxeter skulls perhaps reflect retrospective ritual and that the heads might have belonged to ancestors, still revered in the fourth century AD, or have been those of people who were sacrificed before the Roman authorities banned such activity after the conquest in the mid-first century AD, preserved in a conscious act of memory.

Whatever the precise meaning of the head ritual associated with scalping and defleshing, and whether or not human sacrifice was involved, the evidence points to a pre-occupation with the head in a manner highly reminiscent of both literary and archaeological testimony to head-hunting among the Gauls, at least of the south, during the later pre-Roman Iron Age (Lambrechts 1954; Green 1986, 28-32). The blows to the head of the Folly Lane youth and certain of the bog-bodies (including the Lindow people), together with the evidence for scalping and face-crushing, seemingly contribute to a pattern involving the systematic, arguably ritual, maltreatment of human heads in the late Iron Age and Roman periods in parts of Britain and northern Europe. What the defleshing of skulls does *not* provide evidence for is cannibalism, ritual or culinary. However, in view of the possible, albeit rare, evidence for anthropophagy in later prehistoric Europe (see chapter 2), it is interesting that Parker Pearson (citing Turner *et al.*) identifies a list of criteria for the archaeological identification of cannibalism (1999, 154-6), which include facial mutilation (the woman at Borre Fen), splintering of long-bone shafts for marrow extraction (Eton) and dismemberment (Býči Skála).

Some Irish skull legends

I am indebted to Dr Bill Mahon of the Department of Welsh at the University of Wales, Aberystwyth, for drawing my attention to two Irish tales, part of the repertoire of a storyteller from County Clare named Stiofán Ó hEalaoire, and collected by Séamus Ó Duilearga in the 1930s. Both tales relate to the use of a human skull to test veracity:

> There was an old custom in the country long ago, any person who might be robbed or have anything stolen from him, the old saying they had was to go to the church-yard and to bring the head of a dead person with them. Every man around the districts and the neighbourhood who wished to clear himself before them, he would come and swear an oath with regards to the matter. And the way he would swear would be to kiss the skull of the dead person, and he was cleared then. It was said that if you kissed the skull on telling a falsehood, then the head would stick to you, and then they would have to tell the truth about it.

The second story describes the modification of human skulls for use as drinking-vessels, once again within the context of truth and falsehood. The tale bears interesting resemblances to descriptions of such treatment of enemy-heads by the ancient Gauls as chronicled by Graeco-Roman authors (above):

> In the olden days long, long ago there was a law in this place that anyone who did anything wrong, that they had a cup that was made out of a dead person's skull, and whoever had committed the transgression, if he wished to clear himself, all he had to do was to go and take a drink out of the cup. If he raised it upside-down [i.e. to drink] and was not telling the truth, his mouth would turn to the back of his head, or his eyes would turn crooked in his head.
> (Ó Duilearga 1981, 276; trans. Mahon pers. comm. 2000)

The link between the human head and the search for truth was presumably made because the brain of that skull would be perceived as capable of seeing through mendacious claims. Such tales may owe their ancestry to medieval mythic tales, such as are found in the Ulster Cycle, particularly in the *Táin Bó Cuailnge*, the epic prose tale of the great war between Ireland's two most northerly provinces, Ulster and Connacht. The head of one Ulster hero, Conall Cernach, possessed magical properties; there was a prophecy that if the Ulstermen drank milk from the skull, they would feel new strength flooding into them (Kinsella 1969; Lehmann 1989, 1-10; Green 1992b, 64-5). In the coeval tale of *Mac Da Thó's Pig*, Conall is represented as a great warrior, who always wore the head of the best Connacht warrior at his belt, and in the *Feast of Bricriu*, the hero boasted that he made a habit of sleeping with the head of a Connachtman beneath his knee (Kinsella 1969; Lehmann 1989, 1-10; Green 1992b, 64-5).

Postscript

In 1898, Kitchener finally defeated the Sudanese at the Battle of Omdurman, thereby avenging the death of General Gordon. Queen Victoria and the British population were jubilant at the victory, but they were shocked by Kitchener's act of contempt towards the body of the Mahdi, Islamic Sudan's revered religious leader:

> In Omdurman Kitchener proceeded to establish the honours of victory. The Mahdi's tomb had already been damaged severely by the bombardment, and now the body of the Mahdi himself was dug up and flung into the Nile — not, however, until the head was severed, and this was purloined by Kitchener as a trophy of war. He appears to have had the notion that he might have used the skull for an inkstand or a drinking cup . . .
> (Alan Moorehead, *The White Nile*: London, 1960, 346)

6
Suffocation: drowning, strangling and burial alive

[Certain Germanic peoples] are distinguished by a common worship of Nerthus, or Mother Earth. They believe that she interests herself in human affairs and rides through their peoples. In an island of Ocean stands a sacred grove, and in the grove stands a car draped with a cloth which none but the priest may touch. The priest can feel the presence of the goddess in this holy of holies, and attends her, in deepest reverence, as her car is drawn by kine. Then follow days of rejoicing and merrymaking in every place that she honours with her advent and stay. No one goes to war, no one takes up arms; every object of iron is locked away, and then only, are peace and quiet known and prized, until the goddess is again restored to her temple by the priest, when she has had her fill of the society of men. After that, the car, the cloth and, believe it if you will, the goddess herself are washed clean in a secluded lake. This service is performed by slaves who are immediately afterwards drowned in the lake. Thus mystery begets terror and a pious reluctance to ask what that sight can be which is allowed only to dying eyes.

(Tacitus Germania XL, trans. Mattingly 1948, 133-4)

Drowning, hanging or strangling and burial alive all involve death by asphyxiation, the denial of breath or *anima*: what the Classical world recognised as the vital principle distinguishing humans (and beasts) from the inanimate. In assessing the evidence for suffocatory death in European antiquity, what should be appreciated is that the immersion of human bodies, whether in wet or dry locations, can be perceived as liminal placement, with the pit, marsh or grave reflecting the interstices between earthworld and the realms of the spirits. Additionally, the habitual consignment of dead people to peat-bogs may be associated with the perception of such wild, uncultivable places as 'other', beyond the reach of human control (Borca 2000, 74-82). In terms of archaeological evidence, it is difficult to establish drowning as a cause of death, but it may — perhaps — be inferred for certain of the bog-bodies for which no mark of trauma is apparent. As we shall see, a symbolic element of drowning may be indicated by the stones or hurdles found weighting down certain of these marsh victims. What is more, there exists a body of literary evidence, from such authors as Tacitus and the ninth-century Bernese scholiast on the Roman poet Lucan's epic civil war poem, *The Pharsalia*, for the drowning of sacrificial victims in north-west Europe during the first centuries BC and AD. There is even an iconographic representation of what may be a ritual drowning scene on the cult-cauldron from Gundestrup (*see* below).

Suffocation by obstruction of the windpipe — caused by hanging, strangulation or garrotting — may only be determined archaeologically in the case of Iron Age bog-bodies about whose necks a cord or rope is preserved in place. The testimony from these bodies does suggest that strangling was a recurrent method of dispatching victims of ritual murder. Once again, the observations of contemporary — or near-contemporary — documents serve to corroborate evidence for throttling as a method of killing, and very rare iconography also testifies to such practice. Burial alive is not easy to establish from material culture alone, but some evidence seems to point in this direction. There may also be circumstances suggesting that interment deep underground played a significant role in sacrificial ritual, even if death by burial alive cannot be securely established. Live burial is distinct from any other method of deliberate killing in so far as it could be perceived as indirect or 'proxy' killing: no direct violence is done to the person; indeed no hand is raised against the sacrificial victim. This may be significant either in terms of the perceived symbolic consent of the individual or in apparently leaving the business of dispatch up to the gods, thus effectively absolving human agency from all responsibility — with all its consonant fears of pollution — for the death.

Watery graves

> Mercurius Teutates is appeased in this manner among the Gauls: a man is lowered head first into a full tub so that he drowns there.
> (from a ninth-century commentator on Lucan's *Pharsalia* I, 444-6: Zwicker 1934, 50, trans. M.E. Raybould)

48 The drowning scene on the Gundestrup cauldron. © Paul Jenkins

The great gilded silver cauldron from the Raevemose bog at Gundestrup in Jutland is generally conceded to have been manufactured — probably by Thracian craftsmen — during the second or first century BC (Taylor 1992, 66-71). It is made up of 13 plates decorated in repoussé and engraving, apparently depicting mythic scenes. The outer plates contain the greater complexity, seeming to display a narrative of specific, linked episodes associated with late prehistoric cosmologies. For us, the interest lies in a processional scene represented on an outer plate (Kaul 1991, pl. 17) which depicts an army: in the lower register (right to left) three *carnyx* (war-trumpet) players follow a footsoldier who brandishes a sword and wears a boar-crested helmet; he, in turn, is preceded by six more infantry-men with shields and spears, the one at the head of the line faced by a rearing hound and by a huge anthropomorphic figure who ducks a warrior into a great vat, as if to drown him (**48**). The upper register of the cauldron-plate, divided from the lower by a horizontal tree, depicts four cavalrymen facing away from the vat-man; the first and third horsemen are unarmed and wear animal-crested helmets; the second, a sword-bearer with an antlered helmet; the final rider wears a bird-crested helmet and carries a sword; and the mounted procession is led by a ram-horned serpent. The way the hands of the supranormal being grip the warrior shows that he is definitely pushing the victim into the bucket rather than pulling him out. The scene might, indeed, be testimony to a human sacrificial episode although it could — instead — represent a mythic scene associated with reincarnation, symbolised by the transformation of infantry into cavalry. The Second Branch of the medieval mythic narrative known as the Mabinogion (more correctly the Four Branches or *Pedeir Keinc*) contains a description of just such an episode wherein warriors slain in battle were cooked overnight in a magical cauldron and were thus resurrected so that they fought better than ever the following day (although their inability

114

to speak is significant in reflecting their status as 'undead' zombies, belonging still to the world of the dead):

> And then the Irish began to kindle a fire under the cauldron of rebirth. And then the dead bodies were cast into the cauldron until it was full, and on the morrow they would arise as good fighting men as before, save that they were not able to speak.
> (Jones & Jones trans. 1976, 37)

The north European cult-practice associated with the veneration of Nerthus narrated by Tacitus in his *Germania* (XL), quoted at the opening of this chapter, describes a ritual involving human sacrifice in some detail. Like many sacred sites, for instance Anglesey and Strabo's all-female holy island off the estuary of the Loire (chapter 4) (**colour plate 10**), the ceremony is chronicled as being enacted in an island-sanctuary. The ceremony in honour of Nerthus took place within the context of an agricultural festival. Apart from the sacrifice itself, other elements of interest in Tacitus's account include the emphasis on peace and the eschewing of iron objects, as if the metal carried some kind of pollutant property, perhaps because of its association with weaponry. In the context of Gallic ritual, the significance of iron as a special metal to be avoided is mentioned by Pliny the Elder (*Natural History* XXIV, 62), in his account of the gathering of the *selago* plant whose smoke, when burnt, was considered good for the treatment of eye-disorders. Pliny comments that the plant 'must be gathered *without iron* [my italics] with the right hand, thrust under the tunic through the left armhole, as though the gatherer were thieving'. In his account of the Nerthus ritual, Tacitus makes it clear that the absence of conflict was crucially important when the goddess was away from her temple, as though she were at that time in some way vulnerable to inimical forces.

Most significant of all in Tacitus's description of Nerthus's worship is his observation about the purification of the holy cloth which, carried on a wagon, appears to have represented the deity herself. It was imbued with such sanctity that anyone not of priestly status who handled it had to die, presumably to inhibit the spirit-world from mingling too freely with that of humans and to maintain the secrecy associated with the goddess. This notion of sacred objects being too holy to be touched by profane hands resonates closely with the Old Testament accounts of the Ark of the Covenant, the repository for the tablets inscribed by Yahweh with the Ten Commandments. The *Book of Samuel* narrates a chilling episode concerning the movement of the ark from Gibeah to the city of David:

> And when they came to Nachon's threshing floor, Uzzah put forth his hand to the ark of God, and took hold of it; for the oxen shook it. And the anger of the Lord was kindled against Uzzah; and God smote him there for his error; and there he died by the ark of God.
> (*2 Samuel* 6: 6-7)

The deadly sanctity of particular objects is expressed equally emphatically in certain early Christian episodes: a medieval tale concerning the death and burial of the Virgin Mary records the fate suffered by a Jewish unbeliever who laid impious hands on her coffin; his hands stuck to the wood and, when he tried to pull himself away, they came off at the wrist (Lewis 1970, pl. 22; Gray 2000, 113, pl.13b).

It is significant that the method by which Nerthus's attendants met their deaths corresponded with the use of water for the final part of the ceremonial activity associated with the goddess's festival: the cloth was washed in a lake and the washers were then drowned in the same water. While it is debatable whether the servants were sacrificial victims *sensu stricto*, Tacitus is clearly giving an account of ritual murder. It is worth noting that, in the preceding section of the *Germania* (XXXIX), the Roman author makes unequivocal allusion to the practice of human sacrifice among the confederation of the Suebi: 'The sacrifice in public of a human victim marks the grisly opening of their savage ritual'.

Tacitus's description of the goddess Nerthus's carriage around the countryside on a wagon has consonance with one of the scenes on the Gundestrup cauldron (Kaul 1991, 91), where a female figure is shown flanked by two wheels, as if to represent a cart. It may also be pertinent to draw attention to an Iron Age bog-deposit, of the late second century BC, at Dejbjerg in Denmark, which consists of a ceremonial wagon and an alderwood stool (that has been described as a 'throne') found associated with part of a loom, perhaps reflecting feminine symbolism (Glob 1969, 168-71; Davidson 1993, 133). Similarly, another late Iron Age Danish water-deposit, made in Rappendam fen in North Zealand, also associates carts and females: the assemblage consisted of wagon-parts, placed in discrete groups, associated with the body of a woman, together with those of sheep, a cow, a horse and a wild pig (Glob 1969, 166-8; van der Sanden 1996, 104). Clearly, no direct correlation may be made between Tacitus's account, Danish ritual deposits and a piece of uninscribed toreutic iconography but, nonetheless, the recurrent association of a 'ceremonial' vehicle with women is at least suggestive of some shared cultic tradition within northern Europe in late prehistory. Aside from Tacitus's narrative, we possess no information concerning Nerthus herself, but Old Norse tradition provides evidence for the veneration of a male divinity named Njorðr, an etymological cognate of Nerthus, one of the Vanir, a group of Scandinavian deities associated with fertility (Rives 1999, 293).

Another Classical text that is apparent testimony to ritual murder by drowning concerns the treatment of a 'scapegoat' (Greek *pharmakos*), a familiar theme in ancient Greek myth (Hughes 1991, 139-65) although, as Hughes points out, most narratives dealing with *pharmakoi* make no reference to the death of the scapegoat. In one of two accounts of human scapegoat rituals (see chapter 7) reported to have been enacted by Gauls in the Greek-founded colony of Massilia, the chosen (self-selected) victim was fêted for a year, dressed up in fine clothes, paraded through the town — cursed as he went — and finally thrown into the sea, bearing all the community's evils with him and thereby cleansing the town (Servius *On Virgil Aeneid III*, 57; Petronius *Fragment* I; trans. Heseltine 1969, 386-7).

Archaeological evidence for ritual murder by drowning is generally hard to identify **(colour plate 16)**. One category of human remains, where such a method of arguably religious killing may sometimes be implied, consists of certain bodies deposited in watery locations, particularly those that bear no signs of throttling or penetrative injury.

Furthermore, certain bodies deposited in marshes or pools were found pinned down by great hurdles, as if to keep them firmly under the water (**49 & 50**). Such restraints might be interpreted either as a practical or symbolic means of effecting death by drowning, or as a method of keeping the dead body submerged.

Literary testimony from Tacitus supports archaeological evidence for the pinning down of bodies in water, though he emphasises the punitive context for such behaviour:

> . . . the coward, the shirker and the disreputable of body are drowned in miry
> swamps under a cover of wattled hurdles.
> (*Germania* XII)

Tacitus is specifically describing punishment for anti-social and taboo-breaking conduct rather than ritual murder among Germanic peoples, but it is interesting that he accurately records the use of timbers to cover bodies deposited in bogs. The archaeological evidence demonstrates such recurrent practice in the disposal of persons in north-west European marshes during the later first millennium BC and earlier first millennium AD. Certain bodies seem either to have been pinned down into the bed of the swamp or to have been tied to stakes: individuals from wetland areas at La Tène and Cornaux in Switzerland were apparently tethered to great timber posts (Bradley 1990, 164; Simón 1999, 12), though — at Cornaux — they may have been accidental victims, innocent bystanders who died when the bridge collapsed during a flood. A plump, well-nourished 50-year-old woman was pinned down into the marsh, at Juthe (or Haraldskaer) Fen in Denmark, by hurdles, one of which was driven with considerable force into her knee-joint, apparently causing it to swell — a feature frequently cited as an argument for her being pegged down while still alive (Glob 1969, 70-100; van der Sanden 1996, 99, pl. 131; Hvass 1998), though it is now thought possible that bog-acids could have caused the oedema (**49**). The case for identifying this person as the victim of a ritualised killing is strengthened by her careful deposition over a spring. The link between springs and sacral activity is well-documented in the pre-Roman ritual landscape: witness the elaborate deposition of metalwork around the 'Giant's Springs' at Duchcov in Bohemia where, in the third and second centuries BC, a huge bronze cauldron containing more than 2000 objects, mainly brooches and armlets, was placed as an offering to the spring-waters (Megaw 1970, 20, no. 134; Fitzpatrick 1984, 178-90).

A young adolescent girl from Windeby in Schleswig-Holstein in North Germany apparently died by drowning (**50**) but not accidentally, for she was found wearing a blindfold made from a brightly-coloured woven waistband, and half of her head had been shaved shortly before she was killed. Her body was weighted down with birch-branches and a large stone (a strangled male victim found nearby was also pegged down with several stakes: **64, 65**); the analysis of associated pollen indicates that the girl was deposited in the marsh during the early centuries AD (Glob 1969, 114-16; van der Sanden 1996, 98, 112). Several points of interest arise from the find, not least the treatment of her hair, a feature shared with another young woman found at Yde in the Netherlands and with other bog-bodies, notably the Windeby man and a mature woman from Huldremose in Denmark (**colour plate 2**), who was discovered with her hair placed by her side, one strand wound

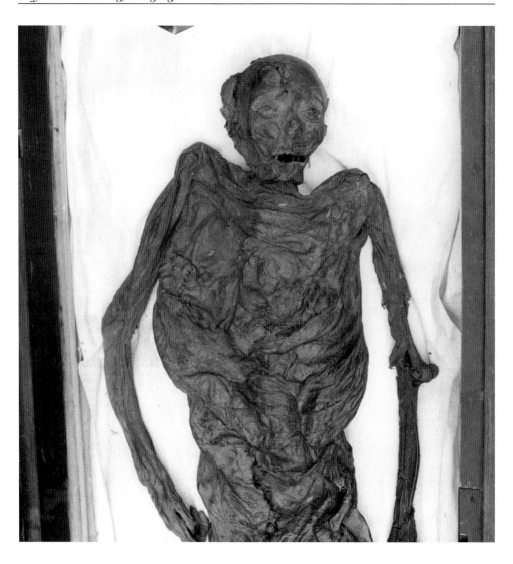

49 *The body of a middle-aged woman, placed in a peat-bog at Haraldskaer, Jutland, in c.490 BC.*
© *Nationalmuseet København*

around her neck (van der Sanden 1996, 164). Tacitus specifically alludes to head-shaving among Germanic communities, once again within the context of punishment:

> Adultery in that populous nation is rare in the extreme, and punishment is summary and left to the husband. He shaves off his wife's hair, strips her in the presence of kinsmen, thrusts her from his house and flogs her through the whole village.
> (*Germania* XII)

50 *A young girl, led blindfold to her death in a peat-bog at Windeby, Schleswig Holstein in the early centuries AD; her body was pinned down in the marsh by great branches and a huge stone.*
© *Stiftung Schleswig-Holsteinische Landesmuseen, Schloss Gottorf —*
Archäologisches Landesmuseum —
Schleswig, Germany

Tacitus nowhere suggests that these unfortunate women were executed, but the literary testimony serves to warn us of the need to exercise caution in attributing death to human sacrifice. What is even more interesting about the Windeby girl is that signs of Harris lines present in her bones attest to her sufferance from several episodes of arrested growth, possibly due to malnutrition caused by famine. Harris lines were also identified on a male bog-victim, killed in the early first millennium BC, from Aschbroeken in the Netherlands (van der Sanden 1996, 112). If the girl drowned at Windeby were to have been the victim of a sacrificial murder, then — on analogy with other ancient traditions where ritual killing was practised (notably some of the Mesoamerican cultures, such as the Moche and Zapotec communities) — one reason for such extreme religious action might have been persistent crop- or livestock-failure. Finally, the presence of the blindfold is interesting: her 'blindness' might — on analogy with certain present-day traditional practices — suggest that, in life, the Windeby girl was a 'seer', a prophetess whose inner sight was enhanced by her physical sensory deprivation (Vitebsky 1995, 146).

Far away from Denmark and North Germany, certain Iron Age bodies from Irish bogs appear to have been similarly treated, in terms of being pegged down and, perhaps, having been drowned. The remains of a woman and an infant were deposited together at Derrymaquirk in Co. Roscommon during the Late Bronze Age or Early Iron Age (according to C_{14} dates), a large stone found in place over the woman's pelvis (Ó Flóinn 1995, 140). Another Irish body, falling within the same date-range and found in a marsh at Kinnakinelly in Co.Galway (*op. cit.* 140), was associated with an upright timber, as if the body had been tethered to it; also present were the bones of red deer as if, perhaps, the animal had been sacrificed with the man. The same region produced a marsh-victim found at Gallagh in 1821; he was a young man who, according to observations recorded at the time of discovery, had long black hair and beard, and was clothed in a deerskin cape. Two pointed stakes flanked his body, as if to restrain him. He may have been drowned but the presence of a band made of twisted willow or hazel wands around his throat may signify an actual or symbolic garrotte. The three C_{14} dates obtained from the deposit put his death in the later first millennium BC (Raftery 1994, 187-8, pl. 77; Brindley & Lanting 1995, 135; Ó Flóinn 1995, 139-40).

Occasionally, human remains are found in ancient wells; these may be interpreted as the result of accidental death, of post-mortem ritual deposition or — perhaps in exceptional circumstances — human sacrifice. In the words of Carol van Driel, 'there are too many Romans tumbling down wells . . . for "accident" to have any credible meaning' (van Driel 1999, 137). The fill of a well at Bavay (Nord) in northern France, of early Roman date, contained three inhumations: a man, a woman and a child, the latter accompanied by a dog (Hénault 1930, 5-9; Merrifield 1987, 43). These deposits do not definitely date from the period of use of the well but were found in subsequent fill, perhaps made even after the well had dried up. The partial human skulls from the Romano-British shrine at Coventina's Well on Hadrian's Wall and a coeval well at Caves Inn, Warwickshire (Allason-Jones & McKay 1985, 34) both belonged to females; the former at least was almost certainly placed in the water as a secondary deposit, perhaps as a mark of respect for human remains that were already old when interred. However, a more likely candidate for ritual killing in a well-context was the owner of a defleshed skull, of second century BC date, from the settlement at Aulnat in the Auvergne (Collis 2000, and see chapter 5).

Several general points should be made concerning watery killings. Firstly, the pinning or weighting down of bodies in aquatic locations has direct analogies with circumstances obtaining in dry pit deposits containing human remains (see below). Secondly, it may occasionally be possible to identify sacrificial substitutes in the archaeological record; one example may be the deposit from Ballachulish in Argyll, where a large wooden female image belonging to the earliest Iron Age was found, according to records made at the time of discovery in the nineteenth century, face-down in peat with signs of having been pinned down with hurdles (Megaw & Simpson 1979, 477; Green 2000a, 18-19) (**51, colour plate 19**). Thirdly, there appears to be a recurrent link between watery ritual murder and the presence of hazel, whether or not drowning is suspected as the cause of death. Thus the male bodies from Windeby and Gallagh wore hazel collars around their necks; another individual, deposited in a Danish bog at Undelev, was associated with three hazel rods (Glob 1969, 68); one of the men from Lindow Moss in Cheshire (Turner 1996, 34; Holden 1995, 76-82), who died in about AD 100 and had been beheaded (either causing or subsequent to his death), consumed a meal of crushed hazelnuts just before he was killed. The presence of hazel may or may not be significant in terms of ritual activity associated with sacrificial murder, but in this context, the wording of a lead *defixio* (curse-tablet) of late Roman date, dredged up from the river Ouse near the Hockwold Roman temple, at Brandon in Suffolk, is of particular interest:

> Whoever . . . whether male slave or female slave, whether freedman or freedwoman . . . has committed the theft of an iron pan, he is sacrificed to the god Neptune with hazel.
> (Hassall & Tomlin 1994, 293-5)

Apart from the link between hazel, sacrifice, Neptune (a Roman water-god) and its riverine context, it is worth noting that sacrifice and punishment seem, according to

51 Wooden female figurine, placed in a marsh and weighted with hurdles, from Ballachulish, Argyll, dating to the earliest Iron Age.
© Paul Jenkins

the inscription, not to have been mutually exclusive. Finally, the symbolic significance of preservation should be appreciated: consignment of bodies (and, indeed, of wooden figurines) to water would have been recognised as a method of halting decay and such choice must have been meaningful both in terms of sacrificial behaviour and perceptions associated with memory and survival beyond the domain of earthworld.

Hanging, garrotting and strangulation

> The traitor and deserter are hanged on trees.
> (Tacitus *Germania* XII)

> To throw away one's shield is the supreme disgrace; the guilty wretch is debarred from sacrifice or council. Men have often survived battle only to end their shame by hanging themselves.
> (*op. cit.* VI)

Tacitus chronicles a range of circumstances under which Germanic communities practised hanging either as suicide or punishment. Archaeology goes some way to corroborating his comments in so far as a number of north European Iron Age bog-bodies exhibit unequivocal signs that they met their deaths by throttling with ropes or cords. As is the case with suspected victims of drowning, it is impossible to be certain that these were human sacrificial deaths; indeed, Tacitus provides us with a set of alternative explanations. Nonetheless, there are sufficiently curious, idiosyncratic features associated with many aquatic deposits of human remains to allow us at least to consider the presence of ritual action. Some victims of strangulation were young, on the threshold of adulthood, and more than one showed signs of disease or deformity, factors that may have influenced their selection for sacrifice. One 16-year-old girl, found in a marsh at Yde in the Netherlands, who had suffered from extreme curvature of the spine (see chapter 7) (van der Sanden 1996, 138), was garrotted with a woven textile band, once used as a belt, similar to the one blindfolding the girl drowned at Windeby in north Germany (**50**). An even younger individual, a boy of not more than 14, was placed in a marsh at Kayhausen in Schleswig-Holstein in the second or first century BC (**59**). His hands had been tied behind his back with strips of woven wool and his feet were bound with a cape; more horrific still, a length of cloth had been passed between his legs and wound around his neck (van der Sanden 1996, 93, 141, pl. 117). Like the girl from Yde, he suffered from a deformity that would severely have affected his ability to walk properly. The lady whose body was found at Elling in Denmark (**52**) was older than these teenagers, being about 30 at her death in the last few centuries BC, by strangulation with her own leather belt, but she, too, had suffered from bone-problems: her skeleton exhibited signs of osteoporosis (van der Sanden 1996, 141), a condition usually affecting post-menopausal women; she was young to be so afflicted.

Deposited in a bog in the same vicinity as the Elling body, but perhaps 70 or so years later in about 250 BC, was the better-known male body known as Tollund Man (**colour**

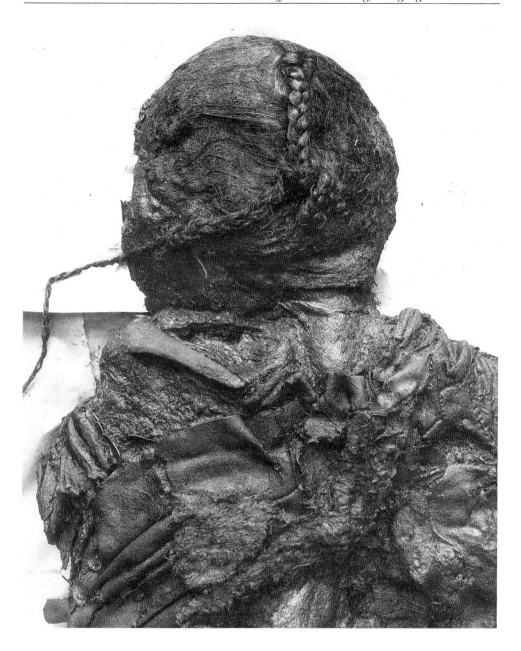

52 *Female bog-body from Elling, Denmark; last few centuries BC. © Nationalmuseet København*

plate 17). His well-preserved face, with its lines and stubble of beard, together with the presence of rheumatism in his thoracic vertebrae, indicate that he died in middle age (between 40 and 50). The presence *in situ* of a noose around his neck, with a knot at the back and a trailing cord, demonstrates his mode of dispatch. He was placed in the marsh naked but for an oxhide belt and a sheepskin cap. It has been suggested that the presence of the strap, made of two plaited leather thongs and tied tightly around the neck, indicates that he killed himself, the argument being that an executioner would have cut the noose and retrieved the garrotte for future use rather than wasting it (Fischer 1999, 93-7; van der Sanden 1996, 155). But this notion does not really stand up to close scrutiny: in the first place, the Tollund body is just one of several found with nooses of various kinds still around their necks; secondly, if human sacrifice were to be the reason for the killings, it may have been important to retain the symbolism of the manner of his death and, at the same time, the instrument of the individuals' demise is likely to have been perceived as polluted and too loaded with meaning for recycling. The man immersed in the Borre Fen, in roughly the same period as the Tollund body, was found with a plaited hempen rope encircling his throat; a male victim from Windeby bore a hazel wand, as thick as a man's finger, bent to form a noose around his neck; the garrotte worn by the young man from the Irish bog at Gallagh in Co. Galway was made of interleaved bands of hazel or willow. Incidentally, it is worth noting that hazel possesses different properties according to the season when it is cut: in summer, the rods are stiff and unyielding, but in winter they are soft and pliable, suggesting that at least the Borremose killing occurred in cold weather (Anne Leaver, pers. comm.).

The bog-body known as Lindow Man (Lindow II), killed in Cheshire in the first century AD (**colour plate 12**) was, like the man from Tollund, thrust naked (but for an armlet made of fox-fur) into the marsh after being garrotted, this time with a noose of sinew, still *in situ* around his neck. Though incomplete, enough of his body was preserved to ascertain that he was about 25 years old and that his neatly-clipped hair and manicured fingernails bore witness to his relatively high rank. He had suffered a 'triple' death: struck hard on the head twice, strangled and his throat cut. The systematic physical abuse he suffered may have served as symbolic degradation, even though the man may have enjoyed relatively high rank during his life: he may even have been a foreign hostage or captive, brought low and ritually slaughtered by an alien community. There is a possibility that his body was painted with blue patterns, although opinion is divided as to whether this was so or if the discoloration was simply due to mineral staining post-mortem. Some time during the Roman period, a male bog-victim was strangled and decapitated at Worsley, also in north-west Britain (Garland 1995). The victims from Lindow and Worsley in Britain and Tollund in Denmark share a further feature, namely their consumption of what may be interpreted as special food, shortly before they died: Lindow Man had eaten bread baked on a griddle, containing a wide range of seeds and grains, and he had also consumed pollen grains of mistletoe; Tollund Man had ingested a seemingly somewhat unappetising gruel or thin porridge (Holden 1995, 76-82). The last meal of the British bog-victim was composed of cereal products, mainly wheat- and rye-bran and barley-chaff, all finely milled to make flour. Electron-Spin-Resonance analysis revealed that the grain had been cooked at a temperature of 200-50°C for a short time, a method consonant with baking rather than boiling for gruel (which requires a maximum temperature of *c.*100°C). The inclusion of mistletoe-pollen in Lindow Man's gut may be significant, given Pliny's comment (*Natural History* XVI, 95) concerning the link between the gathering of mistletoe and druidic ritual, and is seen by some scholars as an indication of a connection between this ritual murder and the druids, especially as a number of Classical writers,

Caesar included, stress the function of this priestly class as perpetrators of human sacrifice (see chapter 9). Tollund Man, by contrast, had consumed a meal of boiled porridge made of barley, wheat and the seeds of wild plants, including flax.

The bog deaths by strangulation considered above all date to the later periods of prehistory, being mainly Iron Age in date. Yet this method of killing had a long ancestry, traceable as early as the Neolithic in northern Europe. Two Danish bodies, from Sigersdel Mose, near Veksø in north Zealand, date to *c*.3500 (cal) BC. Both were young females, one of whom — about 18 years old — had a cord made of vegetable fibre round her neck; the second girl was about 16, and showed no signs of how she met her death. Interestingly, the facial features of both skulls reveal that the two individuals were very probably related; they may even have been sisters (Bennike & Ebbesen 1986, 85-115; Bennike 1999, 30). The phenomenon of families being apparently selected for sacrificial ritual is exhibited very clearly during the later Iron Age at Leonding in Austria (see chapter 3) where several individuals, all suffering from the same congenital and inherited jaw-deformity, were found in a pit, allegedly as the result of repeated fire-sacrifice.

The great majority of archaeological evidence for victims of hanging or strangulation comes from the bog-bodies, but a singular piece of Romano-British iconography strongly suggests the representation of such a killing, though it may simply depict a bound captive. In the British Museum, with a provenance of Brough-under-Stainmore in Cumbria, is a small copper-alloy human figurine, with holes for suspension (as if designed for wear as an amulet, or even as a piece of liturgical regalia) (**colour plate 20**). The statuette bears an uncanny resemblance to the bog-body of the youth found at Kayhausen, in so far as it is the image of a young man with a rope around his neck attached to his bound hands (Green 1978, 48, pl. 138). It is very tempting to interpret this figure not simply as a prisoner but, perhaps, as a sacrificial victim.

Interment underground and burial alive

> To be buried, while alive, is, beyond question, the most terrific of these extremes [of agony] which has ever fallen to the lot of mere mortality . . . *no* event is so terribly well adapted to inspire the supremeness of bodily and of mental distress, as is burial before death . . .
> (Edgar Allan Poe, *The Premature Burial*, 1844)

Killing someone by burying them alive is different from other methods of dispatch, by virtue of its 'passivity' and the 'detachment' of the killers from their victims; in other words it does not involve physical violence in the same way as stabbing, strangling or burning. In a ritual context, burial alive could be perceived as — in some way — leaving the death up to the gods and, perhaps, as a 'voluntary' death, thus absolving the perpetrators from some level of responsibility. Such practice is by no means unknown in European antiquity, and has been recorded further afield. Early seventeenth-century ethno-historical Spanish records describe an incident in which an Inca girl had volunteered to take centre-stage in a sacrificial ritual involving her entombment alive on an Andean mountain-top, as part of a fertility rite, a gift to the sun-god. The ceremony was enacted at the place where the crops were stored and, after her death, the girl was venerated as a goddess of healing and abundance. To be chosen for sacrifice was clearly, in this context, regarded as a great honour: her father was granted permission to offer his child to the divine powers by the Inca authorities in acknowledgement for his public service to his community. It should be remembered that this event took place some time after the Spanish Conquistadors had de-paganised the region (Sillar 1992, 107-23; Parker Pearson 1999, 19). This form of ritual killing may be seen as 'auto-sacrifice', inasmuch as both the girl's father and the girl herself were willing participants. Similar self-sacrifice is recorded far away in the southern Sudan where there is a Dinka tradition wherein particularly prestigious priest-chiefs were allowed to bury themselves alive for the good of their communities (Bourdillon 1980, 19). The right to sacrifice oneself in this manner was conferred as an honour to a highly-regarded leader who wished to do this, in the perception that, only by submitting himself to an unnatural but non-violent end could he avoid losing control over his own life and that of his people. By interring himself alive, he remained with his village and could continue to protect it. A variation on 'voluntary' sacrifice involving live burial is still carried out during village rituals in the Madurai district of Tamilnadu in South India, where children are interred as part of an therapeutic purification rite of 'circling the temple' and are then disinterred unharmed (Foulston 1998). By performing this act of pseudo-sacrifice, the children are ritually dedicated to the goddess who then heals them of their afflictions. In a recent interview conducted at Perayur near Madurai (Foulston pers. comm.), a woman described the ritual associated with the village goddess Mariyamman involving a baby, who was smeared with holy ash, placed in a hole and loosely covered with earth, while its parents walked around the temple; the child was then uncovered but, in this case, the 'sacrifice' did not work and the baby was not cured. Apparently, in some areas, this kind of aversion/healing sacrifice originally involved the live burial of pigs, their place later being taken by babies who were actually sacrificed, their bodies trampled into the earth by cattle (see chapter 2). Jain communities in India possessed a tradition of auto-sacrifice, in which devotees starved themselves to death, leaving memorials to their self-dedication in sacred places, in the form of footprints carved on stone. Such practice, called the *Sallekhana* (the 'religious death') still very occasionally takes place (Kamdar 1993).

In ancient Rome the sacred fire, personified as the goddess Vesta, was kept by a group of celibate priestesses, the Vestal Virgins. These women enjoyed high rank in Roman society, being allocated special seats for watching the games in the arena and possessing privileges, such as the right to conduct business autonomously, normally granted only to men. The Vestals wore white as a sign of their purity, and held their posts for 30 years, after which they retired with a handsome pension and were free to marry. But there were dire penalties for any Vestal who broke her vows of chastity, for her punishment was harsh, as recorded by several ancient authors, including Pliny the Younger writing in the reign of Trajan, in a letter to Cornelius Minucianus, about such an occurrence apparently taking place at the end of the first century AD:

> [Domitian] had made up his mind to bury alive Cornelia, the chief priestess of the Vestal Virgins, with the idea of making his age famous by an example of this kind . . . The priests were dispatched at once to carry out the burial and the execution . . . when she was taken down into the famous underground chamber and her robe caught as she descended, as she turned to free it the executioner offered her his hand; but she drew away in disgust.
>
> (Radice 1963 trans. *The Letters of the Younger Pliny* Letter XI, 6-11, 117-18)

Plutarch's *Life of Numa*, the second king of Rome who allegedly reigned in the seventh century BC, describes an earlier horrific punishment more graphically: Numa is credited by his biographer as having established the College of Vestals:

> . . . But she that broke her vow of chastity was buried alive by the Colline gate. There, within the walls, is raised a little mound of earth, called in Latin *Agger*; under which is prepared a small cell, with steps to descend to it. In this are placed a bed, a lighted lamp, and some slight provisions, such as bread, water, milk and oil, as they thought it impious to take off a person consecrated with the most awful ceremonies, by such a death as that of famine. The criminal is carried to punishment through the *Forum* in a litter well covered throughout, and bound up in such a manner that her cries cannot be heard. The people silently make way for the litter and follow it with marks of extreme sorrow and dejection. There is no spectacle more dreadful than this, nor any day which the city passes in a more melancholy manner. When the litter comes to the place appointed, the officers loose the cords, the high-priest, with hands lifted towards heaven, offers up some private prayers just before the fatal minute, then takes out the prisoner, who is covered with a veil, and places her upon the steps which lead down to the cell: after this, he retires with the rest of the priests, and when she is gone down, the steps are taken away and the cell is covered with earth; so that the place is made level with the rest of the mound. Thus were the *Vestals* punished who preserved not their chastity.
>
> (Plutarch *Life of Numa* 10: trans. Langhorne & Langhorne 1884, 50)

This grisly ritual execution, carried out publicly, in the very heart of the city, was clearly, in a very real sense, a religious death, hedged about with formalised ceremony that involved the very highest cult official (equivalent to the Anglican Archbishop of Canterbury). The strict formula of practice applied appears to demonstrate the sacrificial overtones to the killing, even though it was a punitive rite; to an extent, the defilement caused by the sexual lapse of the victim had to be expiated by a sacrificial rite in which the pollutant was denounced collectively by the citizens of the city. The particular mode of death has a symbolic voluntariness in so far as the errant Vestal was left to make her own way down to her living tomb; furthermore, the presence of food and light served symbolically to deny human agency and allow her executioners to abnegate responsibility for her death. It may even be that these women acted as scapegoats for the more general evils of the Roman city.

Burial alive as a definite sacrificial rite seems also to have taken place in ancient Rome in the heyday of the Republic, during the later third century BC. Several Graeco-Roman authors, Pliny the Elder (*Natural History* XXVIII 3, 2), Plutarch (*Life of Marcellus* 3; *Quaestiones Romanae* 83) and Dio Cassius (*Roman History* XII, 50) among them, allude to the recurrent practice of sacrificing gendered pairs of Gauls and Greeks by burying them alive in the Forum Boarium. In each instance, the rite apparently occurred at a time of great stress to the city; for instance, the ceremony was enacted in 216 BC following the disastrous defeat suffered by the Romans at the hands of the Carthaginians at the Battle of Cannae. Plutarch describes the context in which such sacrificial ritual took place in 228 BC when, following the 22-year-long first Punic War, the Insubres of Alpine Gaul, aided by *Gaesatae* (Gallic mercenaries), threatened the city:

> The Romans do not practise any barbarous or outlandish rites, and in the humane sentiments which they cherish towards their divinities they come nearer than any other people to the Greeks: nevertheless at the outbreak of this war they felt obliged to follow out certain oracular instructions laid down in the Sibylline Books, and to bury alive two Greeks, a man and a woman, and likewise two Gauls in the place known as the Cattle-market; and in accordance with these oracles they still to this day in the month of November perform certain ceremonies, which may not be spoken of nor witnessed by either Greeks or Gauls.
> (Plutarch *Life of Marcellus* 3; trans. Scott-Kilvert 1965, 87)

The Augustan historian Livy (*Ab Urbe Condita* XXII, 57, 6) also admits the practice took place in the past but, like Plutarch, emphasised how unusual — and how unRoman — it was (Green 1998a, 172). This particular rite appears to have been an aversion sacrifice, designed to ward off further catastrophes and, presumably, to placate or propitiate whichever divine powers were perceived to have responsibility for Rome's problems. Pliny the Elder's testimony is particularly striking, for he refers to the enactment of this sacrificial rite in his own day (first century AD):

> Our own generation indeed even saw buried alive in the Cattle Market a Greek man and a Greek woman, and victims from other peoples with whom at the time we were at war. The prayer used at this ceremony is wont to be dictated by the Master of the College of the Quindecemviri, and if one reads it one is forced to admit that there is power in ritual formulas, the events of eight hundred and thirty years showing this for all of them.
> (Pliny *Natural History* XXVIII, 3, 12: trans. Jones 1963, 11)

Archaeological testimony to ritual interment alive is generally equivocal, there being few instances where the evidence is strongly suggestive of such practice. During the 1960s and 1970s, archaeologists investigated a series of geographically contiguous sites threatened by gravel quarrying at Garton Slack, near Great Driffield in East Yorkshire (Brewster 1976, 104-16). The work carried out in 1965 revealed a range of features including four square-ditched Iron Age barrow-cemeteries and coeval single graves. Other excavations unearthed further graves, houses, grain silos, ditches and pits. Several tombs consisted of relatively high-status inhumations — male and female — including a cart-grave (one of a number since discovered). In the ditches of certain enclosures at Garton Slack, several chalk human figurines of later date had been deliberately deposited, their heads removed first (Stead 1988). But most sinister of all (Brewster 1976, 115) was the discovery of two bodies — a young man in his late teens and a 30-year-old woman — interred tightly together, a wooden stake pinning their arms together down into the ground and 'buried in an exact replica of a chariot-grave', with an associated pole-shaft. Beneath the female skeleton was the body of a six-month foetus. Brewster interpreted these remains as those of persons who had been buried alive, the child being expelled from the woman's womb as the result of trauma at the time of burial, while she was unconscious. The assemblage may represent a punitive execution: perhaps the couple were caught in adultery, maybe even incest. But whatever the circumstances surrounding the deaths, they appear to have occurred within a ritualised context. The act of pinning down the limbs with timbers is highly reminiscent both of certain bog-body deaths and the treatment of human remains buried in disused grain storage pits at places like Danebury (see below). The placement of these two bodies away from the main cemeteries may be indicative of their special, polluting deaths (Giles 2001).

Broadly contemporary with the Garton Slack interment was the Irish Iron Age burial of a woman within an embanked enclosure, on a plain known as the Curragh in Co. Kildare. Her body was placed at the centre of the enclosure, which in itself is indicative of special treatment. Barry Raftery comments that her 'strained and awkward position and unnaturally raised skull prompted the conclusion that she had, in all probability, been buried alive' (Raftery 1981, 173-204; 1994, 199). The woman may have suffered a punitive execution for some transgression, but the circumstances of her interment suggest that the killing had ritual overtones and she may even have been a human sacrificial victim.

Gifts to the Underworld

Archaeological evidence testifies to a recurrent ritual practice that may be associated with sacrificial offerings, involving human beings, to the chthonic spirits. The rites in question consist of multiple interments of people deep underground in circumstances that argue against their burial as any kind of 'normative' sepulchral practice. Whilst there is no evidence to suggest that these persons were actually buried alive, it may be that their consignment to the depths of the ground represented their symbolic union with the spirits of the underworld and their reciprocal contribution to the earth's fertility. Examination of two sites, where this kind of multiple interment took place during the European Iron Age, serves to illustrate the tradition: one in Gaul, the other in Britain. But these two are just a small sample of cult-practice that has been identified in several locations in western Europe during this period. Indeed, finds from the Luxembourg Gardens in Paris indicate that similar rites were going on in Gallo-Roman times. Here, in the first-third centuries AD, more than a hundred pits, between 3m and 12m deep, were excavated between 1956 and 1974 some of which contained human burials; in one pit two skeletons were found together and a third body had either fallen or been thrown in on top (Merrifield 1987, 43; Hénault 1930, 5-9).

The settlement of Acy-Romance in the Ardennes was a site where curious ritual activity, involving people, occurred during the second and first centuries BC (Lambot 1998, 73-87; 2000, 30-6). The centre of the village appears to have been designated as public cult-space, focused on a large D-shaped ditched enclosure. In the ditch itself there was evidence that cattle and horses had been slaughtered for feasting; their remains had been deliberately placed in discrete groups, cattle in the southern half, horses to the north. Access to the interior was through a portico, apparently decorated with cattle-heads. Along the western edge of the enclosure ditch five rectangular structures — identified as temples — were erected, the largest of which covered a square pit 7.6m deep. In front of this building was a terrace below which a total of 19 young adult men had been entombed in the earlier second century BC, after having been subjected to a bizarre set of rituals (**colour plate 18**). First, the dead were placed in a seated position, their backs doubled forward and their heads resting on the ground between their outstretched feet. The bodies were then desiccated before their final interment: they appear each to have been placed in wooden containers *c.*75cm square while their flesh shrank and dried out. The body, folded in on itself, was then re-interred in the terrace. The deep pit in the central temple appears to have been the temporary repository for each box; the caskets rested in turn on two lateral joists about 2m up from the bottom of the shaft. After a period of time, the box would have been raised, the body removed to complete the drying process and then buried. This rite was repeated several times, probably at regular intervals. Three other men, one a mature adult, were found interred all in a line in square pits adjacent to one another; each was, like the others, desiccated, perhaps subjected to excarnation first, and placed deliberately orientated towards the rising sun. They were buried in a seated attitude, the trunk in an upright position.

The hypothesis that all these young men were sacrificial victims is supported by a number of features. It is clear from the range of cemeteries associated with the settlement at Acy that cremation was the normal burial-rite for the inhabitants of the village (some 130 cremations have been recorded). The seated inhumations seem, therefore, to be special, a view strengthened by the curious — and repetitive — circumstances of their interment, their central location in association with an arguably cultic precinct, and the absence of any grave-goods (a feature in direct contrast with many of the cremations). The seated position of these bodies (**53**) (particularly the upright ones) is, to my mind, significant also: the fact that they were not laid out flexed or extended, but sitting, may be indicative that they were placed in a 'lifelike' attitude, as if to symbolise their burial alive, whether or not this was actually the cause of death.

While the remains of these seated bodies bear no sign of how they died, another male burial found nearby exhibits clear evidence for violent death: he sustained a brutal axe-blow to his head in about 100 BC. This man was older than most of the others, perhaps as much as 30 years of age; he was buried in a shallow grave, lying on his back with his head bent backwards and his hands behind his back, one wrist over the other, as if he had been bound. The blow that killed him was struck from above and behind; the inference

53 Bronze figure, seated cross-legged, from the 'sanctuaire de la Bauve' (Seine-et-Marne); fourth-first centuries BC, in association with ritually-destroyed weapons. The Gaulish shrine was succeeded by a Gallo-Roman temple. Antoine Maillier © Centre archéologique européen du Mont Beuvray

is that he was kneeling when attacked. The excavator, Bernard Lambot, is of the opinion that this man was slaughtered some time after the formal sacrificial rites at the central temple had ceased, perhaps when human sacrifice had become officially forbidden. One significant point about this death is that the mark left on his skull by the axe-blow is an exact fit with the blade of a curious transversely-perforated weapon found in a rich cremation-grave on the site, one of a group tentatively identified as those of religious officials and distinguished by the presence of special knives and buckets (*see* **72**).

Lambot interprets the sacrificial rituals, involving seated individuals, as taking place at Acy-Romance over the space of a century or less. The ceremonies seem to have been accompanied by public feasting on cattle and horses as the victims were interred. Sheep were consumed as well, and the remains of a lamb-foetus indicate that some animals were slaughtered in mid-winter. The whole ceremony appears to have been related to rites associated with fertility, the nourishment of the earth and with linkages between the sun and the underworld. The chthonic forces received the life-essence of the young men's bodies released as they decomposed, together with the remains of ritual feasts. The drying-out pit identified in the main temple building is reminiscent of the great central decomposition pit found at the shrine of Gournay-sur-Aronde in Picardy, where elderly oxen were interred for a time and their bones then redeposited in the ditch surrounding the sacred enclosure (Brunaux 1988; 1996, 69-77). It is interesting to speculate on the identity of the young men selected for sacrifice at Acy. It is almost inconceivable that these individuals belonged to the community itself; if they did, then the village was repeatedly engaged in sacrificing its most valuable resource: vigorous young men in the prime of their fighting- or farming-lives. The lack of grave-goods and the bound hands (of one man) suggest that they may, instead, have been persons of low status: slaves, criminals or war-captives, analogous to those sacrificial victims mentioned by Caesar and other Classical writers on Gaulish ritual behaviour (see chapter 7). This idiosyncratic form of cult-activity was not confined to this one settlement in the Ardennes; in 1998, excavations at the ancient port of Geneva revealed evidence for similar rituals: the seated inhumation of an adult man, about 20 years old, interred in the third or second century BC, exhibited signs of controlled desiccation closely resembling the treatment of people at Acy and, once again, with no grave-goods. Other human remains, from the town gate, suggest further sacrificial activity (Haldimann & Moinet 1999, 170-81).

The second case-study relevant to chthonic and, arguably, sacrificial ritual activity is the Iron Age hillfort of Danebury in Hampshire. In the course of his investigations over 20 years, Barry Cunliffe excavated a series of grain silos which, following their period of practical use for storage, became the repositories for a range of 'special' burials, both human and animal. The human remains consisted of entire and partial skeletons; some bodies were deposited in groups of two or three. They were generally placed at the base of the disused pits once they had been cleaned out; the absence of significant levels of erosion-silt beneath the bodies argues for their prompt deposition in the silos very shortly after their clearance, presumably especially for the purpose of interment. Certain features of the human and animal pit-burials possess elements in common, suggesting a shared ritual tradition: these include the selection of particular body-parts — notably the head (in the case of animals, this custom applies mainly to horses), multiple deposition and the crushing and/or weighting down of the bodies with blocks of flint or chalk.

The 'pit-tradition' at Danebury probably lasted from the eighth/seventh to the first century BC; Cunliffe (1992, 69-83; 1993a; 1993b) has estimated that the human silo-burials took place on average once every six years or so (**54**), making this an exceptional rite rather than part of a normative burial tradition. The ritual activity focused on these pits is probably best interpreted as being closely linked with the original business of the silos, namely storage of seed-corn over the winter and the disturbing of the ground that took place in order to construct them. The curated deposits of human and animal remains, together with inanimate pit-assemblages (such as metalwork and, probably, perishable organic material) appear to relate to repetitive, complex ceremonies which should be seen as the end-product of elaborate symbolic episodes, beginning with the gathering of the corn and the digging of the pits. In all likelihood, the apparently mundane process of corn-storage was an integral element in the expression of fundamental and sophisticated beliefs concerning reciprocity, asking and thanking the supernatural guardians and producers of the crop, and constant reinforcement and acknowledgement of the dependence of people upon the spirit-world.

Certain features of the human burials themselves suggest that their deposition came about as the result of cult-activity. The position of certain bodies, tightly flexed with hands together, implies that these individuals may have been bound. The crushing and pinning down of some bodies exhibits a similar pattern of restraint and violent attitudes to the

54 One of the bodies interred in grain silos at Danebury. © Danebury Trust

victims to that discerned in the bog-bodies, some of whom also were bound. Such treatment could mean that these individuals were either genuinely or symbolically buried alive; the damage done to the bones might even point to symbolic cannibalism, a ritual that may serve to honour or insult the dead (Lewis 1996, 88-104); it is interesting to note the implication of cannibalistic activity at one or two British Iron Age sites (chapter 2).

The two sites of Danebury and Acy-Romance share elements in common, most notably the bias in selection of victims, in each instance, towards young adult men. It is also significant that the status of the candidates chosen for ritual killing may, on both sites, have been low: at Danebury, several of the skeletons show signs of malnourishment (just as is displayed by many of the bog-bodies); at Acy, the absence of grave-goods (also the case at Danebury) and the disposal by inhumation have been argued as marks of inferior rank. Such a notion fits well with the binding of certain individuals at both sites. Classical writers emphasise the low status of Gallic sacrificial victims (Caesar *de Bello Gallico* VI, 16; Diodorus Siculus *Library of History* V, 32, 6).

If people were sacrificed at Danebury, the rite may have been enacted according to strict criteria of victim-selection and seasonality. Particular groups of persons might have been marked out for such a fate, by virtue of status, appearance, foreign-ness or deviant behaviour (chapter 7). Deposition in the pits clearly relates to an underground location, a region perhaps perceived as a liminal, threshold space between earth and underworld. Such boundary-symbolism may be extended to the time of year when the pit-rituals may have been carried out, at the liminal period between the harvest and the sowing of the new crop. The symbolic death of the buried seed and its rebirth in the spring perhaps prompted cult-behaviour designed as negotiative action to ensure the continuance of the earth's regenerative properties and in acknowledgement of the supernatural dimension of seasonal cyclicity and germination (Bloch & Parry 1982, 1-44). Indeed, victims of ritual murder could symbolically mimic the burial alive of the corn seed itself. Additionally, the interment of the bodies might serve to link the community to the land that supported it, in so far as the flesh of the victims would nourish and form part of the earth within which it decomposed. It is significant that some human remains in the Danebury silos comprised only one or two bones as if, perhaps, the linkage between the community and the chthonic forces could be maintained by the interment of a token portion of an individual, an ancestor maybe, whose body was first subjected to excarnation rites and a fragment buried in a pit *pars pro toto*. In this manner, the ancestors retained a stake in the community and served to help reinforce the longstanding, unbroken relationship between past, present and future (the latter signified by the investment, through sacrifice, in the land's continued fertility).

In any attempted interpretation of the 'special' human remains in the Danebury pits, cognisance must be taken of the perceived socio-cultural context of the site and others like it. A central question relates to the function of hillforts in central-southern England within the surrounding countryside. Were they 'central places', proto-towns, with dense permanently-settled populations, or were they special, with a particular ceremonial role within society? J.D. Hill (1995b, 53) has argued persuasively that sites such as Danebury may have been special locations for public expressions of ritual and for reaffirming social ties, similar to the great assemblies, described in early medieval Irish historico-mythic texts, at Tara, Emhain Macha and elsewhere (Bhreathnach *et al.* 1997). In support of this thesis, Hill cites the differences between formal, structured deposits on hillforts and open sites, the way in which the human element in such deposits is represented on hillforts, by a greater bias towards young adult males and the presence of isolated skulls (*see* **11**), together with the identification — at Danebury, Maiden Castle, South Cadbury, for instance — of centrally-positioned buildings interpreted as shrines. If Danebury and cognate sites were special, that would fit well with a model of repeated sacrificial activity, perhaps associated with a professional clergy and serving to express public, collective devotional linkages with the spirit world, on behalf of a community over and above the inhabitants of the hillfort itself. The Danebury pit-bodies may, in this way, be regarded as analogous to the seated, boxed bodies at Acy-Romance and — maybe — to bog-sites like Windeby and Lindow Moss, where several persons were consigned to a single discrete area of marsh in episodic activity, taking place over a period of time.

7
Selecting
the victims

The Gauls believe that the gods prefer it if the people executed have been caught in the act of theft or armed robbery or some other crime, but when the supply of such victims runs out, they even go to the extent of sacrificing innocent men.
(*Caesar* De Bello Gallico VI, 16)

The question of choice is crucial to understanding the perceptions that underpin the use of people as sacrificial victims. There is a substantial body of both literary and archaeological evidence that, in antiquity, the selection of the victim took place according to prescribed rules: status, gender, age and physical condition all appear to have been important factors in determining which members of communities were likely candidates for ritual murder. Persons of high or low rank, children, slaves, criminals and prisoners-of-war are mentioned by Classical authors as victims; archaeological testimony adds other categories, including adolescents, young men and those with disabilities. There is abundant evidence, from human remains in the Iron Age and Roman periods in northern Europe, to suggest that state of health and the presence of blemishes or deformity could act as a trigger for sacrificial choice.

Certain of the above-mentioned groups may share a common feature, namely marginality or exclusion from the community in which they dwelt. Slaves and war-captives are quite likely to have been foreigners, who did not belong. Similar principles might apply to the disfigured or handicapped, particularly those whose disability was highly visible or prevented them from functioning efficiently. Children equally may not have been considered as full members of society; those at the threshold of life-stages — such as pubescent teenagers or menopausal women — may have been perceived as special and as symbolic of transformation, of boundary-crossing between earth- and spirit-worlds. Young men who met their deaths violently and were interred in idiosyncratic locations, such as disused grain silos, appear to flout the rules of exclusion or marginality, but it should be acknowledged that — in many non-western traditions — certain vigorous young males were set apart from their group, particularly before battle or the hunt (Chaudhri 1996, 166-77; Blacker 1996, 178-85).

Some sacrificial victims, especially prisoners-of-war, criminals, slaves and children may have been selected according to the principle of substitution or surrogacy, whereby persons considered as of lesser worth were sacrificed in place of the sacrificer. The apogee of a human sacrificial gift would, perhaps, be perceived as being the life of the individual making the offering but, since this person could not benefit by his or her own death, a surrogate victim might be chosen, a life nearly as valuable as that of the supplicant but deemed more expendable: a good example is the Greek drama *Alcestis*, where Euripides presents the *mores* of Athenian society in the late fifth century BC, in which it was considered 'right' for a wife to sacrifice herself in place of her husband. Social outcasts (on whatever criteria applied within the particular society), outsiders, enemies, foreigners could all legitimately be dispatched in acts that combined religious veneration, expediency and reprisals (Green 2000b). It is of extreme interest that new research into Iron Age and Gallo-Roman material culture is revealing that substitution may affect inanimate objects too (**colour plate 19**): at late Iron Age sites, such as Corent, in the Auvergne and Lyon (Collis; Guichard pers. comm.), the presence of sword-cuts on chopped-up sherds suggests that wine amphorae were sometimes 'sacrificed'. These tall, double-handled jars do bear a resemblance — in colour and general shape — to human beings, and the analogy is enhanced by the resemblance between flowing blood and spilt red wine. It is tempting, therefore, to interpret this deliberate destruction as mimicry of ritual murder. Additionally, some of the purposely damaged Iron Age swords, especially those with anthropomorphic hilts, could also be surrogate people: one sword-scabbard (unprovenanced: Musée de la Civilisation Gallo-Romaine at Lyon) actually has a small pair of human feet near the base, as if the whole weapon was designed to imitate the human form (temporary exhibition 'Les Druides Gaulois' at the Musée de Bibracte, AD 2000) (**55**).

Prisoners and slaves: literary testimony

Criminals

In the ancient world, people lost their freedom as a consequence of warfare, enslavement or transgression of legal or social rules. Julius Caesar's comment (the opening quotation for this chapter) relates to criminal activities and to the — on the face of it — curious statement that such persons were positively desirable as sacrificial vctims. Diodorus Siculus makes a similar observation concerning Gaulish sacrificial custom; he says:

> For their criminals they keep prisoner for five years and then impale them in honour of the gods, dedicating them together with many other offerings of first-fruits and constructing pyres of great size. Captives also are used by them as victims for their sacrifices in honour of the gods.
> (Diodorus Siculus *Library of History* V, 32, 6)

Both Caesar and Diodorus (after Poseidonios) were describing a perfect example of substitution, combined with retaliation, aimed at the social outcast. But there may have been another reason for the deliberate choice of such malefactors. Occupying the margins of society, these persons were quite likely to be perceived as charged with special energy (albeit of a negative nature), a force that could benefit the community if channelled, as a gift, toward the supernatural world. On the one hand, then, wrongdoers could usefully be disposed of with an easy conscience, legitimately ridding society of troublesome misfits; on the other, such people may have been sought out as especially effective votive offerings.

Prisoners-of-war

War-captives are generally foreign enemies. In antiquity, they may have possessed ambiguous status: to their victorious opponents, they were of lesser worth, by virtue of their alien-ness and their representation of a defeated people, yet they may have been high-ranking individuals in their own communities. Therefore they might, on occasions, have been perceived as particularly efficacious sacrificial victims.

There exists a mass of literary and material evidence for the sacrifice of war-captives in ancient Europe, not only in the 'barbarian' west but even in Greece itself. According to Plutarch, the Athenian war-leader Themistocles was responsible for the sacrifice of Persian prisoners during the great war against Xerxes. In 480 BC, just before the Battle of Salamis, he obeyed an oracle which announced that the gods demanded human

55 *Silver-inlaid iron sword in an iron, enamel-inlaid scabbard, with a pair of small human feet decorating the sharp end of the latter; provenance unknown (in the Musée de la Civilisation Gallo-Romaine, Lyon). Third-first century BC. Antoine Maillier © Centre archéologique européen du Mont Beuvray*

sacrifice as the price of victory over the Persian fleet. The passage is worth quoting in full for it contains a great deal of interest concerning principles governing victim-selection:

> Meanwhile, Themistocles was offering sacrifice alongside the admiral's trireme. Here, three remarkably handsome prisoners were brought before him, magnificently dressed and wearing gold ornaments. They were reported to be the sons of Sandauce, the king's sister, and Artayctus. At the very moment that Euphrantides the prophet saw them, a great bright flame shot up from the [animal] victims awaiting sacrifice at the altar and a sneeze was heard on the right, which is a good omen. At this, Euphrantides clasped Themistocles by the right hand and commanded him to dedicate the young men by cutting off their forelocks and then to offer up a prayer and sacrifice them all to Dionysus, the Eater of Flesh, for if this were done, it would bring deliverance and victory to the Greeks. Themistocles was appalled at this terrible and monstrous command from the prophet, as it seemed to him. But the people, as so often happens at moments of crisis, were ready to find salvation in the miraculous rather than in a rational course of action. And so they called upon the name of the god with one voice, dragged the prisoners

to the altar, and compelled the sacrifice to be carried out as the prophet had
demanded.
(Plutarch *Life of Themistocles* XIII, 2; trans. Scott Kilvert 1960, 90-1)

The Persian war-captives were young, male, foreign, good-looking and of noble birth.
The idea of human sacrifice was repugnant to Themistocles but, in the stress of warfare,
his warriors clamoured for this cathartic ritual act, believing the prophecy that such an
event would result in victory and, no doubt, anxious for an excuse to exact vengeance on
Xerxes for all the Athenians killed in the war.

   The sacrificial episode before Salamis, if indeed it were not simply a figment of an
author's fertile imagination, occurred within the context of a desired outcome: victory for
the Greeks against the Persians, the need to overcome the threat of foreign conquest. The
emphasis on foreign-ness recurs in other ancient texts, including those relating to the
Punic Wars with Republican Rome, when aversion sacrifices were carried out in the centre
of the city of Rome itself, involving foreigners — pairs of Greeks and Gauls — buried alive
in ritual response to the threat posed by Carthaginian power (see chapter 6).

   According to contemporary texts, high-ranking prisoners-of-war were occasionally
sacrificed in acts of reprisal following the killing of heroes in battle. The death of the
Greek Patroclus, close friend of Achilles, in the Trojan Wars, was avenged by the sacrifice
of 12 youths belonging to the enemy, for his comrade's funeral pyre:

> Nine dogs had the prince, that fed beneath his table, and of these Achilles cut
> the throats of twain, and cast them upon the pyre and twelve valiant sons of the
> great-souled Trojans slew he with the bronze — and grim was the work he
> purposed in his heart — and thereto he set the iron might of fire, to range at
> large. Then he uttered a groan, and called on his dear comrade by name: 'Hail,
> I bid thee, O Patroclus, even in the house of Hades, for now am I bringing all
> to pass, which aforetime I promised thee. Twelve valiant sons of the great-
> souled Trojans, lo all these together with thee the flame devoureth . . .
> (Homer *Iliad* XXIII, lines 175-84; trans. Murray 1963, 507-9)

A parallel episode is found in Virgil's Roman epic poem the *Aeneid*, which drew heavily
on Homer for its inspiration and form. Aeneas's comrade-in-arms, Pallas, son of the
Etruscan king Evander, is slain by Turnus, principal hero of the Latins against the Trojan
incomers led by Aeneas. In the preparation of Pallas's funeral pyre, Aeneas includes
human sacrificial victims:

> Steeds too he adds, and darts from foemen . . .
> And captives he had bound, hands lashed behind,
> To send as offerings to the shade, and, slain,
> Dash with their blood the fire . . .
> (*Aeneid* X, lines 59-93; trans. Rhoades 1957, 243)

In the foregoing passages from Homer, Virgil and Plutarch, it is the foreign, noble war-captive who is sacrificed, within the context of reprisals and the principle of a life for a life or — more accurately — several foreign lives for one 'home' one. This last is significant for, despite the high rank of the victims, it is clear that we are witnessing substitution in action: the enemy lives are inferior and therefore more must be killed to compensate for the one killed in battle.

The sacrifice of war-captives is attested repeatedly in Graeco-Roman documentary sources pertaining to Gaul, Germany and Britain. Strabo (VII, 2, 3) alludes to the blood-sacrifice of prisoners-of-war among the Cimbri, whose throats were cut by elderly barefoot, white-clad priestesses, the blood collected in cauldrons. Similarly, Tacitus (*Annales* XIV, 30-1) makes specific reference to the sacrifice of British war-captives by the Druids on their sacred island of Mona (Anglesey) in the mid-first century AD: 'for it was their religion to drench their altars in the blood of prisoners'.

It is possible that the captive state of sacrificial victims was itself loaded with symbolic meaning, over and above issues concerning status, victory and foreign-ness, but linked additionally with restraint and fettering, a theme which is picked up later, in the context of archaeological evidence. There is a curious comment by Tacitus relating to Germanic rituals among the Semnones, in sacred groves, that supports this notion of the symbolic significance of bondage

> In another way, too, reverence is paid to the grove. No one may enter it unless he is bound with a cord. By this, he acknowledges his own inferiority and the power of the deity. Should he chance to fall, he must not get up on his feet again. He must roll out over the ground. All this complex of superstition reflects the belief that in that grove the nation had its birth, and that there dwells the god who rules over all, while the rest of the world is subject to his sway.
> (*Germania* XXXIX; trans. Mattingly 1948, 132-3)

In this way, the priest or religious official is acting the part of a prisoner, in reflection of his subservient status relative to the supernatural power resident in the grove. In a sense, the dedicant is playing the part of a bound sacrificial victim, helpless in the presence of the supernatural. Additionally, the binding of victims might have relevance to the use of the human body as a social metaphor for the community, and the projection of corporeality and anonymity, as opposed to individual identity, as important symbolic constructs (E. Hill 2000, 317-26) (**colour plate 20**).

Slaves and persons of low status
By definition, slaves in antiquity were prisoners, people detained against their will, often in a foreign land, where they enjoyed virtually no human rights (Wiedemann 1992, 5-6; Bradley 1989, 20). Their status as captives and aliens, outside society, gave them much in common with prisoners-of-war; their inferiority may have meant that they were a favourite form of surrogate sacrificial victim. Attitudes to foreign slaves were complex, in so far as many would have forfeited their liberty in the context of warfare, and — as argued above — may have enjoyed high rank at home. The abrupt change in circumstances and

dramatic drop in rank may have charged slaves with metaphoric meaning and that may have prompted their selection as candidates for ritual murder. Julius Caesar specifically describes a Gaulish funerary custom that had become obsolete shortly before his campaigns of the mid-first century BC. He observes that:

> Not long ago slaves and dependants known to have been their masters' favourites were burned with them at the end of the funeral.
> (*De Bello Gallico* VI, 19; trans. Wiseman & Wiseman 1980, 124)

The killing of slaves in 'retainer' or 'attendant' sacrifice was by no means unknown in antiquity. Michael Parker Pearson (1999, 1-3), for instance, draws attention to a text known as the *Risala*, a contemporary account of a noble Viking burial in AD 921/2, whose ritual included the voluntary death of a slave-girl. After several days of pleasure, the girl was intoxicated with liquor, stabbed and strangled, before being placed on her master's funeral pyre (Jones 1968, 423-30).

Slaves as ritual murder victims are mentioned by Tacitus, in his description of ceremonies enacted in honour of the Germanic earth-goddess Nerthus (*Germania* XL). The deity's slave-attendants were drowned in a sacred lake after they had handled her holy cloth, the explanation for such a fate being that intimacy with a supernatural being could only be permitted to those whose lives were forfeit. There is a clear implication here that these unfortunate servants stood as surrogates for the priest; they were expendable victims who, at one and the same time, acted as gifts to the goddess and were silenced so that the secret rites should not be disclosed to profane ears.

The lowly scapegoat

The treatment of the slave-girl in the Viking *Risala* is reminiscent of the alleged sacrificial rituals, described in Classical texts, associated with the scapegoat (Greek *pharmakos*). The scapegoat — or 'emissary victim' — was known in several ancient Greek city-states as a purificatory device used symbolically to cleanse the community and avert disease, particularly during spring-ceremonies. In Greece, the victim was of low status; like the Viking slave-girl in the *Risala*, he was decorated and made much of before being cursed and driven out, bearing away with him all the evils besetting the town (Hughes 1991, 139-65). The victim was not killed but his expulsion — presumably — represented his symbolic death, for he was an outcast and may well have perished unless accepted into a distant community elsewhere. Greek *pharmakoi* were often chosen because of some physical defect, the perception being that their resentment, against society and the gods for their afflictions, made them appropriate victims (Garland 1995, 23). Interestingly, in his play *Andromache*, Euripides refers to a female scapegoat whose foreign status made her eminently suitable for such a role (Girard 1977, 80); again, the notion of substitution comes into play. Herodotus, too, refers to an Egyptian oracle who stated that famine in that land would cease if a stranger were sacrificed every year to Zeus. The ruler Bousiris first killed the prophet and then any foreigner who landed in Egypt (van Straten 1995, 40-7; Herodotus II, 45). Apart from being human, the Greek *pharmakos* had a function closely resembling the Judaic scapegoat described in the Old Testament (*Leviticus* 16, vv 21-2): in this tradition, a he-goat was selected from the herd, laden with the sins of the Israelites and cast into the wilderness, presumably to starve or perish from thirst.

The link between the scapegoat and human sacrifice occurs only in Graeco-Roman accounts of *pharmakos* rituals taking place in the Greek city of Massilia in southern Gaul, where a poor citizen volunteered himself as a victim on behalf of the town. For a year before his death, this person was looked after and cosseted by his fellow Massiliotes before being dressed up in a sacred robe and leaf-crown, led through the city, collecting imprecations as he went, and then murdered. The precise manner of his death varies between two accounts: in one (Petronius *Servius on Virgil Aeneid III*, 57; Petronius Frag. 1, trans. Heseltine 1969, 386-7), the *pharmakos* was thrown into the sea to drown. In the second (Lactantius Placidus, commentary on Statius's *Thebais* 10, 793), the human scapegoat met his end by stoning outside the town walls (Hughes 1991, 139-65).

These two accounts are interesting in so far as the culmination of the ceremony represents a significant divergence from the Greek *pharmakos* theme, where the victim is not actually put to death (though his death, like that of the Judaic goat, may be implied). Either the tradition was deliberately distorted to include the Gaulish practice of human sacrifice, in a literary convention designed to contrast the civilised Classical world with the 'barbarian' world of Gaul or, alternatively, the rite itself was changed in Gaul precisely because human sacrifice was a practised rite there (Green 1998a). In most of the accounts of *pharmakos* ritual in the Classical sources, it is significant that the victim offered himself, that he was of low status, and that he was fêted prior to his expulsion or death. Like that of the *Risala* slave-girl, the lavish treatment of the Massiliote *pharmakos* may, in part, have been compensatory behaviour, indulging the victims in order to make up for their deaths and thus reduce the community's responsibility for the killing. More important, though, may have been the perceived need to treat the sacrifice as if he were of noble rank thereby, perhaps, symbolically enhancing the value of the divine gift.

Sacrifice and status: archaeological evidence

Archaeological testimony is bound to be equivocal in the identification of prisoners-of-war, or other captives, as sacrificial victims. It is sometimes possible to determine that certain individuals met their deaths while bound, usually with their hands tied, but this may carry little significance in that anyone faced with the prospect of violent death might have required restraint. But it is tempting to interpret the little amulet-figure of a bound man from the Romano-British site of Brough-under-Stainmore (**colour plate 20**) as a human sacrificial victim.

Danebury and Acy-Romance: slaves or prisoners-of-war?
The remains of young adult men have been discovered on European Iron Age sites in circumstances suggesting their identity as sacrificed war-captives or as belonging to some other socially marginalised group. The idiosyncratic 'box burials', dating to the second century BC, at Acy-Romance in the Ardennes (chapter 6) consisted of young males whose inhumed bodies were encased in containers before being lowered into a pit to dry out

(**colour plate 18**); the desiccated remains were then re-interred in a central cult-area within the settlement. The normative funerary rite, accorded to a number of high-ranking individuals here, was cremation. The choice of inhumation for this particular section of the Acy population, together with the absence of grave-goods, may indicate that these were persons of low status. While there is no specific evidence on the bodies themselves that they died violent and untimely deaths as the result of sacrificial practices, one other, unboxed, inhumation found in the settlement, suggests this may have been the case: an extended male burial showed signs of dying with his hands tied behind his back (Lambot 1998; 2000).

The pit-burials at Iron Age Danebury in Hampshire bear certain resemblances to those at Acy (**56**). Most of the human remains deposited in disused grain silos at the hillfort comprised young adult men; although a few women and children were disposed of in this manner, there is a statistically significant bias towards males in their twenties. Twenty-five complete bodies, together with many partial ones, skulls and disarticulated limbs, were interred during the 'pit-tradition' at Danebury (seventh-first century BC). Some of the complete bodies had tightly flexed limbs, as though they had been bound, like prisoners (**57**). Certain remains, especially the heads, exhibit evidence of injuries consistent with those sustained in warfare. One horrific find consisted of a pelvic girdle with clear signs of butchery (**25**); the pelvis and femur-heads had been cut away from the legs and torso with a thin, sword-like blade while the flesh was still intact. It was impossible to tell whether this occurred post-mortem or took place in the process of slaughter (Walker 1984, 442-63); the thought of the latter is a chilling one. Interestingly, some of the skeletal remains from Danebury displayed evidence of poor nourishment, a situation commensurate with low, even servile, status.

Sacrifice and honour

Some young men interred at, for instance, Danebury and South Cadbury in Somerset, may have been honourable battle-dead, for they were buried behind the ramparts of their hillforts, as if both to celebrate their bravery and symbolically to reinforce the protective strength of the defences. At the latter site, a young male was deposited tightly crouched, as if once bound, and 'crammed head down in a small pit' in the rear of the late Iron Age bank. The excavator noted that the body showed no sign of injury or physical abnormality to account for his premature death, though — of course — his skeleton would not necessarily exhibit evidence for sustainment of a war-injury. His interpretation was that 'the general character of the burial suggested that it was a dedicatory sacrifice intended to bless the later rampart' (Alcock 1972, 103, pl. 31).

Some of the Iron Age bog-victims from northern Europe may have been persons of high status. The middle-aged woman from Haraldskaer (**49**), who died in *c*.490 BC, was well-nourished and incredibly fit for her age, suggesting that she had been, to some extent, protected from the rigours of peasant-life. Like many marsh-bodies, she was naked when she was consigned to the water, but her clothes were placed nearby (Hvass 1998). It may, indeed, be that her nakedness played a significant role in the sacrificial ceremony, perhaps because both the bog and human skin were perceived as significant boundary places.

56 One of the Danebury pit-bodies, perhaps that of a captive or slave. © Danebury Trust

57 Flexed body with hands possibly once bound at the wrists, from one of the grain silos at Danebury. © Danebury Trust

Bondage, slaves and sacrifice: some archaeological studies

> As for the common folk, they are treated almost as slaves, venturing naught of themselves, never taken into counsel. The more part of them, oppressed as they are either by debt, or by the heavy weight of tribute, or by the wrongdoing of the more powerful men, commit themselves in slavery to the nobles, who have, in fact, the same rights over them as masters over slaves.
> (Caesar *De Bello Gallico* VI, 13; trans. Edwards 1986, 335)

An Iron Age grave at Ohnenheim in Germany contained the secondary burial of a headless man who has been interpreted as a servile attendant to the higher-status person for whom the tomb was built. In another German grave, in the Upper Palatinate region, four decapitated male bodies were interred in the main burial area, one still with his hands tied behind his back (Simón 1999, 6; Maringer 1942-3, 80). One further piece of circumstantial evidence is that of the slave-gang chains that occur on some late Iron Age sites in Gaul and Britain, such as Llyn Cerrig Bach on Anglesey and Verdun-sur-le-Doubs

148

58 Iron slave-gang chain found at Le Petit Chauvort, Verdun-sur-le-Doubs (Saône-et-Loire) in 1999; second century BC. Antoine Maillier © Centre archéologique européen du Mont Beuvray

(Saône-et-Loire) (**58**). These wrought-iron chains are the product of a huge investment of material, time and skill, and it has recently been suggested (Guichard pers. comm.) that the function of such valuable objects may have been other than the simple conveyance of slaves or prisoners but may, instead, have been associated with human sacrifice. Such an interpretation makes sense, for instance, in terms of the votive context of the Llyn Cerrig gang-chains (**colour plate 21**) (Macdonald 1996, 32-3; Parker Pearson 2000, 8-11), particularly given the possibility that human bones formed part of the ritual assemblage.

Evidence for the sacrifice of slave-prisoners in northern European antiquity is paralleled further east, in the Grecian world, notably in ancient Crete during both the Minoan and Archaic-Geometric periods (early second and first millennia BC). To the latter belongs the grave of a warrior from Eleutherna, whose cremated remains occupied the main position in the tomb. At the edge of an unlit funerary pyre lay the inhumed body of a decapitated man; his body had been tightly bound and his limbs perhaps mutilated before he died. The excavator considered this individual to have been a slave-attendant, sacrificed to accompany the warrior-hero to the next world (Stampholidis 1996, 164-73). But other interpretations have been put forward as to the identity of this person, including the possibility that his sacrificial death was a vengeance-killing by the kin of the cremated individual. The inhumed man was denied the privileges of noble Cretan burial: the provision of grave-goods and the rite of cremation on a funeral pyre. These features may indicate either that he was of lowly rank or the desire to insult the corpse and the dead man's memory. It may be significant that he was of similar age and robust physique to his cremated companion. So this secondary burial could represent retaliation essentially similar to the reprisal killings mentioned in Homeric epic (for instance, in the *Odyssey*, 23-4). In the *Iliad* (11, 145ff; 12, 202ff), revenge for the death of kin took the form of decapitation (Stampholidis 1996, 173-89).

Another, much earlier Cretan site, which belonged to the Middle Minoan period (1750-1650 BC) exhibits clear evidence for sacrificial ritual involving a human captive, possibly — though not necessarily — a person of low status. Commanding superb views over the surrounding countryside at 400m elevation was the temple at Anemospila, in the Archanes region, a location that must have been selected for its special position. The sanctuary was destroyed by an earthquake and the great fire that followed it, and there are indications that a human sacrifice was carried out by religious officials there just before the catastrophe, in a desperate attempt to avert it. The temple building consisted of a tripartite ante-chamber with three rooms behind. The west room contained the sparsest assemblage of finds but in it were the remains of three people: a female in her late 20s, a man of about 37 and a youth of about 18. The first two appear to have died in the collapse of the shrine's roof and to have lain where they fell. But the young man's death was different: he lay on an offering-table, a bronze spear-head on top of him, stretched out, with his legs tied together; his jaws were clamped shut, seemingly also bound tightly to each other. A curious feature of the bones was the discrepant colouring of the two halves of the skeleton: the right half was blackened, the left bleached white, as if he had suffered a huge loss of blood to that part of his body, commensurate with a wound to the carotid artery in the left side of his neck. The older man lay in the position that the 'sacrificer' might have adopted, standing just behind the victim (Sakellarakis & Sapouna-Sakellaraki 1997, 269-311).

War sanctuaries in Iron Age Gaul

> To Mars, when they [the Gauls] have determined on a decisive battle, they dedicate as a rule whatever spoil they may take. After a victory they sacrifice such living things as they have taken, and all the other effects they gather into one place. In many states heaps of such objects are to be seen piled up in hallowed spots, and it has not often happened that a man, in defiance of religious scruple, has dared to conceal such spoils in his house or to remove them from their place, and the most grievous punishment, with torture, is ordained for such an offence.
> (Caesar *de Bello Gallico* VI, 17)

Two sanctuaries in Iron Age Gaul deserve especial mention, since their investigations have revealed startling information concerning the cultic disposal of the dead, the majority of whom may have been sacrificed enemies. During the early Roman period, a vast temple-precinct was constructed at Ribemont-sur-Ancre (Somme), but it was preceded by a great Iron Age religious complex demarcated by a rectilinear enclosure, constructed in the third century BC. The most remarkable feature of the Iron Age shrine was the presence of a series of 'ossuaries' or 'bone-houses' in the corners of the enclosure. Two of these altar-like structures survive but they may once have been placed one in each of the four angles. These ossuaries were built, log-cabin fashion, from human long-bones; the leg-bones of horses were arranged around the edge of the human remains. The latter belonged mainly to robust men in the prime of life, fully mature but less than 40 years old, and the state of the skeletal material implies their deposition as the culmination of a complicated 'taphonomy', involving the decapitation of the bodies (no skulls were found) and their dismemberment while the bones still retained their flesh: the preservation of small foot-bones indicates that this was so. What is more, the nature of the cut-marks, made by a sword-like instrument, suggested to the excavators that the bodies had been hung upside-down prior to being butchered, although Chris Knüsel (pers. comm.) has cast doubt on the validity of drawing such conclusions from the osteological evidence. Each ossuary represents the remains of about 200-50 people so, if there were originally four such structures, around a thousand men may once have been disposed of in this manner (Cadoux 1984; Brunaux 1988; 1996, 77-90; Brunaux *et al.* 1985; Smith 2000, 152-63). If the Ribemont corpses were hung upside-down, it is interesting that similar inversions are apparently represented on a Bronze Age rock-carving at Hamn in southern Sweden, where a group of people is shown suspended by their feet from a horizontal pole (Coles 1990, fig. 24).

So who were the men whose headless bodies were suspended in the Ribemont temple before being cut up and built into charnel-houses of human limbs? The weapons may provide a clue, for they originated from a wide area of Gaul and Germany; their presence, together with the age and gender of the dead, is highly suggestive of the construction of battle-trophies to the victors' gods. These dead warriors may have already been killed before they arrived at the shrine, their corpses then offered up in triumph in the sanctuary of their conquerors. But it is possible that they were prisoners-of-war who suffered a shockingly brutal sacrificial fate on holy ground, paying a harsh price for defeat.

Ribemont is by no means alone in its evidence for the dedication of human war-trophies in an Iron Age Gallic shrine. The sanctuary of Gournay-sur-Aronde (Oise) was the focus of martial rituals that included the deposition of thousands of deliberately broken or bent weapons (*see* **23**) and shields, along with the bodies of sacrificed horses and cattle and the debris of feasting on young pigs and lambs. The human dead of Gournay differed from the Ribemont bodies in so far as their heads were not taken away from the temple, but their remains, particularly their heads, seem to have been hung from the entrance, eventually falling into the ditch enclosing the holy ground. Once again, the deceased comprised, for the most part, young men of fighting age, whose bones were carefully selected to include heads and limbs; the rest of their bodies must have been disposed of elsewhere. The choice, for cult-deposition, of the heads and long-bones at Gournay (Brunaux 1988; 1996, 69-77; Brunaux *et al.* 1985; Simón 1999) closely resembles the pattern of interment observed in parts of Iron Age Celtiberia (Sopeña Genzor 2000), where many human burials (at Numancia and Tiermes, for instance) are represented solely by skulls and thigh-bones. The Gournay bodies may, as suggested for the dead of Ribemont, have been sacrificed enemies. That they were not simply warriors killed in action is indicated by the presence of three women, presumably non-combatants, which perhaps supports the notion that human sacrifice did, indeed, take place here rather than honourable disposal of battle-dead (Simón 1999).

Age of the victims

Sacrificing the future: children as ritual victims

> And God said, take thou thy son, thine only son Isaac, whom thou lovest, and
> get thee into the land of Moriah, and offer him there for a burnt offering upon
> one of the mountains which I will tell thee of.
> (*Genesis* 22, v. 2)

The ritual slaughter of children seems — to a modern western viewpoint at least — to represent an act of 'ultimate concern', for in carrying out such action, the perpetrators are, literally, sacrificing the future. There are complexities here in so far as — according to the principle of substitution — children, according to a short-term perspective, might be considered expendable, perhaps because they were neither economically useful nor were they able to reproduce or bear arms nor, to an extent, were they necessarily regarded as full members of their communities (Diemberger 1993, 88-127). Conversely, since children, particularly healthy children, were the future of those communities they may, indeed, have been considered as its most valuable resource and, as a corollary, have represented the most precious offering available for dedication to the supernatural forces. In such a context, they may have been sacrificed at critical times, when a settlement was threatened with extinction through war, famine, disease or other impending disaster. Classical literature contains a number of incidents involving the sacrifice of offspring: on his way home from the Trojan Wars, the Cretan Idomeneus is said to have pledged to sacrifice the first being he met on landing, after surviving a storm at sea, and it was his son (Servius *Aen.* III, 121; XI, 264); Pausanias (*Guide to Greece* IX, 33.3) recounts a similar event (this time associated with a toponymic myth), in which the ruler of Haliartus in Boeotia consulted the Delphic Oracle concerning a serious drought afflicting his land; she instructed him to sacrifice the first person he saw on his way home; thus, he was forced to stab his son, Lophis, to death, and the boy's flowing blood became the river of that name (Bradley 2000, 21).

In assessing the archaeological evidence for child-sacrifice, it is important not to confuse its identification with neonatal or stillborn deaths nor with the pragmatic practice of infanticide. The presence, for instance, of multiple perinatal deaths on late Romano-British sites (Mays 1993, 883-8) argues for the occurrence of the latter. Children are at their most vulnerable during the first few weeks of life but the archaeological evidence for the deaths of older children sometimes raises questions concerning deliberate and sacrificial killing although, of course, epidemics might equally account for mass juvenile mortality.

In western European antiquity, the evidence for child-sacrifice is rare, and there are few textual references to such cult-practice, but further east there is an accumulation of both documentary and material sources which are persuasive. The greatest body of data comes from Phoenician sites in North Africa, Sardinia, Sicily and elsewhere in the Punic southern Mediterranean, where there is both literary and archaeological testimony apparently relating to the sacrificial deaths of infants aged between two months and five years. Considerable debate surrounds the interpretation of this material: some scholars are convinced that Punic human sacrifice involving children occurred on a regular basis over about a millennium, from the eighth century BC to the third century AD. Others take the view that the sources have been misunderstood, arguing that the ancient Graeco-Roman texts exhibit barbarian stereotypic bias and that the human remains in the child-cemeteries are explicable in terms of natural death and discrete disposal of the bodies. My own view is that, given the accumulation of data suggesting the occurrence of human sacrifice in antiquity, together with the combination of repeated and varied textual and material evidence from the Phoenician world, admittance of child-sacrifice in Punic cities is at least highly plausible.

The observations of authors from the Classical world and archaeological testimony combine to present indications that the Phoenicians offered children to the gods, killing them with knives and interring their cremated remains in urns within special cemeteries called 'tophets' (see chapter 3). The texts and the inscriptions from stone stelai sometimes erected over the inurned remains mention dedications to Baal Hammon, either alone or with Tanit, in the pre-Roman period, and later to a North African deity given the name of the Graeco-Roman Kronos or Saturn. Diodorus Siculus (XIII, 86, 3) described how the great Carthaginian leader Hamilcar sacrificed his own son to Kronos, according to an old-established cult. Elsewhere, the writer commented that, on one occasion — when their city was besieged by the Syracusans — the Carthaginians sacrificed 200 of their noblest offspring to the god and pledged 300 more, being convinced that Kronos was angry with them for having substituted lowborn children for their own, in past ceremonies (XX, 14.6). In his *De Superstitione* (XIII, 171d), Plutarch gives quite detailed information on the enactment of child-sacrifice in the city of Carthage, mentioning that infants were stabbed to death at the foot of altars, the area being filled with musicians in order that their cries could not be heard. The author remarks that the child's mother would be present at the ceremony but would not cry or protest. He also alludes to the purchase of children from the poor by childless couples to kill as offerings (de Vaux 1964, 79-81; Brown 1991, 159-62). Certain Christian writers provide graphic accounts of Punic child-sacrifice; but here we have to exercise particular caution in that there may well be polemical, ideological perspectives affecting their reporting. Two of these authors, Tertullian — who was born near Carthage — and Minucius Felix, are especially condemnatory. Felix (*Octavius* XXX, 3) comments that the doomed children were kissed to prevent them crying out (presumably because their wails would be perceived as ill-omened); Tertullian (*Apologeticus* IX, 2-4) observed that the ritual murder of children continued in secret long after its official ban by the Romans, even to his day (in the early third century AD).

A number of child-cemeteries has been discovered at the sites of major Punic cities, from North Africa to southern Italy. The pattern of behaviour, exhibited at this series of graveyards comprises the interment of the cremated remains of children in exclusive burial-grounds or 'tophets', in urns sometimes marked by inscribed stones. The urn-cemetery at Carthage was particularly important, containing a great many stone monuments and evincing sacrificial practice that lasted from the eighth century BC until the destruction of the city by Rome in 146 (Brown 1991, 13-15, 37-55). The identification of these infant burial-grounds as evocative of special religious ceremonies depends partly on the formality with which the interments were made; 'normal' child burials were usually carried out with less formality and were mixed with the graves of adults. The Motya tophet was respected when the community built a wall across the island in the fifth century BC, although the regular cemetery was not, suggesting that the child cemetery had special significance. Furthermore, it is meaningful that the tophet burials were not the remains of newborns but of older, 'established' children. The inscriptions on the stelai refer specifically to the dedication of the children to the indigenous deities Baal Hammon and Tanit and, later, to Kronos or Saturn, the Graeco-Roman names for Baal. It could be argued that children dying of natural causes might thus have been 'given' to the gods, but it is interesting that a group of Latin inscriptions to Saturn at N'G'ous in North Africa clearly state that lambs were being substituted as offerings in place of children (de Vaux 1964, 73-9). On occasions, the urns in the tophets are found to contain a blend of children's cremated bones and those of young lambs or kids (Brown 1991, 13-15). It seems clear that, in the later burials, animals were either partially or wholly substituted for infants as sacrificial gifts. In my opinion, it is significant that the dedicated offerings — whether human or animal — were *young* creatures, as if this were the crucial factor determining the selection of the gift; if this were so, then it supports the interpretation of sacrifice.

A small collection of iconographic material appears to reinforce the argument for the dedication of Punic children as victims of ritual murder. Although none of the gravestones bears images of the sacrificial act itself, a stele from the Carthage tophet carries the depiction of a man, wearing a ceremonial headdress, holding an infant in the crook of his left arm and raising his right hand, as if in a hieratic gesture (Brown 1991, 306, fig. 64c) (*see* **31**). A second image, on a stone of third century BC date from Monte Sirai in Sardinia, consists of a woman holding a small child (*op. cit.* 303, fig. 61c) (*see* **32**).

There is a small, but significant, body of evidence for the sacrifice of children in ancient Europe, including Iron Age and Roman Britain. The Iron Age hillfort at Wandlebury in Cambridgeshire is an impressive monument set in a landscape containing few such sites. The excavation of a series of shallow pits in the interior revealed in one (pit 2) the partial body of a child aged about six. Only the upper half was present, the lower limbs having been severed with a sword-like blade before burial, at a time when the flesh of the torso had not yet decomposed. The state of the *ilia* indicated that the limbs may have been removed at the time of death and perhaps constituted the fatal injury. The mutilated corpse was then wrapped in a sack fastened by a bronze needle and placed face-down in the pit, with no accompanying grave-goods (Hartley 1957, 14-15, 26). A similarly grisly fate seems to have been suffered by a 12-year-old boy on an early Iron Age site at Hornish Point in the Western Isles (**colour plate 22**): his body was cut into quarters and placed in four pits together with the butchered remains of two young cattle and two sheep, in what seems to have been a foundation deposit prior to a house being erected on top of the pits (Barber *et al.* 1989, 773-8).

The remains of children, generally babies, associated with buildings may be the burials of infants selected as foundation offerings, to bless a new house or shrine with an appropriately new life. Iron Age and Romano-British temples seem sometimes to have been constructed with rituals involving child-sacrifice. Buried just outside the entrance of a circular building, interpreted as a sanctuary, at Maiden Castle was the body of a child (Cunliffe 1991, 512). The structure was rebuilt during the Roman period next to a rectilinear temple of Romano-Celtic type, suggesting its religious use. But it is less clear whether a second infant found in association with a late Iron Age or early Romano-British building died as the result of a ritual killing or met a natural end (**colour plate 23**) (Sharples 1991, 101).

Romano-British shrines sometimes contain infant-burials, once again interpretable as foundation-offerings. The great multi-shrine complex at Springhead in Kent has revealed evidence for the recurrent deposition of infants associated with the construction of temple buildings: babies' bodies were placed in postholes dug to take a line of timber uprights within the cult-area, and some of these holes also contained the skulls of cattle and horses, reinforcing thereby the ritual nature of the skeletal material (Isserlin 1997, 91-100). Beneath the foundations of Shrine IV were the remains of four more children, one of whom had been decapitated (Penn 1960, 121-2). Testimony to the presence of child-sacrifice in non-temple contexts comes from a series of late Romano-British aisled farm buildings, identified as corn-drying installations, probably relating to the malting process (Scott 1991, 116-17). This seems to have occurred, for instance, at Barton Court Farm (Oxon) and at Winterton (Lincs), where four children were interred beside the walls. Eleanor Scott has interpreted these burials as foundation sacrifices, arguing for the deliberately-deposited remains of ritually-slain children as part of a 'revitalizing' fertility ritual.

Liminal age-groups

> Lady, thou know'st, I trow, the host's resolve,
> And the vote cast, yet will I tell it thee:
> The Achaeans will to slay Polyxena
> Thy child, upon Achilles' grave-mound's height.
> Me they appoint to usher thitherward
> And bring the maid: the president and priest
> Of sacrifice Achilles' son shall be . . .
> (Euripides *Hecuba*, lines 220-5; trans. Way 1959, 265-7)

So spoke Odysseus to Hecuba, wife of King Priam of Troy before the sacrifice of her maiden daughter Polyxena by Neoptolemos at the tomb of his father Achilles (*see* **10**). The sacrifice apparently took place in order to placate Achilles' shade so that a fair wind would be granted to sail the Greek ships home after the Trojan War. The episode is depicted on Greek vase paintings, of which the most evocative is an Attic black figure ware *krater* showing Polyxena being hoisted aloft by three named warriors — Amphilochos, Antiphates and Aias — so that she is suspended, face down over the altar, while Neoptolemos plunges his sword into her throat and her blood flows down in a great stream (Durand 1989, 87-118, fig. 7; van Straten 1995, 113-14).

The sacrifice of Polyxena is one of several episodes in Greek mythology in which a young girl was sacrificed, usually by her father, in order to affect the fortunes of war. The best-known of these mythic virgin-victims is Iphigeneia, daughter of King Agamemnon who conducted the sacrifice at Aulis in order to to persuade the virgin goddess Artemis to allow the Greek fleet to sail for Troy (Euripides *Iphigeneia in Aulis* lines 1547-97; Aeschylus *Agamemnon* lines 198-248). Euripides and Aeschylus differ in their presentation of Iphigeneia's attitude to her impending death. In *Iphigeneia in Aulis*, the girl approached her father as a willing victim, and it is he who wept. But Aeschylus's version describes a girl pleading for her life:

> So he hardened his heart to sacrifice his daughter that he might prosper a war waged to avenge a woman, and as an offering for the voyaging of a fleet! Her supplications, her cries of 'Father', and her virgin life, the commanders in their eagerness for war reckoned as naught . . .

A third event, alleged as historical fact rather than myth, concerns the lame Spartan Agesilaüs who became king in spite of an oracular decree that his infirmity made him ineligible for royal appointment. Agesilaüs was appointed as overall commander of the panhellenic forces against the Persians and, in the spring of 397 BC, while the army was assembling, he stayed overnight in Aulis. On hearing a voice bidding him emulate the sacrifice of Agamemonon's daughter, he agreed but offered a slaughtered hind as a surrogate gift: the expedition failed (Plutarch *Life of Agesilaüs* VI, 4-6); unlike the Biblical episode of Abraham and Isaac, the substitution of an animal for a human sacrifice was presumably unacceptable because it was Agesilaüs's decision rather than the result of divine intervention.

The ancient Greek accounts of female human sacrifice have in common the notion that a virgin girl was deemed the most fitting ritual victim but the ultimate offering was that of a daughter by her father. In discussing this, Aeschylus makes the interesting comment that a maiden was chosen, in part at least, in expiation for the 'avenging of a woman', the seizing of Helen which was the official excuse for the Trojan War. It is surely significant, in terms of mythic metaphor, that Iphigeneia was sacrificed to the virgin goddess Artemis: virginity in a sacrifice may have been highly prized not only because such a girl represented, simultaneously, unsullied purity and undissipated sexuality, and stood as an allegory for a 'first fruits' gift, but also because — in a sense — a virgin occupied a boundary position in her social group, being neither child nor woman; this ambiguity, the threshold state between life-stages, may have been a potent factor in judging the efficacy of a divine gift.

Hélène Foley (1985, 21) observes that the human sacrificial events in Greek myth constitute responses to situations 'in which an idealistic youth sacrifices herself or himself to resolve a cultural crisis'. She also suggests that myths may preserve 'the uncomfortable memory of human sacrifice' (*op. cit.* 39). But what of the archaeological evidence for young adult or adolescent sacrifice? A body of data points to the selection of youths and young girls as ritual victims, both in ancient Europe and further afield. An example of such practice in the Aegean is the body of the teenage youth, bound and stabbed to death in the Minoan temple of Anemospila in Crete and discussed earlier in this chapter (Sakellarakis & Sapouna-Sakellaraki 1997, 269-311). The deposition of the deliberately defleshed skull of a Romano-British youth in a pit outside a shrine at Folly Lane, St Albans in the second century AD has already been considered (chapter 5) (**47**). The head had been placed 2m down on the pit-floor, in a fresh, unweathered state, the condition of the base suggesting its display on a pole either for a short time out of doors or indoors before its final deposition. The head was found associated with the bones of a young dog (Niblett 1999, 86) and this inclusion of the animal remains is interesting for, like the mixed bones of children and lambs in the Carthaginian tophet, the symbolism of youth may be reflected in the offering of both beast and human.

A range of Iron Age bog-bodies from northern Europe belonged to adolescent youths and females. The young girl whose head was shaved on one side and then was led, blindfold, into the marsh to drown at Windeby in Schleswig-Holstein (**50**), was about 12 or 14 years old (Glob 1969, 114-16; Coles & Coles 1989, 187; van der Sanden 1996, 98, 112). Slightly older, at about 16, was the girl from Yde in the Netherlands, half her head also shaved, who was strangled before being placed in the bog (van der Sanden 1996, 138). The bound and sacrificed boy from Kayhausen in North Germany (**59**) was likewise an adolescent, about 14 when he died (van der Sanden 1996, 93, pl. 117).

The selection of pubescent teenagers or very young adults for sacrificial rites might be significant as an especially effective gift, with its investment of value in terms of reproductive and economic potential together, perhaps, with the inherent symbolism of liminality, of belonging to the worlds of childhood and adulthood and to neither. Similar choices were seemingly made elsewhere in antiquity, for instance in the Inca lands of South America, where young people were recurrently sacrificed on the summits of mountains (Parker Pearson 1999, 18). The perception of these youthful victims, on the threshold of maturity, may have contained powerful metaphors relating to the community itself and the desire for fertile prosperity. It is interesting that the Inca victims were traditionally deposited in the liminal landscape of mountains, which may have been perceived as belonging to both land and sky. The North European bog-victims may similarly have been deliberately placed in uncultivable locations that were seen as boundary places: half water, half-land (envisaged, maybe, as half earthworld, half spiritworld). But in the following section, we shall see that other, even more disturbing factors may have influenced the singling out of the North European teenagers for ritual immolation.

Deformity and disability: sacrificing the afflicted

> . . . unnatural progeny we destroy; we drown even children, who at birth are weakly and abnormal.
> (Seneca the Younger *De Ira* I.15.2)

In ancient Greek and Roman society, physical imperfections were generally regarded as unacceptable. There is abundant literary testimony to the effect that parents were encouraged, sometimes coerced by law, to do away with malformed and handicapped babies. In promoting what was, in effect, the ancient equivalent of eugenics, Aristotle

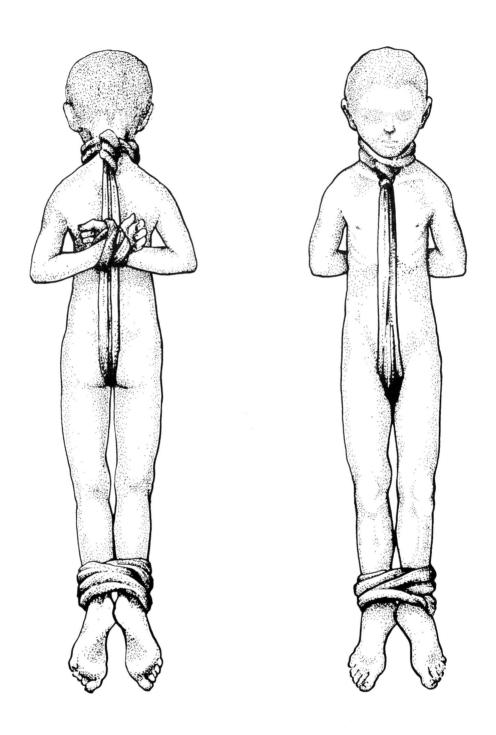

59 The Kayhausen boy, from Schleswig-Holstein, who died, bound hand, foot and neck and placed in a peat-bog in the second or first century BC. © Anne Leaver (after van der Sanden 1996)

(*Politeia* 7, 1335b, 19-21) argued for laws to prevent parents from rearing their handicapped offspring. The Twelve Tables of Roman law instructed the *paterfamilias* (or male head of the family) to destroy any malformed children (Garland 1995, 13-17). Robert Garland (1995, 12) estimated that 'a substantial minority of the population suffered from hereditary deformity' in antiquity with, quite possibly, much higher incidences than are present in modern populations. In terms of acquired disabilities, malnutrition was probably the main culprit: in his *Gynaecology*, the second century AD Greek author Soranos identified the presence of disorders in children related to poor diet, causing them to develop twisted thigh-bones (Garland 1995, 21).

A significant proportion of human bodies from Iron Age Europe, suspected as having been victims of ritual killing, exhibit signs of deformity or disability. We should remember, too, that only conditions affecting the skeleton would normally be identifiable to archaeologists (Molleson 1999, 69), although the armless people depicted on Bronze Age rock-carvings from Sweden (Coles 1990, 27) *may* represent mutilated ritual victims. We should take cognisance also of the possibility that attitudes similar to those of the Classical world obtained in temperate Europe; handicapped persons might have simply been killed because they were abnormal. But, if this were so, we should not expect to find the adult or near-adult remains of disabled bodies because these persons would have been killed in infancy. The bog-bodies of the girl from Yde and the boy from Kayhausen (**59**) both had mobility problems: the Yde girl suffered from extreme curvature of the spine (idiopathic scoliosis), which could have affected her posture and gait, and the Kayhausen boy suffered from a hip defect that would have caused him to walk with considerable difficulty. The bones of the young girl from Windeby (**50**) indicated that she had suffered from periods of arrested growth induced by poor food, perhaps because of famine. Several of the Danebury bodies exhibited signs of osteoarthritis: one 35-year-old woman had an arthritic hip that had not yet inhibited mobility but her walking would have been limited and painful, like that of the beheaded Romano-British woman interred at Guilden Morden (chapter 5). One of the pits at Danebury contained the body of a young man who had a deformed left hip caused by Perthes' Disease, a disorder usually afflicting children between five and ten years old. The condition lasts about two years but leaves a permanent disability; the Danebury sufferer would have always walked with a pronounced limp (Hooper 1984, 463-74). One of the late Iron Age longbones from the 'cannibal' cave at Alveston (Cox pers. comm.) showed signs that its elderly owner was afflicted with Paget's Disease, which would have resulted in a shuffling 'simian' walk. The Danish female bog-body from Huldremose (**colour plate 2**) showed signs of having broken her leg in early adulthood, an injury which would, once again, have caused a permanent limp (Coles & Coles 1989, 188). In the mid-first century AD, a large ceremonial enclosure was built to surround a high-status cremation burial at Folly Lane, St Albans. The bodies of three women were placed in the enclosure-ditch, near its entrance, at the time of its construction (Niblett 1999, 20), the inference being that they were sacrificial victims, killed in honour of the dead chieftain. It may be significant that all three of these women had hip-deformities (Niblett pers. comm.); they may even have been related. The group of 12 individuals, whose charred remains were found in a fire-pit in the Iron Age settlement at Leonding in Austria, all suffered from a hereditary malformation of the jaw that prevented them from speaking (Simón 1999, 10); is this why they were chosen as sacrificial victims? The Leonding deposit is not the only example of the simultaneous death of a likely family-group; the late La Tène burial at Hopstädten in the Moselle Valley contained what appears to be an entire family (Wightman 1970, 242, and see chapter 8). The body deposited, without its head, at Lindow Moss in the second century AD apparently suffered from no disability but his selection as a human sacrifice may have something to do with the vestigial extra thumb on his surviving right hand (Turner 1996, 34-5). The burial of a female dwarf, about 22 years old, deep in a pit at the Roman fort of Newstead, Scotland, may be significant in terms of sacrificial ritual. She was interred beneath the bones of nine horses (Curle 1911, 383-4). Again, the Worsley man, killed violently in the Roman period, had a deformed right ear.

The choice of victims on the grounds of physical abnormality is strongly suggested by some of the evidence. The reasons for such selection may relate to complex and equivocal attitudes to people who stood apart from their peers. They may have been considered cursed or blessed, as persons of good or ill omen; expediency, in terms of the reduced fighting or economic capacity of the disabled, might be a factor and the principle of substitution thus perhaps came into play. The ancient Greeks and Romans particularly admired physical perfection and beauty; their sacrificial animals and their priests had to be without defect. The ancient Jews could also only sacrifice perfect animals and food items in the temple (*Leviticus* ch. 1, v. 3). The Greeks believed that some defects in humans were considered the result of divine intervention; in their attitude to certain handicaps, for instance in the lame Greek god Hephaistos or blind seers, like Teiresias, there was a perception that disability could sometimes be 'redeemed' by a compensatory talent (Garland 1995, 61, 99), such as skill in smithing or prophecy. It could be that being singled out as a sacrificial victim was considered a sacred gift.

In seeking to understand the archaeological evidence from Iron Age temperate Europe, we must be aware of the need to employ relativistic approaches to interpretation of meaning: the values obtaining in ancient Greece were not necessarily relevant in lands to the north and west. But the number of young individuals with archaeologically identifiable physical abnormalities who met apparently untimely, possibly sacrificial deaths in north-west Europe during the Iron Age and Roman periods may be meaningful in terms of the reasons behind their ultimate fate as offerings to the spirit world.

8
'Pattern and purpose': some reasons for ritual murder

When a king dies, they dig a great square pit, and, when it is ready, they take up the corpse, which has been previously prepared . . . the corpse is laid in the tomb on a mattress, with spears fixed in the ground on either side to support a roof of withies laid on wooden poles, while in other parts of the great square pit various members of the king's household are buried beside him: one of his concubines, his butler, his cook, his groom, his steward, and his chamberlain — all of them strangled. Horses are buried too . . .

At the end of the year another ceremony takes place: they take fifty of the best of the king's remaining servants, strangle and gut them, stuff the bodies with chaff, and sew them up again . . . Fifty of the finest horses are then subjected to the same treatment . . . When the horses and riders are all in place around the tomb, they are left there, and the mourners go away.
(Herodotus *Histories* IV, 72-3; trans. de Sélincourt 1965, 264-5)

So wrote the fifth-century BC Greek historian in his account of Scythian customs and ceremonies. Herodotus is describing an extreme form of 'attendant' or 'retainer' sacrifice, wherein dead nobles were accompanied to the afterlife by persons considered as of lower rank (whether members of the deceased's family or servants). In this Scythian funeral rite, the bodies of the slaughtered people and horses were stuffed and reinforced with poles so that the royal tomb could appear to be surrounded by guardian horsemen.

Herodotus gives us a rare insight into the context and circumstances within which human sacrifice could take place. In seeking to establish motive for ritual killing, the testimony of ancient texts is likely to provide more answers than archaeological evidence, which is inevitably equivocal. Both kinds of source have to be treated cautiously: written observations and material culture can both be misread and misinterpreted. In any case, the specific reasons for sacrificial ritual are contingent upon the symbolic context of the society enacting the sacrifice.

Attendant sacrifice

The deliberate dispatch of a human being to accompany another is predicated on the simple principle of relative worth: thus, in the Hindu practice of *suttee*, a widow is burnt on the funeral pyre of her husband; the converse never occurs. An analogy to this perception of gender-value is presented in Euripides' play *Alcestis*, in which Apollo makes a bargain with the sick Admetus that his life shall be restored if a substitute be found; his wife, Alcestis, willingly sacrifices herself in his place; this was the right thing to do, according to the Classical Athenian *mores*, in which women were automatically of lower social status (Vellacott 1974, 15-17). Similarly, a slave might be killed at the grave of his or her master; needless to say, a nobleman is never slaughtered to accompany a servant to the next world. The Scythian grave-rite recorded by Herodotus appears particularly elaborate but there is strong evidence for similar practices in the archaeological record. During the second and first millennia BC, lower-status people were interred with their dead leaders in the great royal tumulus burials at Kerma, in the northern Sudan. In these Nubian tombs, there is a great distinction in the quantity and value of the funerary goods differentiating the main burial from the satellite graves (Connah 1987, 37-8, fig. 33; O'Connor 1993, 54-5, fig. 4.2; Shinnie 1967, 150). But it may be that the paucity of the material accompanying the attendant bodies may merely symbolise low rank *relative* to the main burial rather than servitude (Green 1998a, 181).

In his observation of Gaulish customs, Julius Caesar described something very similar to the evidence from both Scythia and Kerma:

> Although Gaul is not a rich country, funerals there are splendid and costly. Everything the dead man is thought to have been fond of is put on the pyre, including even animals. Not long ago, slaves and dependants known to have been their masters' favourites were burned with them at the end of the funeral.
> (Caesar *de Bello Gallico* VI, 19; trans. Wiseman & Wiseman 1980, 124)

Caesar's comment here is interesting, for he observes that the practice of attendant sacrifice had become obsolete shortly before his Gallic campaigns began, in 58 BC.

There is some archaeological evidence that, on occasions, attendant sacrifice was practised in the European Iron Age. However, we need to be careful in so interpreting this kind of data: Dennis Hughes reminds us that the occurrence of multiple, coeval interments might sometimes be equally understood as the result of 'grief suicide' (Hughes 1991, 18-24). We could read either way the presence of what appears to have been an entire family, interred together in a late Iron Age tomb at a cemetery in the vicinity of a small hillfort at Hoppstädten-Weiersbach in the Moselle region of Belgic Gaul (Wightman 1970, 242; 1985, 102), unless they all died almost simultaneously in an epidemic or a massacre.

In the sixth century BC, Hallstatt chieftains in parts of central Europe and eastern France were buried with great ceremony in wooden mortuary chambers beneath huge mounds. In some of the tombs, principal, centrally-situated graves were accompanied by peripheral and lesser interments, suggesting that high-status individuals were buried with others, who were perhaps ritually slain for this purpose. One such grave-mound was at Hohmichele, in the vicinity of the Heuneberg hillfort, near Hundersingen in the Upper Danube; the inference is that the dead of Hohmichele may have once lived in the stronghold. Archaeologists investigating the tomb found that the large primary burial chamber had been robbed of its contents, but its size suggested it was designed for two bodies. However, a second main chamber was discovered, containing the remains of two people, a man and a woman, lying on their backs, side by side on animal-pelts, the rich accompanying grave-goods implying that the pair were of equal rank. The mound also housed several secondary interments (Frey 1991, 75-92). The tumulus at Hohmichele has two significant features: a pair of main chambers, one with two bodies, the other heavily robbed but of comparable size, and the presence of satellite burials. If coeval with the main graves, the latter may be interpretable as those of attendants, but what of the bodies in the primary chambers? What was the relationship between the two chambers and between the two bodies once lying in each? The presence of two main funerary locations in the one mound may signify the use of a dynastic or family 'mausoleum'; more enigmatic is the juxtaposition of the two bodies found in one of the main chambers and suggested as once present within the other. The treatment of the couple in the undisturbed grave suggests that they were interred in a single episode; if that were so, either they died at about the same time, perhaps because of disease, or one committed suicide so as not to be parted by death, or one — the man or the woman — was sacrificed in a ritual equivalent to *suttee*.

Sometime during the late Iron Age, two people were interred together in a pit at Viables Farm, near Basingstoke in south-east England. Both bodies were those of women and it is of particular interest that the grave-goods accompanying them were, for the most part, paired: they included the remains of two sheep and two horses, two terret-rings (one of silver-washed bronze and one of antler) and four antler combs (two decorated, the others plain), one 'set' apparently inferior to the other. The women were interred so as to display the asymmetry of their relationship one to the other: the younger woman lay in an extended position; crouched on top of her legs, was the body of an older female, her head resting on the younger one's pelvis (Merrifield 1987, 66). It is tempting to interpret the bodies as those of a young, high-ranking woman who was interred with her faithful older attendant, the grave-goods of each reflecting their discrepant status. This kind of 'retainer sacrifice' might be the reason for other double burials noted in the British and European Iron Age: the pairs of bodies from southern England found at sites such as Westhampnett in Sussex and Latchmere in Hampshire; the adults and children interred together at the Irish cemetery of Carrowjames in Co. Mayo; and the two male bog-bodies from Weerdinge, near Bourtangermoor in the Netherlands (van der Sanden 1996, 101-2). In the context of paired burials, it is interesting to speculate on the circumstances surrounding the two Iron Age cart-burials at Soissons, each of which was accompanied by a funeral cortège including pairs of oxen, horses and goats (Green 1992a, 105-6; Meniel 1987, 101-43) (*see* **16**).

Attendant sacrifice seems a highly likely interpretation for the presence, at Folly Lane, St Albans, of three women interred in the enclosure ditch surrounding the cremation burial of a Catuvellaunian chieftain who died in about AD 55 (Niblett 1992, 917-29; 1999, 20). The bodies were deliberately placed, unburnt, by the entrance to the funerary precinct at the time the ditch was dug; they may have been selected according to age: one was perhaps no more than 20, the second over 35 and the third possibly as old as 50; all suffered from disabilities affecting their ability to walk properly. In terms of their relationship with the nobleman burned on the central funerary pyre, it is probably significant that they were not cremated but inhumed; inhumation may sometimes have been symbolic of inferiority, as has been argued for the burials without grave-goods at Acy-Romance (Lambot 1998) in Iron Age Gaul (**colour plate 18**). The same kind of ranking was present elsewhere in antiquity: at Eleutherna in Archaic Crete, for instance, a cremated warrior-hero occupied the central position in a grave, with a tightly-bound, perhaps mutilated male body lying, unburnt, on the edge of an unlit pyre (see chapter 7).

Foundation and fertility sacrifices

All over the world human sacrifice seems to be closely linked with the mystery of food-production.
(Merrifield 1987, 23)

Sometimes the context of a ritualised death provides clues as to intention. This is true of so-called 'foundation' sacrifices, the deposition of human remains during the construction of buildings or other structures. The purpose of such burials was arguably linked with gaining approval from the supernatural powers, perhaps in particular those on whose territory the building was raised, together with magically endowing the structure, and its builders, with good luck, prosperity and longevity.

The ramparts of several hillforts in southern England were associated with deliberately placed inhumations. At Danebury (Hants) and South Cadbury (Somerset), the bodies of young men were positioned within or behind the earthen defences (see chapter 6); similar practice was noted at Sutton Walls in Herefordshire, and at Hod Hill, Dorset, the crouched remains of a woman had been buried beneath the small outer bank of the hillfort (Merrifield 1987, 51-2). A late Iron Age cemetery at Harlyn Bay in Cornwall contained a circular stone structure under whose foundations were the bodies of an adult and a child (*op. cit.*). Human and animal remains were deposited in the bases of Iron Age bridge piers at La Tène in Switzerland (Bradley 1990, 157, 164).

The practice of placing human remains in foundation contexts did not die out with the Roman occupation. In the late first or second century AD, a timber bridge was constructed over the river Nene at Aldwincle in Northamptonshire. When the site was investigated in the early 1970s, four human burials were discovered; one was demonstrably of Anglo-Saxon date (the form of iron knife found in the ribs belongs to the seventh century AD). Of the other three, only one is contemporary with the building of the bridge. No details are available as to the gender or age of the individual, but the body had been placed in a trench dug into the bank of the river to take the side-timbers of the bridge abutment, and was lying on its back, arms and legs stretched out (Jackson & Ambrose 1976, 46-7). The remains could be those of someone involved in the construction-work, who perhaps died in an accident and was interred within the structure in order to avert evil befalling the bridge or the builders. Alternatively, there could be a more sinister explanation: the person could have been deliberately chosen to die so that the bridge and its local community would flourish, just as may have happened in the construction of the Iron Age bridge at La Tène.

Plenty of other buildings in Roman Britain may have been blessed by the deposition of bodies, who may even have been sacrificed for the purpose. The remains of infants are recorded as being placed in the foundations of a barrack block at the Reculver Roman fort in Kent; the extension to the public bath-suite at Wroxeter was associated with the interment of a child, its body in two parts, buried under the floor in the corner of the room; in the Silurian capital of Caerwent, an adult was found under a wall, with the head reposing in a niche deliberately left in the wall for it (Merrifield 1987, 51-2). Infant-burials in the foundations of Romano-Celtic temples, such as Springhead in Kent (Penn 1960), were treated in precisely the same manner as animal- and bird-remains deposited at other shrines, like Hockwold in Norfolk (Green 1976, 212; Lewis 1966, 135), where at the foot of each of the four brick column-bases of the *cella* had been placed ritual deposits of pigs and birds. The dismembered child, whose quartered remains were interred in four pits beneath an Iron Age house at Hornish (chapter 7), may equally be interpreted as a foundation sacrifice, even if there had been a significant interval between the deposition and the erection of the dwelling (**colour plate 22**).

The burial of infants in late Romano-British rural buildings such as Winterton in Lincolnshire and the Star villa at Shipham, Somerset (Scott 1991, 115-21) has been connected to the function of the structures themselves: these are generally interpreted as being associated with corn-drying, specifically with malting. Eleanor Scott has interpreted the child-burials as part of a 'revitalizing' ritual, concerned with fertility and crop-growth. In discussing the meaning of infant-burials in association with dwellings in Iron Age western Spain, Jésus Alvarez-Sanchis (2000, 74) interprets such practice as 'a custom which demonstrates concern for the fertility and possession of the land'. Fertility-rites are almost certainly also involved in the deposition of people and animals in the disused grain-storage pits at Iron Age Danebury and other cognate sites. Human and faunal remains were habitually interred in the bases of these silos, alone or in groups of two or three, shortly after the pits had been cleared out (**60**). Barry Cunliffe (1992; 1993b) has argued with conviction that the linkage between the primary use of the pits for storing seed-corn and their secondary function as graves is by no means fortuitous, and that the human and animal deposits are likely to have been associated with fertility-rites and the desire to propitiate the supernatural forces of the underworld, into whose space the pits had penetrated. The pits might be seen as threshold spaces, occupying the interstices between earth and otherworld, where the corn was placed at the liminal time between the harvest and germination of the grain. The burial of people and animals in the silos, whether resulting from sacrifice or natural death, might be perceived as acts of sacred reciprocity, giving something to the gods in order to ensure the crops' protection from contamination by air, water or vermin.

Classical literature seldom refers to human sacrifice specifically for fertility purposes, but there is a curious allusion, by Diodorus Siculus (V, 32-6) to a Gaulish sacrificial ritual involving malefactors:

> For their criminals they keep prisoners for five years and then impale in honour of the gods, dedicating them together with many other offerings of first-fruits.

In the second century AD, the Greek author Arrian wrote a treatise about hunting, entitled the *Cynegetica*. In it, he refers to hunting rituals among the Gauls, which included payment to the spirits of the natural world for the 'theft' of animals taken in the hunt, in a reciprocal, life-for-a-life exchange (similar to the principle recounted by Caesar (VI, 16), where he alludes to the Gauls' belief that one human life had to pay for the preservation of another). Arrian (XXIV) mentions a hunter-goddess to whom sacrifice of a domestic animal was made, together with the first-fruits of the hunt, on the occasion of her birthday. Clearly, then, the idea of 'first-fruits' was closely bound up with reciprocity and the abundance provided by the natural world. The incarceration of wrongdoers for long periods of time, as recorded by Diodorus, is not easy to comprehend, but one reason for such practice may have been the symbolic accumulation of value invested in these social outcasts as represented by their maintenance — particularly the provision of their food —

60 Multiple pit-burial at Danebury. © Danebury Trust

for years before their sacrifice. Similar perceptions may have informed the sacrifice of aged cattle at Gournay or the pampering of the *pharmakos* for a year before he was expelled from the city or ritually murdered.

Aversion and appeasement

> For who does not know that to this very day they [the Gauls] retain the monstrous and barbarous custom of sacrificing men? What then, think you, is the honour, what the piety, of those who even think that the immortal gods can best be appeased by human crime and bloodshed?
> (Cicero *Pro Fonteio* 31)

The self-righteous outrage expressed by Cicero, writing in the first century BC, is somewhat ironic, given that human sacrifice was only outlawed in Rome in 97 BC (Balsdon 1979, 246) and — according to certain early Christian writers (for example Porphyry II, 56) — it was not officially banned in the empire as a whole until the reign of Hadrian in the early second century AD. During the period of the Roman Republic, human sacrifice was the occasional response to critical situations, when the security of the city-state itself was under a threat that required dire means to avert or neutralise it. Such was the context for the ritual murder, by burial alive, of Greek and Gaulish couples in the Forum Boarium, during the Second Punic War, after Rome suffered a severe defeat at the hands of the Carthaginians. The foreign-ness of the victims probably salved the consciences of those responsible; aliens were not quite as human as Romans (see chapter 7). Indeed, it is recorded in the third-century compilation known as the *Augustan Histories* that the emperor Aurelian is alleged to have demanded that a supply of prisoners from different nations (foreigners again) be kept in case of sacrificial need (Vopiscus *Aurelian* XX).

The aversion of catastrophes by appeasement of the divine was a common pretext for human sacrifice in antiquity. Thus the Old Testament king, Mesha of the Moabites, pledged his son as a sacrifice when the city of Moab was besieged by the Israelites (2 *Kings* III. 27), and Jephthah's daughter was similarly promised as the price of victory (*Judges* XI. 30-40). Diodorus (XIV, 4-6; XX) describes how in 310 BC, when the Punic army was facing defeat by the Syracusans, the Carthaginians believed that their god Kronos was angry because he had been cheated of his due of child-sacrifices, which the people had withheld by deception and replaced by substitute gifts. Under the threat of disaster, 200 children from the noblest families were ritually slaughtered for Kronos, and 300 more were offered (de Vaux 1964, 79-81). In the context of Carthaginian child-sacrifice (Brown 1991, 22), three main reasons for such practice are given in the literary sources: to placate the gods, to appease or avert their displeasure and for personal gain; the bigger the favour asked, the more valuable the sacrifice had to be. In discussing Gaulish ritual practice, Julius Caesar makes a similar point, observing that those suffering from life-threatening illness, or facing the dangers of war, conducted human sacrifices in order to persuade the gods to protect them (VI, 16). Marcus and Flannery (1994, 59) have noted precisely this relationship between request and reward: in the Zapotec ritual traditions of ancient Mexico, the value of a sacred offering was predicated on need or the amount of gratitude deemed appropriate for divine favours. Anticipation and thanksgiving were both occasions for human sacrifice; the aversion of earthquakes was an important context for ritual murder in Oaxaca, just as seems to have been the case at the temple of Anemospila in ancient Crete (see chapter 6). The prediction of events and their avoidance or encouragement were contexts for human sacrifice in ancient Gaul and Britain, according to chroniclers like Diodorus (V, 31. 2-5) and Strabo (IV, 4.5), who speak of its perpetration in divinatory ceremonies. Similarly, if we believe the chroniclers of human scapegoat sacrifice in ancient Massilia, the rite was carried out in order to cleanse and purify the town, perhaps following an epidemic or a run of ill-luck.

61 Iron sword with anthropomorphic
hilt, inlaid with gold, perhaps used
in sacrificial ritual, from Saint-
André-de-Lidon (Charente-
Maritime). Antoine Maillier
© Centre archéologique européen du
Mont Beuvray

Reprisals, vengeance and compensation

Four warriors hereupon from Sulmo sprung,
As many reared by Ufens, he takes quick,
To slay as offerings to the shade, and drench
The blazing funeral-pyre with captive blood.
(Virgil *Aeneid* X, 506-36; trans. Rhoades
1957, 258) (**61**)

Virgil's epic poem, in which he sought to
contextualise the foundation of Rome and its
development as a world-power, was modelled on
Homer's two heroic sagas, the *Odyssey* and the *Iliad*.
The passage quoted above is the finale of the episode
in which the eponymous hero Aeneas takes revenge
against Turnus and the Latins for the death of his
companion-in-arms Pallas. The story is clearly
closely inspired by Achilles' grief-retaliation after the
death of Patroclus, where he sacrifices 12 Trojan
youths at his friend's funeral. So, the sepulchral rites
surrounding the deaths of Patroclus and Pallas
included reprisal sacrifices, thereby avenging death in
battle of comrades and at the same time both
providing fit company for the dead heroes in the
afterlife and offering valuable gifts to the chthonic
spirits so as to ease their passage from earthworld to
the underworld. There is a sense, too, in which these
sacrificial acts served to compensate both the
bereaved friend, the dead hero's kin and his gods.
This kind of reciprocity may have been in the mind
of Julius Caesar when, in the mid-first century BC,
he spoke of the Gauls' belief that:

the power of the immortal gods can be
appeased only if one human life is exchanged
for another, and they have sacrifices of this
kind regularly established by the community.
(*de Bello Gallico* VI, 16)

A combination of revenge, reparation and sacrifice
might also provide the context in which men were
sacrificed at war-sanctuaries like Gournay and
Ribemont.

The link between reprisals, punishment and sacrifice is clearly demonstrated in a late Romano-British context, by the inscription on a lead curse tablet or *defixio* dated (by the form of cursive script) to the fourth century AD, found in silt dredged from the river Ouse at Brandon in Suffolk; its message is clear (chapter 6) in demanding sacrifice in revenge for theft, in the name of Neptune (Hassall & Tomlin 1994, 293). If we are to take the mention of sacrifice at face value, the late Roman date of this inscription is significant in so far as ritual murder had been illegal for centuries. But even if the phraseology is metaphorical, the connection between punishment and sacrifice is interesting; clearly the two are not necessarily mutually distinct.

Human sacrifice and the gods

> And those who propitiate with horrid victims ruthless Teutates, and Esus whose savage shrine makes men shudder, and Taranis, whose altar is no more benign than that of Scythian Diana.
> (Lucan *Pharsalia* I, 445-6; trans. Duff 1977, 35-7)

62 Gallo-Roman relief carving of Esus, from Trier (Germany). © Paul Jenkins

Lucan, writing of deities encountered by Caesar's army in southern Gaul, gives no clue as to the functions and responsibilities of these Gaulish gods, although the ferocity of each is clearly indicated. Teutates may be a title cognate with early Irish 'tuath', meaning tribe; Esus's name may mean simply 'lord'. The ninth-century Bernese commentator on the text (Zwicker 1934, 50) alludes to equations between Teutates and Esus (**62**) and the Roman gods Mars and Mercury; in this early medieval glossary, Taranis is linked with Dis Pater, but on altars of Roman date from western Europe (Green 1982) his Gaulish name is coupled with Jupiter; moreover, his function is

*63 Anthropomorphic sword-hilt on a gold-decorated sword from Saint-André-de-Lidon (see **61**). Antoine Maillier © Centre archéologique européen du Mont Beuvray*

indicated by the 'taran' root, meaning 'thunder' (*see* **29**).

Archaeological evidence can rarely link the practice of ritual murder with specific, named deities, although the Brandon curse-tablet appears to provide just such a connection. But literary sources sometimes allude to the need to placate particular divinities by means of human sacrifice. The two types of divine being most frequently associated with this kind of offering in ancient Europe are war-gods and sky-gods. Herodotus, Strabo and Dio Cassius each allude to the dedication of human sacrificial victims to warrior-deities. Herodotus speaks of the Scythian practice of slaughtering war-captives to Ares (the Greek god of war) (*Histories* IV, 62). He recounts how one prisoner out of every hundred would be selected, wine poured over his head and his throat cut over a bowl; the blood was then poured out over an ancient iron sword, which represented the god himself (**63**). The ritual took place at a 'temple' comprising a heap of brushwood, levelled off to form a platform, on which the sword was placed upright. Sacrificed with the men were cattle and horses. Herodotus' observations are interesting in so far as blood and wine appear to have had a cognate symbolism, perhaps associated with either life-force or purification; the use of a sword as a surrogate image is also significant, particularly if we recall the anthropomorphic hilts on many Iron Age swords.

Herodotus was describing a 'barbarian' custom taking place, during the fifth century BC, in Scythia, beyond the civilised world. In similar vein, Strabo (*Geographia* III, 7) recounted the Celtiberian custom of sacrificing prisoners and horses to Ares. More surprising is a passage in Dio Cassius's *Roman History*, in which he refers to ritual murder on the Campus Martius (the Field of Mars) in the very heart of Rome itself in 46 BC. The context for the episode is given as the extravagant behaviour of Julius Caesar, on his return from defeating Pompey, which led to riots among the army. Caesar intervened and one agitator was summarily executed and 'two others were slain as a sort of ritual observance'.

Dio explains further:

> The true cause I am unable to state, inasmuch as the Sybil made no utterance
> and there was no similar oracle, but at any rate they were sacrificed in the
> Campus Martius by the pontifices [official state priests] and the priest of Mars,
> and their heads were set up near the Regia.
> (Dio Cassius *Roman History* XLIII, 24.4; trans. Cary 1969, 257)

Dio was born more than a century after this alleged event but, if he was recording a
genuine occurrence, then human sacrifice, of a kind, took place in the city of Rome 50
years after its official prohibition. The location of the ritual is significant, as is the presence
of the *Flamen Martialis*; it may be that the association with Mars lay in the identity of the
rioters as army personnel. Dio makes another allusion to ritual activity that, by
implication, involved a variety of ritual killing, this time in Britain. He narrates the story
of the Boudican Rebellion in AD 60, when the consort of the dead client-king Prasutagus,
ruler of the East Anglian Iceni, took revenge on the Romans for humiliations and the
seizure of Icenian assets, by sacking the three most developed Romano-British cities:
London, Verulamium and Colchester. During the attack on London, Boudica committed
various atrocities on the population in the name of Andraste, a goddess of victory (Dio
Cassius LXII, 7, 1-3), including the mutilation and murdering of Roman women:

> While they were doing all this in the grove of Andraste and other sacred places,
> they performed sacrifices, feasted and abandoned all restraint (Andraste was
> their name for victory and she enjoyed their especial reverence).

Although Dio does not say so, there is a sense in which the unfortunate women of London
were reprisal sacrifices: according to his text, they were treated with indescribable savagery,
being impaled on sharpened timbers, their severed breasts forced into their mouths, as if
in a parody of the rape suffered by Boudica's daughters by Roman officials (Green 1995,
32-3; Wood 1992, 123-5). Andraste is unknown in the epigraphic record, but the cognate
name Andarte belonged to a goddess worshipped by the Gaulish tribe of the Vocontii
(Duval 1976, 59).

There is some archaeological evidence to support the association between war-deities
and human sacrifice. The remains of people deposited, along with weapons and other
battle-trophies, at war-sanctuaries such as Gournay and Ribemont, are suggestive of such
a link. Another, more overtly significant find is the altar from Apt (Vaucluse) in southern
Gaul, inscribed with a dedication to Mars by worshippers with Gaulish names, erected on
top of a deposit of human skulls (Isserlin 1997, 97). It is tempting to interpret such a cache
as a sacred gift.

The Roman Jupiter was both lord of the heavens and the spirit of Rome itself; as the
all-conquering Iupiter Optimus Maximus, he was venerated by the Roman army. In
Gallo-Roman religion, the sky-god was frequently manifested as a warrior-deity: he
appears thus on the Jupiter-Giant columns of eastern Gaul and the Rhineland
(Bauchhenss & Nölke 1981), and on many other images where he is accompanied by his

indigenous Gallic solar symbol of the wheel (Green 1991, 95-6). So it should not surprise us to find a recurrent connection between celestial deities and human sacrifice. Lucan alludes to the thunder-god Taranis, and the medieval Berne commentator on his text speaks of sacrificial offerings of people who were burnt alive in his honour. It has been suggested (chapter 3) that the human bodies burnt in a fire-pit at Leonding in Austria might have been dedicated to a sky- or sun-god, maybe even Taranis himself.

A number of late Roman texts make links between the worship of Jupiter and ritual killing although, since some of the authors were Christians, we need to be wary of their ideological bias. Indeed, the context in which the early Christian writers attacked pagan human sacrifice was in defence of their own faith which, according to its detractors, included the killing and consumption of people (Rives 1995). The African writer Lactantius, born in the mid-third century AD, had this to say on the subject, claiming the survival of ritual murder until the second century:

> In Salamis of Cyprus Teucer sacrificed a human victim to Jove. And the sacrifice he handed down to posterity, and it was recently abolished during the reign of Hadrian.
> (*Divinae Institutiones* I. 21; trans. Hughes 1991, 133)

Another Christian author, Minucius Felix (*Octavius* XXX), writing in the early third century, refers to the dedication of ritual murder victims to Jupiter Latiaris 'in his own day', as do Tertullian, a Christian of Carthaginian origin, in his *Apologeticus*, written in *c*.AD 197, and Tatian (*Oratio ad Graecos* 29, 1), who links Latiaris with Diana Nemorensis, an Italian goddess venerated at Lake Nemi, near Aricia. Felix's *Octavius* is an elegant 'dialogue' between a pagan, Natalis of Cirta in North Africa, and the eponymous Christian Octavius, in which they argue the relative merits of the two systems. Jupiter Latiaris was an ancient Latin deity to whom a white heifer was sacrificed at a festival called the *feriae Latinae*. The association between Latiaris and human sacrifice may have originated in an alleged practice in which his altar was anointed with the blood of people killed in his sacred games (Rives 1995, 75). Porphyry alludes to human sacrifice to Zeus and its association with ritual cannibalism (*de Abstinentia* II, 27; Brown 1991, 147-58). The Christian message is clear: human sacrifice was an outrageous practice, fit only for pagans. Ironically, this was precisely the same argument used by earlier Graeco-Roman writers about the uncouth ritual customs of 'barbarians' like Gauls, Britons and Phoenicians.

Of the other gods linked to ritual killing in the ancient texts, one of the most prominent in the Classical literature is the Punic deity known as Baal Hammon, or by his Graeco-Roman equivalent Kronos-Saturn who, interestingly enough, had a link with sky-gods: Baal was a lord of high places and the Greek Kronos was the father of Zeus (in Roman equivalence Saturn and Jupiter). As already discussed (chapters 3 and 7), there is a great deal of literary and archaeological evidence to suggest that this Phoenician divinity was placated by means of child-sacrifice, although some of the Classical writers, in seeking to cite the barbarity of Carthaginian ritual, may well have exaggerated the practice, in so far as the sacrifice of children might be considered the most shocking and uncivilised behaviour of all.

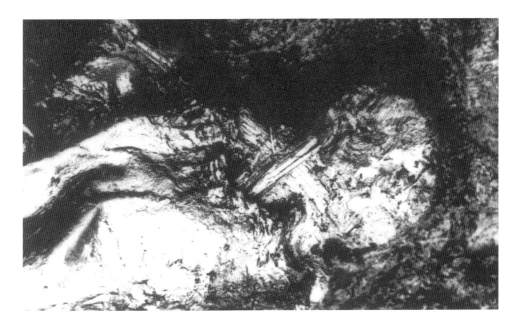

64 *The body of a man interred in the marsh at Windeby, Schleswig-Holstein, not far from the find-spot of the Windeby girl, in the first few centuries AD. © Stiftung Schleswig-Holsteinische Landesmuseen, Schloss Gottorf — Archäologisches Landesmuseum — Schleswig, Germany*

65 *Hurdles pinning down the Windeby man in the peat. © Stiftung Schleswig-Holsteinische Landesmuseen, Schloss Gottorf — Archäologisches Landesmuseum — Schleswig, Germany*

Context and circumstance

In attempting to gain some understanding of the circumstances under which the sacrificial killing of humans took place, some mention should be made of context. There is a body of testimony to the enactment of human (and animal) sacrifice during major festivals, which was conducted, sometimes on a regular basis, perhaps according to the seasons or some other cyclical criterion. But there were clearly other rites that were responses to crises and disasters, such as the death of a ruler, plague, drought or defeat in war, or favourable events, like victory in battle, the birth of a royal baby or a bumper harvest. Tacitus says this of a Germanic Suebian tribe, the Semnones:

> At a set time all the peoples of the blood gather, in their embassies, in a wood hallowed by the auguries of their ancestors and the awe of ages. The sacrifice in public of a human victim marks the grisly opening of their savage ritual.
> (*Germania* XXXIX)

This kind of regular ceremony is suggested at temple-sites like Gournay, where people and animals appear to have been sacrificed about every 10 years, perhaps at times of major festivals. If the victims at these shrines were prisoners-of-war, it could be that they were kept incarcerated until the right occasion for their ritual execution, as mentioned by Diodorus, when he describes the Gaulish treatment of criminals: 'for their criminals they keep prisoners for five years and then impale them in honour of the gods . . .' (V, 32-6) (**colour plate 25**). The repetition of sacrifice at particular locations did not only take place at formal shrines: the multiple depositions of bog-bodies at sites like Tollund, Borremose, Windeby (**50, 64 & 65**) and Lindow Moss (**colour plate 12**) show that place was important to the sacrificial rite, even if it was enacted in the open air, with no physically demarcated space.

Festivals, as contexts for human sacrifice, are significant occasions, in so far as the period of their celebration could be perceived as outside earthworld rules. They were times when norms were flouted and inversions occurred. The Roman Saturnalia is a good example of the latter: staged at the winter solstice, the festival included a tradition wherein servants and masters changed places (Adkins & Adkins 1996, 200). Other inversions included transvestism: Plutarch (*Quaestiones Graecae* 58) commented that on the Greek island of Kos, the priest of Herakles donned female attire in preparation for sacrifice. Likewise, Tacitus (*Germania* XLIII) spoke of cross-dressing by a priest of a Germanic tribe called the Nahanarvali, in a sacred grove. Religious festivals provide an opportunity to behave in a manner contrary to normal custom. They therefore would have afforded a fitting backdrop to ritual murder, perhaps one of the least normative aspects of human behaviour.

9
The sacrificers

Human sacrifice is generally considered to be directed at supernatural entities and carried out under the auspices of religious specialists.
(Parker Pearson 1999, 17)

. . . the barbaric gods worshipped here [in the grove] had their altars heaped with hideous offerings, and every tree was sprinkled with human blood . . . Nobody dared enter this grove except the priest.
(Lucan Pharsalia *III, 372-417)*

Priests and cult activity

The Classical chroniclers of religious custom in ancient Gaul and Britain, towards the end of the pre-Roman Iron Age, all emphasise the involvement of priests — specifically the Druids — in all sacrificial activity, including (indeed, especially) ritual murder. This chapter explores the literary and archaeological evidence for the association between religious practitioners and human sacrifice in the late first millennium BC. It considers the observations of Graeco-Roman historians, together with the material culture relating to cult-officials; in certain circumstances, it is even possible to make close archaeo-logical linkages between clergy and the enactment of sacred murder. Classical historians speak not only of the role of professional priests in human sacrifice but also of 'auto-sacrifice', where the holy man or woman became the victim. In addition, there exist rare examples of iconography that appear to show human sacrificial victims accompanied by religious functionaries.

It is almost a commonplace that ceremonial officials are associated with sacrifice, however such activity is manifested. In virtually every religious tradition — past and present — for which there is specific evidence for ritual practice, one individual or a group of special people are identified as being responsible for cult-activity and for mediating between humans and the spirit world. But we need to be

66 Reconstruction of Diviciacus, the Druid, friend of Caesar and Cicero in the mid-first century BC. Musée de Bibracte. Antoine Maillier © Centre archéologique européen du Mont Beuvray

careful in making a case for the existence of a professional and exclusive priesthood, for is is likely that, in late Iron Age Europe at least, the distinction between religious and political power could be blurred, with certain individuals having dual responsibility for earthly and spiritual leadership. In his *de Bello Gallico*, Caesar makes repeated reference to

179

67 Gallo-Roman altar from Autun (Burgundy) dedicated by a local priest, called a gutuater. The inscription reads 'Norbaneius Thallus, gutuater. Dedicated to the Divine Augustus and to the god Anvallus'; first century AD. Antoine Maillier © Centre archéologique européen du Mont Beuvray

his Gaulish friend and ally Diviciacus (**66**), ruler of the Burgundian polity of the Aedui, and his anti-Roman freedom agitator brother Dumnorix who, according to Caesar's text, declined Caesar's 'invitation' to accompany him to Britain on account of his religious duties at home. While Caesar himself does not refer to Diviciacus' s role as a holy man, Cicero (*de Divinatione* I, 90) identifies him as a Druid, describing him thus on the occasion of their meeting at Rome in 60 BC, and commenting on Diviciacus's particular skill at divination. In another treatise, written to Julius Caesar in 45 BC, Cicero defends the Galatian king Deiotarus against an accusation raised by the king's own grandson, of conspiracy to assassinate Caesar; in extolling Deiotarus's virtues, Cicero alludes to his role in religious affairs (*Pro Deiotaro* 8). The third-century AD writer Dio Cassius speaks similarly of Ambigatus, chief of the Bituriges, who embraced both political and sacred leadership (Millar 1964, 178; Fr 50, 2-3; Fr. 57, 6b; Brunaux 1996, 135).

Apart from the probability that certain Gaulish priests were also influential in the political arena (**67 & 68**), it is highly likely that a hierarchy of religious practitioners existed in the European Iron Age, of whom the Druids may have been the most

68 Pot inscribed with a graffito in Gaulish, reading 'Vergobretos readdas' (donated by a vergobret), a title given to a Gaulish magistrate, from Argentomagus (Indre); earlier first century AD. Antoine Maillier © Centre archéologique européen du Mont Beuvray

prominent, at least in Gaul and Britain, where they are specifically situated by Classical writers of the first centuries BC and AD. On analogy with societies documented in anthropological literature, the Druids — at the apex of the clerical hierarchy — may well have enjoyed sole responsibility for human sacrifice. In the Zapotec rituals of ancient Oaxaca (Mexico), special priests were in charge of human and animal sacrifice (Marcus & Flannery 1994, 60). Indeed Strabo alludes to three categories of 'learned' men in Gaul in the first century BC: the Druids, the Bards and the *Vates*, seers who were particularly involved with sacrificial matters (*Geographia* IV, 4, 4). It might be that the individuals who actually engaged in the praxis of sacrifice, and dispatched the victims — whether animal or human — were of lower status than the high priests, the Druids themselves. Indeed, such practitioners might have been regarded 'as mere technicians' (Bourdillon 1980, 11). Jean-Louis Brunaux (2000, 26-9) comments that several classes of cult official were probably involved in Gaulish sacrificial practice, including the Druids and a variety of more lowly assistants who did the slaughtering and cleaned up after this messy business, maintained and repaired the buildings and ritual equipment, and tended the sanctuary precinct and its gardens.

There is archaeological evidence for the use of liturgical regalia and ceremonial paraphernalia in the western European late Iron Age and Roman periods, including wands, headdresses and special cult-instruments. Moreover there is an array of material culture indicative of a well-orchestrated and highly complex pattern of ritual behaviour that makes sense only in the context of the presence of professional clergy, or at least the designation of certain individuals within each community to control the management and enactment of sacrificial and other ceremonial activity. In the Roman period, we know that priests officiated in sanctuaries, for we have epigraphic evidence for their presence: at the great healing sanctuary dedicated to the hybrid Brittano-Roman goddess Sulis-Minerva, for instance, we know of a resident priest of the cult, Calpurnius Receptus, immortalised by an inscribed tombstone erected by his wife, the freedwoman Calpurnia Trifosa (*R.I.B.* 155). Calpurnius is described on the stone as *'sacerdos deae Sulis'* ('priest of the goddess

181

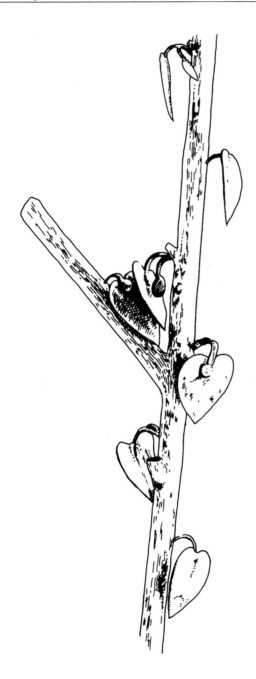

Sulis'); he lived a long time for a Roman Briton, dying when he was 75 years old. Romano-British priests probably avoided using the term 'Druid' (or were discouraged from so doing) because it was loaded with a not entirely happy meaning for the Roman administration.

This is not the proper place to examine in detail the evidence for religious regalia; this has been done recently elsewhere (Green 1997, 60-3). It is sufficient here merely to point to some of the most prominent material which proves, beyond reasonable doubt, that professional clergy were present in Gaul and Britain during the later Iron Age and Roman periods. The 'warrior' buried at Deal in Kent in the late third or early second century BC wore a headdress that was certainly not a soldier's helmet; furthermore, the garment in which he was interred was fastened at the knee by a brooch, suggestive of a long flowing garment rather than armour (James & Rigby 1997, 19-24; Parfitt 1995). The so-called 'cult tree' found at the great *oppidum* of Manching in Bavaria (**69**), and used during the third century BC, consists of a gilded wooden staff with gold-washed bronze leaves, each about 5cm long, attached (Perrin 2000, 21-2). It is difficult to interpret this curious object as other than a piece of liturgical equipment, used by cult officials in religious ceremonies. Similar model leaves have been recorded on sacred sites, such as the sanctuary at Saint-Maur (Oise) (Green 2000a, 11; Maier 1990, 249). Interestingly, the Manching 'tree' has now been identified as a climbing

69 Model of a climbing plant, possibly convolvulus (the seeds of which have hallucinogenic properties), from a cult-place in the oppidum of Manching, on the Danube in Bavaria; third century BC.
© *Paul Jenkins*

70 Part of a set of six diadems or crowns from the Romano-British temple at Hockwold-cum-Wilton, Norfolk. © Paul Jenkins

plant, probably a convolvulus, the seeds of which have hallucinogenic properties (Paddy Coker, pers. comm.); it is tempting to infer that such psychotropic plants were used by priests in transcendental rituals.

To the Roman period belong sets of ceremonial headgear and cult sceptres repeatedly associated with sanctuaries. The rural temple at Hockwold-cum-Wilton in Norfolk, built in the second century AD, has produced no less than six bronze crowns (**70**) or diadems, some fitted with adjustable headbands to allow for use by a range of individuals; a hoard of similar headdresses comes from Cavenham, also in East Anglia. Three chain headdresses come from the shrine at Wanborough in Surrey, two of which have a wheel-motif worn on the crown of the head, in a fashion remarkably similar to the head-ornament on an antlered human face depicted on a late Iron Age silver coin from central England (Boon 1982, 276-82). Wands or sceptres have been identified at British temples such as Farley Heath in Surrey, where a thin bronze band, once encircling a staff, had been incised with a series of cult-figures and motifs belonging to a recognised repertoire of divine figures identified in Gallo-British cosmologies (Green 1976, 219; Goodchild 1938, 391ff). A similar, though plain, binding has been identified as part of the Llyn Cerrig Bach late Iron Age ritual assemblage, along with part of a ceremonial trumpet (Savory 1976, 84, 93).

In seeking to establish the presence of priests in pre-Roman antiquity, the circumstantial evidence of complex, clearly staged patterns of ritual behaviour are as evocative as the presence of liturgical equipment in religious contexts. It is clear from the formalised complexity of cult-practice identifiable in evidence-rich well-excavated Gallic sanctuaries, such as Gournay and Ribemont in northern France, that some kind of organised religious praxis was in place. We shall see later that such controlled orchestration is evident in the context of human sacrificial ritual. At Iron Age Ribemont, a sacred site occupied from the third century BC until the Augustan period, vast quantities of human leg-bones were arranged in 'log-cabin' type structures, probably one positioned at each of the four corners of the cult enclosure (two have been excavated), with the long-bones of horses carefully placed around the edge of each 'ossuary' and the whole edifice associated with assemblages of weapons (*see* **22**). There is a notable absence of human skulls at the site, suggesting that they were deliberately deposited elsewhere. The whole pattern of deposition at the site shows unequivocal signs of having been controlled rather than the result of haphazard and random activity. It is significant that the Iron Age sanctuary was replaced by an enormous Gallo-Roman religious complex (Cadoux 1984, 53-78; 1991, 156-63; Brunaux 1996, 77-90). The cognate-free Gaulish shrine at Gournay equally shows evidence of carefully stage-managed ritual events, again implying the presence of professional, probably resident, clergy; here, there were regular episodes of cattle-skull deposition at the entrance (Brunaux 1988; 1996, 69-77). Military trophies were displayed in the sanctuary before being buried in the enclosure ditch, along with the remains of people and animals, placed in carefully-arranged and discrete groups. The sacrificed cattle were kept until they were old, then slaughtered according to a prescribed ritual, involving precise blows to the nape of the neck and post-mortem sword-slashes to the muzzle (**17**). The carcasses were then placed in a decomposition-pit in the centre of the precinct and later re-deposited in the ditch surrounding the shrine after the connective tissue had decayed. Horses were sacrificed and interred entire, but other beasts — notably young pigs and lambs — were butchered for religious feasting and the culinary debris placed in the ditch. Human skulls were suspended from the entrance-way and eventually fell into the ditch. The evidence for precise and formulaic ritual action at sites such as Ribemont and Gournay — whether or not human sacrifice was involved here — testifies to the presence of presiding officials who controlled access to the *locus consecratus* and what took place there (Brunaux 2000, 26-9). Both sanctuaries appear to have been foci for the offering of slain enemy battle-victims and their weapons to the gods of the victorious army; Gournay seems to have been located in the territory of the Bellovaci but — significantly perhaps — close to the boundaries of two other polities, the Viromandui and the Ambiani.

There exists another category of evidence for the presence of priests in the later Iron Age and Roman period in western Europe, namely the material culture and skeletal record from certain cemeteries. A number of rich Gaulish graves have recently been identified, albeit tentatively, as those of religious officials, partly on the grounds of the accompanying grave-goods which are suggestive of activity associated with sacrifice and/or healing. In a tomb of second-century BC date at Saint-Georges-les-

71 Set of iron surgical instruments, including a combined pincers and scalpel, together with a knife, from the cemetery at Tartigny (Oise), perhaps the possessions of a priest-physician; second half of the third century BC. Antoine Maillier © Centre archéologique européen du Mont Beuvray

Baillargeaux (Vienne) a knife, some 32cm long, had been deposited with a set of razors and a whetstone (**colour plate 26**). A group of six high-status cremation-graves, dating to the third century BC, at Tartigny (Oise) comprised elaborate funerary chambers within quadrangular enclosures. In the tombs small surgical instruments lay with the dead (**71**); these and others found at Saint-Georges, are essentially similar to those identified in the broadly coeval 'surgeon's grave' at Obermenzing in Germany (Lejars & Perrin 2000, 37-40) and in the rich first-century AD British cremation-grave at Stanway near Colchester (Essex), where curious 'divining' rods, four of bronze and four of iron, were also found (Crummy 1997, 337-41). The surgical instruments from these tombs are almost invariably of iron; at Stanway, though, most were made of ferrous metal, some were bronze. It is possible that the materiality is itself significant in terms of cult and symbolism: both Pliny (*Natural History* XXIV, 62) and Tacitus (*Germania* XL) make reference to iron as a symbolic metal, though both suggest its negative rather than positive properties. On analogy with many non-western traditions, the alchemy and magic involved in the manufacture of iron is likely to have been charged with meaning (Green 2000b), so the seeming deliberation with which iron was chosen for certain cult-objects may well be important. In the northern Gaulish graves, the sets of surgical instruments are frequently associated with special vessels, including wooden, metal-bound buckets (**72-3**) and, sometimes, pairs of spoons that Fitzpatrick (2000, 47-9) has suggested may have been used in divinatory ritual, in so far as the

72 *Bronze-decorated yew-wood bucket, bronze bowl and iron surgical instruments from the priest-surgeon's grave at Tartigny (Oise). Antoine Maillier © Centre archéologique européen du Mont Beuvray*

dished surface of one is divided into quadrants and the other has a hole drilled through it, as if to take a powder or liquid that would trickle onto the quartered surface (**colour plate 27**). We shall see later that, at one site — Acy-Romance in the Ardennes — it is possible to make a direct and persuasive connection between high-status cremation graves of 'priests' with human sacrificial activity. This site has produced a series of rich cremation-graves, containing buckets, special knives, tweezers, razors and metal-bound wooden chests; deliberately broken weapons were found with some of these high-status burials.

One further piece of circumstantial — and highly enigmatic — evidence for the presence of priests' tombs has come to light in excavations at Baldock in Hertfordshire, a site that has produced a series of five cemeteries ranging in date from the first century BC to the sixth century AD. Keith Matthews (1999, 141-61) has compared the age-at-death profile of two burial-grounds here, Wallington Road and Royston Road, and observed the presence of notable discrepancies in the pattern of life-expectancy between them. The age-profile revealed by examination of the bodies buried at Wallington Road 'seemed to be what one might expect of an essentially rural Romano-British population'; a number of infants and a high proportion of young adults, particularly women, who had presumably succumbed to the hazards of childbirth, with an average life-expectancy of 26 years. The picture at Royston Road was very different: here there were few infants; young adults formed a very small percentage of the population (3.5%); the largest group comprised older adults, more than 45 years of age, and the life-expectancy here was 41.3 years. Matthews's opinion is that the Royston Road cemetery was special and was, perhaps, exclusive to special members of the community (**74**). He comments that the 'women seem to have sailed through their years of fertility with almost no life-threatening problems, almost as if they were not bearing children' (**75**). The age-profile here is actually analogous to that obtaining in some Anglo-Saxon nunneries and, on this basis, Matthews has suggested that the Royston Road cemetery might have been 'the burial ground of a largely celibate religious community'. The notion that the dead interred here were special is supported by the relative wealth and elaboration of the graves, particularly in the later phases; some of the activity accompanying the funerals seems to have involved exotic rituals, including decapitation. Clearly, we cannot prove the existence of an exclusive cemetery for clergy at Baldock, but the evidence is suggestive and it is difficult to dismiss the anomalous survival rates of people into what, for antiquity, would count as old age.

Druids, priests and human sacrifice:
the evidence of Classical literature

Francisco Simón (1999, 1-15) argues that human sacrifice, in the late pre-Roman Iron Age in Gaul and Britain, was a ceremonial form of killing associated with a unique feeling of collective responsibility that demanded orchestration by and presence of the Druids. Indeed, Classical writers on the religious customs of Gaul and Britain emphasise the involvement of the Druids in sacrificial ritual, particularly ritual murder. Strabo and Diodorus Siculus each comment on the necessity of a Druidic presence at the sacrifice of human beings to the gods. According to Strabo:

> They [the Gauls] used to strike a human being, whom they had devoted to death, in the back with a sword, and then divine from his death-struggles. But they would not sacrifice without the Druids.
> (*Geographia* IV, 4, 6)

Diodorus similarly describes human sacrifice by stabbing, adding the remark:

> And it is a custom of theirs [the Gauls] that no one should perform a sacrifice without a 'philosopher'; for thank-offerings should be rendered to the gods, they say, by the hands of men who are experienced in the nature of the divine, and who speak, as it were, the language of the gods.
> (V, 31, 2-5)

These two texts provide interesting information concerning the context of Druidic involvement in human sacrifice, Strabo emphasising the divinatory element, the telling of the future by observing the manner in which ritual victims died, in order to control the supernatural forces and thus events, such as the outcome of battles. Diodorus presents a somewhat different contextual scenario in so far as he specifically alludes to the purpose of sacrificial offerings as thanksgiving. Moreover, he explains that the presence of the Druids was necessary because they were in tune with the spirit world and could therefore

187

73 *Bronze-bound yew-wood bucket from a tomb at Fléré-la-Rivière (Indre); first century BC. Antoine Maillier © Centre archéologique européen du Mont Beuvray*

74 *Gallo-Roman stone relief of a man with birds perched on his shoulders: possibly a shaman with his animal-helpers; from Moux, Burgundy. © author*

mediate between humans and the gods. It is noteworthy that Diodorus describes the role of the Druids in a manner highly reminiscent of the responsibilities of the holy person or shaman in many non-western religious systems of the present or recent past (**74, 76**) (Vitebsky 1995).

Other texts of the first century BC endorse the link between the Druids and ritual murder. In his defence of Fonteius against the Rhône Valley tribe of the Allobroges (*Pro Fonteio* 31), Cicero accused the Gauls of practising human sacrifice, implying the involvement of the Druids, and making the point that the word of people capable of such barbarity should not be taken seriously. The purpose of this passage in Cicero's text is to castigate the Allobroges and their leader, Indutiomarus, thereby negating their reliability as witnesses against Fonteius. Although not stated in so many words, it is clear that Cicero lays the responsibility for ritual murder upon Indutiomarus himself, and it is permissible to consider whether the Allobrogian ruler might himself have been a Druid. Julius Caesar is our most prolific source for this period: Book VI of his *de Bello Gallico* is devoted to the customs of the Gauls (among whom he spent a decade), and he took an especial interest in the Druids for whom, quite clearly, he had considerable respect. But we should remember that it is only in the ethnographical digression of Book VI that Caesar mentions Druids by this name; elsewhere, he refers to holy men as *sacerdotes*, the generic label for priests in the Roman world. Caesar comments that:

> The Druids are concerned with the worship of the gods, look after public and private sacrifices, and expound religious matters.
> (*de Bello Gallico* VI, 13)

75 *Romano-British bronze figurine of a female flute-player, from Silchester, Hampshire. © Paul Jenkins*

He elaborates on the particular circumstances surrounding decisions to conduct ritual killing, explaining that

> . . . those who are suffering from serious illness or are in the midst of the dangers of battle, either put to death human beings as sacrificial victims or take a vow to do so, and the Druids take part in these sacrifices . . .
> (VI, 16)

189

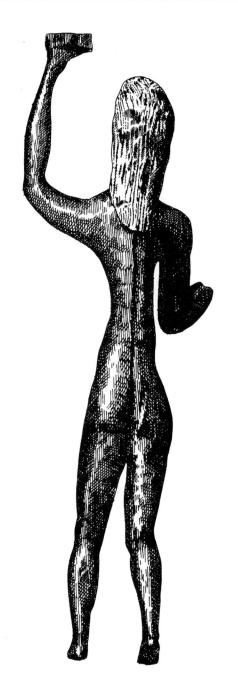

76 Bronze figurine of a female dancer, possibly in an ecstatic state, from the sacred hoard of bronzes found at Neuvy-en-Sullias (Loiret), and originally from a shrine; end of pre-Roman Iron Age. © Paul Jenkins

Interestingly, Caesar does not say that the Druids were the initiators of such proceedings, only that their presence was required in order, perhaps, to ratify the sacrifice or to ensure its acceptability by the gods. It is likely, in fact, that underlings undertook the praxis of sacrificial slaughter and that the community or its leader, rather than the Druids themselves, often 'commissioned' the killing (Green 1997).

Tacitus, Lucan and Suetonius wrote a century or so later than Caesar, in the first-second century AD; all corroborate his avowal of the connection between the Druids and human sacrifice. In his *Life of Claudius* (25), Suetonius comments that the emperor 'completely abolished the barbarous and inhuman religion of the Druids in Gaul'. Lucan's epic poem, the *Pharsalia* contains an allusion to the presence of Druids in the sacred groves of southern Gaul, encountered by Caesar's army as it marched to meet Pompey's forces in 48 BC; Lucan writes that 'the Druids, too, took advantage of the armistice to resume the barbarous rites of their wicked religion' (I, 422-65). In describing the Roman attack on the holy Druidic island of Anglesey, led by Suetonius Paulinus in AD 60/61, Tacitus refers to the association between this priesthood and the sacrifice of war captives in north-west Britain:

> Close by stood Druids, raising their hands to heaven and screaming dreadful curses . . . The groves devoted to Mona's barbarous superstitions he demolished. For it was their [the Druids'] religion to drench their altars in the blood of prisoners. (*Annales* XIV, 30-1)

So the Druids are firmly linked with human sacrifice in the Classical sources, so much so that they have retained a reputation for savage barbarism over two millennia, although several ancient texts refer also to their wisdom, intellect and peacemaking activities (Green 1997, 40-53). But the Druids were not the only religious group to have been associated with ritual murder by their contemporary chroniclers. Strabo and Tacitus each provide an account of human sacrifice at which cult officials presided. Strabo describes the practice among Cimbrian priestesses of killing prisoners-of-war in order to inspect their innards for divinatory purposes:

> They were grey with age, and wore white tunics and over them, cloaks of finest linen and girdles of bronze. Their feet were bare. These women would enter the [army] camp, sword in hand, and go up to the prisoners, crown them, and lead them up to a bronze vessel which might hold some 20 measures. One woman would mount a step and, leaning over the cauldron, cut the throat of a prisoner, who was held over the vessel's rim. Others cut open the body and, after inspecting the entrails, would foretell victory for their countrymen.
> (Strabo *Geographia* VII, 2, 3)

This short passage contains a great deal of information, not least in terms of the religious practitioners themselves. They were female, they were elderly, and there was more than one of them. They were carefully dressed in pure white; they used a cauldron; there was task-based differentiation between those that dealt the death-blow and others whose job it was to eviscerate the body for divination. The gender and age of these cult officials deserve a little attention: in his lengthy description of the Druids, Caesar never mentions women, but he does emphasise that it took as long as 20 years to complete Druidic training, suggesting that these priests were of mature years when they matriculated. Other authors do allude to female Druids, notably in the obscure group of third-century AD texts known as the *Scriptores Historiae Augustae* (the Augustan Histories), where the reigns of several Roman emperors are correctly predicted by Gaulish Druidesses. The bare feet of Strabo's Cimbrian women may be significant: Carol van Driel (1999) has argued that feet may be regarded as liminal parts of the body, able to touch the Otherworld and the means of transition between earth and spirit dimensions. If this were so for these priestesses, then the lack of shoes would mean more direct contact with the chthonic powers underground. Finally, the use of a cauldron as a blood-container is worthy of note. Strabo may have taken this idea from ancient Greek animal sacrifice, where the *sphageion* was used as a vessel for catching the blood when the victim's throat was cut. Indeed, we could read Strabo's text as a deliberate pastiche of Mediterranean ritual, in which humans are substituted for beasts and women for men in a deliberate attempt at barbarisation. Aside from that, though, the cauldron is significant for it is generally seen as a transformatory vessel (Green 1998b; 2001b), a symbol of death and regeneration; cauldrons are frequent finds in Iron Age material culture as cult deposits, often in watery or marshy contexts which themselves may have been perceived as threshold spaces between worlds.

There is a passage in Tacitus's treatise known as the *Germania* in which he describes an agricultural ritual associated with the north European goddess Nerthus (see chapter

6), which culminates in the death of the two slaves whose job it was to wash the goddess's holy cloth in a sacred lake. Tacitus makes it clear that a priest officiated at the ceremony:

> In an island of Ocean stands a sacred grove, and in the grove stands a car draped with a cloth which none but the priest may touch. The priest can feel the presence of the goddess in this holy of holies, and attends her, in deepest reverence . . .
>
> (Tacitus *Germania* XL)

This passage serves to stress the role of Nerthus's priest as a mediator between the goddess and her devotees; only he had sufficient sanctity to make direct contact with her and her attendant slaves had to be ritually killed because, of necessity, they handled the holy cloth to wash it in the sacred lake. So the unfortunate servants, presumably the very lowest in the hierarchy of cult officials, were considered to be too impure to remain in earthworld after having been close to the goddess; to leave them alive perhaps constituted an insult to the divine presence which would bring ill-luck to the community. Additionally, it may have been perceived as peculiarly appropriate to sacrifice persons already touched by the spirit essence, who were perhaps treated as surrogates for the priests themselves. The context of the ceremony is important, for it was enacted not only within a sacred grove but in the liminal location of an island in the sea, in a similar place to the Druidic grove-sanctuary on Anglesey.

Two further references to an association between religious officials and human sacrifice bear comparison with Tacitus's narrative, with regard to its enactment in sacred groves, although in all other respects the contexts are widely divergent one from the other. Lucan's first-century AD account of the Massilian grove — defiled by the axes of Julius Caesar's army in the mid-first century BC — contains a comment that

> the barbaric gods worshipped here [in the grove] had their altars heaped with hideous offerings, and every tree was sprinkled with human blood . . . Nobody dared enter this grove except the priest.
>
> (*Pharsalia* III, 372-417)

In his *Apologeticus* (IX, 2-4), written in about AD 197, the Christian author Tertullian refers to the Punic practice of child-sacrifice to a North African god known by the name of the Roman god Saturn, as still continuing openly to his own day, despite its longstanding prohibition under Roman law (Brown 1991, 22-6). Tertullian gives an account of the arrest of Phoenician priests perpetrating this outrage and their crucifixion on the very trees of their temple. We need to exercise caution in evaluating early Christian homilies since their authors were clearly writing to a specific anti-pagan agenda. However, we should not dismiss the allusions to sacred groves in this and other texts, such as those of Lucan and Tacitus, since Cicero speaks of such *loci* as being fitting contexts for Roman rural cult-practice while built temples, he says, were more appropriate for urban worship (*de Legibus* 8). What is more, there is a body of archaeological and epigraphic evidence for the importance of groves and trees in Gaul and Britain in the later Iron Age and Roman periods (Green 2000a, 8-17).

Priests and self-sacrifice

> And you Iphigeneia, must be priestess of this goddess [Artemis] at the holy meadow of Brauron. When you die, you will be buried there, and people will dedicate to you the beautifully woven dresses that women in life-destroying labour leave behind in their houses.
> (Euripides *Iphigeneia among the Taurians*, lines 1462-7)

In this version of the Iphigeneia myth, when the maiden is condemned to be sacrificed to the goddess Artemis by Agamemnon, in exhange for the lifting of the curse that prevented his fleet from sailing (Holst-Warhaft 1992, 137), Iphigeneia's fate is deflected by the intervention of Artemis herself who, instead, consigns the girl to live among the Taurians, presiding as priestess over their habitual practice of human sacrifice. In a sense, then, the story of Iphigeneia is a myth of self-sacrifice. We should remember that, for the ancient Greeks, ritual murder was safely confined to the realm of mythic fantasy. Euripides was particularly fond of using drama to explore metaphors of society that was out of kilter with itself; such treatment is very apparent in his play *The Bacchae* that examines the theme of chaos and was, significantly, composed against the backdrop of civil war between Athens and Sparta.

But what of genuine evidence for auto-sacrifice among religious officials? Strabo refers in considerable detail to such an occurrence (chapter 4); interestingly, like Tacitus's island shrines on Anglesey and Nerthus's holy place, this account of self-sacrifice among holy persons was set on a sacred island, situated off the mouth of the river Loire (**colour plate 10**).

> It is their custom once a year to remove the roof from their temple and to roof it again the same day before sunset, each woman carrying part of the burden; but the woman whose load falls from her is torn to pieces by the others; and they carry the pieces around the temple crying out 'euoi', and do not cease until their madness passes away; and it always happens that someone pushes against the woman who is destined to suffer this fate.
> (Strabo *Geographia* IV, 4, 6)

The passage is unique in its presentation of the sacrifice of a priest by fellow cult officials; moreover, the inference is that, unlike auto-sacrifice as documented in some anthropological literature, Strabo's holy victim — one of an all female 'guild' — does not appear to have connived at her fate, which seems to have been an aversion sacrifice at a time of the temple's vulnerability in its roofless state, perhaps perceived as a 'time of no being' when maleficent spirits could invade the unprotected sanctuary. Although Strabo does not say so, it may even be that the victim acted as a kind of scapegoat, purifying the sanctuary and its attendants by her death: there may be an analogy to be made with the punishment meted out to errant Vestal Virgins in Rome, who reneged against their vows of celibacy; in a sense, these hapless holy women were sacrificed as a means of turning ill-fortune away from the city. The implication of Strabo's report is that, during the ceremony, the holy women were possessed by their god, in the same way as Dionysus's Maenads were maddened by divine intoxication, and tore their fellow priestess apart whilst in the frenzy of their altered state of consciousness.

Archaeological evidence for self-sacrifice in the European Iron Age is not easy to come by. However, Parker Pearson has made an interesting suggestion which serves to link some human remains, that were arguably victims of sacrifice, with an observation in Tacitus's *Germania*. The Roman writer comments that

> . . . the shirker and the disreputable of body are drowned in miry swamps under a cover of wattled hurdles.
> (*Germania* XII)

Parker Pearson wonders whether some of these individuals were perhaps 'special' people, even sacrificed shamans (Parker Pearson 1999, 70-1) and whether some of the bog-bodies known from northern Europe might, indeed, be prophets or seers themselves. He argues that the deformed or disabled — as were the Netherlands finds of the Yde girl, with her deformed spine, the woman from Zweeloo, who had exceptionally short forearms and the two men from Dojringe, one with a short right arm and spina bifida and the other with a short left arm — form a high proportion of these watery burials (see also chapter 7) and that it may have been these people that were perceived as being touched by the spirits and were therefore chosen to be shamans. It is of especial note that the Grauballe Man (**colour plate 13**), whose throat was slit before his deposition in a Danish marsh, had ingested a quantity of ergot, a substance that would cause hallucinations and then convulsions (Parker Pearson 1999, 68), a feature that may mark him as a shaman, seeking to achieve an altered state of consciousness in order to gain spiritual access to the Otherworld. There is plenty of evidence in the Classical literature for the ancient linkage between seers or divine beings and disability: blind Teiresias as depicted, for instance, in the Greek dramatist Sophocles's plays *Antigone* and *Oedipus Tyrannos*, was a prophet whose ability to 'see' the future was enhanced by his inability to see in earthworld (Garland 1995, 29, 34); the Norse god Oðin's one-eye disfigurement (Page 1990, 36) signalled his special supernatural status and, what is more, he underwent a form of self-sacrifice by being hung on the World Tree, in order to gain perfect wisdom (Davidson 1993, 98). The blindfolded Windeby girl (chapter 6) may, indeed, have been a seer.

Self-sacrifice of religious leaders is not unknown in non-western traditions, although it is rare that some kind of substitution is not invoked. An example of voluntary auto-sacrifice can be found among the Dinka of the southern Sudan, where the chief of a village, also its highest cult official, chooses to sacrifice himself and perceives the act of interring himself alive as a great honour (Bourdillon 1980, 19). By burying himself alive at a time of his choosing, he can die in his own village and remain with his people, continuing to protect them from beyond the grave.

A different kind of self-sacrifice is chronicled in the ethnohistories of the Spanish Conquistadores relating to pagan religious systems they found in Oaxaca (Mexico), among the Zapotec people (Marcus & Flannery 1994, 55-74). According to these sixteenth-century texts, the priests of these Central American communities used incense and narcotics to send themselves into a transcendent state in which they could communicate with royal ancestors and spirit beings. Blood was central to Zapotec cosmology and their priests practised human sacrifices, tearing the still-beating hearts out of living victims. But they also enacted a kind of auto-sacrifice which did not involve their own deaths, by letting small quantities of their own blood, using special and elaborate instruments including the spines of stingrays or obsidian imitations, sharks' teeth, lancets made of obsidian or flint, or the spines of the *agave* cactus to cut their skin and veins. The accounts of Spanish colonists are supported by archaeological evidence which traces the instruments used in auto-sacrifice back to the beginning of the first millennium BC, with the discovery of implements identical to the auto-sacrificial instruments recorded in the early modern texts (Marcus & Flannery 1994, 60-2).

The evidence of archaeology

The material culture of the western European Iron Age provides both direct and indirect evidence for the involvement of professional clergy in human sacrificial ritual. The rich cremation-grave discovered at the settlement of Acy-Romance (Ardennes), containing an axe with a curious, transversely-perforated blade, might be that of a priest, for an inhumation-burial from another part of the settlement contained the body of an adult man, his hands behind his back, as though once bound, and his skull displaying signs of a wound that corresponds exactly to that axe-blade (Lambot 1998; 2000, 30-6; Simón 1999, 1-15). It is clear from a series of 'boxed' inhumations (see chapter 6) that human sacrifice took place on a regular basis at Acy (**colour plate 18**) during the second century BC; the man attacked with the axe probably met his death in about 100 BC, and Lambot suggests that he may have been the victim of clandestine, subversive cult-activity at a time when human sacrifice had become officially obsolete (chapter 6).

The formulaic ritual involving human sacrificial victims at Acy provides indirect evidence of its orchestration by professional religious officials. There is a marked difference in status reflected in the rich cremations, on the one hand, and the inhumations, which are without grave-goods, on the other. The manner in which the 20 young adult men were, over a period of time, placed in boxes, dried out in a deep pit beneath the communal cult building at the centre of the village, then raised and placed in a well-ventilated location to complete the drying process, and finally re-interred in a seated position on a terrace in a central public cult area, has to have been the result of carefully-managed ritual behaviour. Furthermore, three more young men were buried in specially aligned positions, again manifestly carried out according to strictly prescribed rules.

Other ritual activity at Acy demonstrates the complexity of ritual activity here very clearly, supporting the notion that a resident hierarchy of religious officials were in control. Cattle and horses were slaughtered for feasting but their remains were carefully interred with cattle placed in the southern half of the central cult-enclosure and horses to the north. One of the features of the site was a huge circular subterranean offering-place, strongly reminiscent of a Roman *favissa* (an underground temple-vault in which sacred offerings were stored), in which a large quantity of miniature iron spears had been deposited. Even though Acy-Romance was by no means a large urban Gaulish centre, it is evident that the settlement supported special religious officials who were involved in highly complex ritual action, including regularly repeated human sacrifice.

Elsewhere in Gaul and Britain, the evidence is not quite as dramatic as that exhibited at Acy-Romance. Nonetheless, other sites where ritual killing is suspected supports the argument for priestly involvement. The defleshed skull of the young Romano-British boy, found placed in a deep pit outside a temple after apparently having been displayed on a pole may have been the focus of professional religious activity (*see* **27, 47**). The skull is of especial interest because of the excessive number of knife-marks that indicate defleshing, suggesting deliberate corporate, presumably organised, involvement (chapter 5). This Folly Lane evidence is strongly reminiscent of the skull-fragments from the later Iron Age site at Roissy-en-France (Val d'Oise) (*see* **44**), which were pierced for suspension, and the front part of a skull, of third-century BC date from Montmartin (**colour plate 15**), which had been made into a kind of mask which, so the excavators suggest, might have once decorated the walls of a religious area within a high-status dwelling (Boulestin & Séguier 2000, 38). Finally, we should not forget that the complex 'triple killing' of Lindow Man (**colour plate 12**) is clear evidence for a collective, organised method of ritual dispatch, as are the repeated human bog-deposits in specific locations, clearly demarcated as sacred spaces.

The archaeological and ethnohistorical records relating to Zapotec ritual in the Oaxaca region of Mexico provide direct information about the role of religious officials in human sacrifice. These holy men, known as *bigaña*, like many non-western shamans, used incense and narcotics (including *datura* and tobacco) to try and communicate with the ancestors and the supernatural world (Marcus & Flannery 1994, 59). The *bigaña* lived in the inner cell of their two-roomed temples, and kept their sacrificial equipment there. In a shrine at Cuilapan, a sacrificial deposit, placed beneath the floor, contained a child-sacrifice and 17 jade figurines; a temple-building, belonging to the phase *c*.AD 100-200 within the great cult-precinct of San José Mogote, had a cistern or basin sunk into the floor in the inner sanctum, perhaps used for washing sacrificial instruments or even as a blood-container. In another shrine, a group of sacrificial knives was found *in situ* on the floor (*op. cit.* 66-7). Documentary sources for the Zapotec describe the use of flint or obsidian daggers to sacrifice slaves and prisoners-of-war by priests; they record that specially-trained priests had responsibility for cutting out the hearts of their living victims with these tools (*op. cit.* 71, 60).

There is a body of anthropological literature that supports the association between special religious functionaries and human sacrifice. Tierney (1989, 20, cited by Parker Pearson 1999) claims that human sacrifice is still practised, on occasions, by shamans in parts of South America who wish to avert or bring about particular events. It is even reported that their powers of communication with the spirit world are used by traffickers in cocaine, who 'sponsor' shamans to enact ritual murder in order to promote their illicit trade. In the 1880s, Robert Louis Stevenson encountered human sacrifice and — worse still — ritual cannibalism carried out by priests in the Marquesas Islands of Polynesia (Bell 1994, 57-8). Stevenson recorded high places of sacrifice in the forest, in the presence of a sacred banyan tree, in the vicinity of which the hapless victims were incarcerated in a subterranean cell until the feast day. 'He [Stevenson] imagined drums throbbing and a crescendo of dancing and singing as the priests sanctified the brutish feast' (Bell 1994, 58).

Human sacrifice in action: images of priests

A very small amount of European Iron Age iconography exists depicting what may be interpreted as religious practitioners actually engaged in ritual killing. A scene in the rock-art of Camonica Valley in northern Italy may be testimony to such activity: a central 'victim' is flanked by two figures, each of whom is clad in 'shamanic' animal pelts and wields a knife (*see* **30**) (Green 1997, 77; Anati 1965, 185). More persuasive still is the tableau displayed on one of the inner plates of the great gilded silver cult-cauldron from Gundestrup in Jutland (Olmsted 1979, pl. 3E), which depicts an army-scene of infantry and cavalry in the company of a huge being, towering above the rest, in the act of drowning a man in a vat (*see* **48**). The interpretation of this individual as a priest rather than a god may be supported by the strange headdress he wears, which is broadly analogous to the ceremonial cap (known as an *apex*) shown on the heads of Roman priests on the *Ara Pacis* at Rome (Croom 2000, 68, 70, fig. 25.1). Both of these pieces are open to conjecture as to their interpretation. There is nothing from Iron Age Europe on the scale of certainty offered, for instance, by the iconography of Carthaginian stelai; one of these images, from Carthage itself, depicts a holy man, holding a child about to be sacrificed in the crook of his left arm, while raising his right hand, as if in benediction (*see* **31**) (Brown 1991, 123-45). The evidence of the Punic iconography is borne out by both archaeology and the testimony of Classical literature.

Despite the paucity of iconography relating to the sacrificers of Iron Age Europe, the body of circumstantial evidence reviewed in this chapter strongly suggests that people with a special religious role within their communities, probably professional clergy, were involved in ritual murder. The testimony of Classical literature is well-supported by both archaeological and ethnographical material culture. In all probability, there was a strict hierarchy of praxis and we can imagine the existence of rigorous selection and training of individuals who possessed the power to control and speak to the spirit world by means of human offerings.

Epilogue:
Confronting
the victims

*These human sacrifices have done much injury to the Druidical character, among us,
who never practise them in the same way . . . If one of these old Druids could have slept,
like the seven sleepers of Ephesus, and awaked, in the nineteenth century, some fine
morning near Newgate, the exhibition of some half-dozen funipendulous forgers might
have shocked the tender bowels of his humanity as much as one of his wicker baskets of
captives in the flames shocked those of Caesar.*
(*Thomas Love Peacock,* The Misfortunes of Elphin, *1829)*

As this book draws to a close, it is appropriate to reflect upon the societies that may have enacted human sacrifice and on the identity of their victims. For much of the pre-Roman Iron Age, what is now western Europe was essentially rural, in which communities, large or small, lived by farming, trading and pursuing specialist crafts, such as smithing and carpentry. Iron Age Europe is now acknowledged as embracing considerable regional and chronological diversity and, as such, it would be quite wrong to attempt to present any kind of unified image either of societies themselves or their cosmologies during the later first millennium BC. However, within pre-Roman temperate Europe, it is possible to identify the results of habitual behaviour that may recur over comparatively long time- and space-perspectives. Sometimes such behaviour only makes sense within an interpretative framework of ritual activity, and may be regarded as a form of cognitive response to a world perceived as being inhabited by supernatural forces that might be malign or benign, depending on how they were treated. This book presents arguments suggesting that ritual human killing was a rare but persistent aspect of this cognitive response, something that communities practised at times of great stress, crisis or relief, a form of behaviour designed to appease or control the spirits residing in the natural and supranatural worlds. Most of the European Iron Age was non-literate and this means that we can have little notion as to the identity of these spirits, although the deposition of precious objects in lakes, marshes and rivers leads us to suspect that their divine recipients were perceived as the numinous personifications of such features in the landscape. The impingement upon parts of 'barbarian' Europe of the highly literate Classical world, from about the second century BC onwards, provides some names and contexts for ritual activity, including sacral murder, though — as the prologue makes clear — we need to be careful how we use this testimony. It is not until the Roman occupation of Gaul and Britain that a complex network of deities and cosmologies emerges in an epigraphic and iconographic expression of interrelated hierarchical religious systems. The archaeology of the pre-Roman Iron Age presents us with dim glimpses of cosmologies that, nonetheless, can be recognised as involving sophisticated and profound negotiations with the spirit-world. Human sacrifice appears to have contributed to this discourse, and such practice may even have continued in Roman provincial society. It may not be without significance that there seems to have been a concentration of 'extreme' ritual activity in Britain just before or during the Roman conquest: Lindow, Alveston and Folly Lane exemplify this burst of sacrificial energy. It is as if the disruption of the new Roman presence goaded people to seek special favours from the gods.

It is seldom possible to confront ancient individuals directly but I was granted such a privilege during the writing of this book, when I was asked to contribute to the re-examination of a Danish bog-body, that of a middle-aged woman from central Jutland, the so-called 'Juthe Fen' or 'Haraldskaer' woman (**colour plate 28**). The project enabled some reinterpretations to be made and some old claims about her to be discarded. The body was found in 1834, pinned down with hurdles, in a bog near the modern town of Vejle. At the time of her discovery, she was identified as the Norwegian Viking queen Gunhild and was given a suitably 'royal' and Christian burial by the Danish king of the time (Lone Hvass pers. comm.). The king had an ornate oak coffin specially constructed for her (**colour plate 29**) and arranged for her to lie at rest in the twelfth-century church of Saint Nicolai at Vejle (where she reposes to this day) (**colour plate 30**). At the time of her discovery, this female body was subjected to a post-mortem, which suggested that she had suffered a horrific death by being pegged into the waters of the bog while still alive, the main thrust of this argument being that one knee-joint had swollen around the timber that had been rammed through it. To add spice to the story, it was reported at the time that, when the woman was found, she had an expression of terror on her face, a feature whose significance has now been discredited by pathological study. The state of forensic and archaeological science in the early nineteenth century led to the disposal of the woman's internal organs unstudied, thus losing vital clues as to the nature of her life and the manner of her demise.

In the winter of 2000, the Haraldskaer woman was subjected to new research by a team consisting of the University of Århus department of Forensic Science, Dr Lone Hvass of the Elsinor Museum and myself, the initiation of the study being the result of the making of a television documentary by Electric Sky. It has now been revealed that the woman might have already been dead when her body was pegged into the bed of the marsh, and that the swelling of the knee could have been caused naturally by acids in the bog. The other injuries to the limbs, noted at the time of her discovery, are now interpreted as having occurred post-mortem. However, close examination during the new autopsy revealed a very faint groove around the throat, which may represent evidence for a garrotte. The Århus team also found that, unlike many Iron Age bog-victims, the Haraldskaer woman, although between 40 and 50 years old, was incredibly fit for her age and time, having apparently suffered from no degenerative diseases such as arthritis, which afflicted so many people in the first millennium BC. Most importantly of all, a new radiocarbon date puts the date of her death at approximately 490 BC, during a time when sepulchral evidence suggests that high-ranking women were beginning to assert themselves as independently powerful in the Iron Age socio-political arena (Arnold 1995, 153-68).

The results of the 2000 study of a well-known bog-body have thus put paid to a number of old assumptions and, at the same time, have raised other significant issues, not least that of how she came by her death. She was undoubtedly pinned into the marsh, but she may have died first. Nonetheless, it is highly likely that the circumstances surrounding her death and interment were associated with ritual action: she was placed in the marsh virtually naked, but her clothes were deposited nearby, suggesting that, perhaps, her nakedness was symbolically significant. Her body was pegged down into a very specific location within the bog, as though it were a sacred spot and it was therefore important that she remain there for all time. Indeed, it is significant that she, like other bog-bodies, was inhumed rather than being cremated — the normative burial-rite of the time and region. The opportunity to re-examine this famous bog-body, using sophisticated forensic science, has enabled new interpretations to be made and old assumptions discarded. Whether she was killed specifically for sacrificial purposes remains a matter for debate, but it is a sobering thought that, if the Haraldskaer woman becomes the subject of further scientific study in a hundred years' time, the picture of her life and death will, almost certainly, change dramatically once again.

The Haraldskaer woman's age and apparent fitness suggests that she may have led a privileged life within her community. She was plump and well-nourished and showed little sign of having undertaken manual labour. She may have lived a special life and certainly was interred in a special way. Between her life and her burial, she met a death that may, itself, have been special, a death that may have been influenced by who she was in life. Noblewoman, hostage or priestess, she was consigned to the local marsh as a gift to the spirits. In all probability, she was chosen as a sacrificial victim, killed as part of a complex ceremony, perhaps witnessed by the whole community, the intention being to preserve her body for eternity. Although no evidence survives as to the time of year she died, having visited this sombre place on a bleak December morning, it is tempting for me to imagine that her placement in the marsh was staged for maximum dramatic impact, in midwinter, just as the sun rose over the horizon and illuminated her watery grave, 'a space of darkness and cold shade' (Lucan *Pharsalia* III, 399-400).

Bibliography

Adkins, Lesley & Adkins, Roy 1994. *Handbook to Life in Ancient Rome*. New York: Facts on File.

Adkins, Lesley & Adkins, Roy 1996. *Dictionary of Roman Religion*. New York: Facts on File.

Alcock, Leslie 1972. '*By South Cadbury is that Camelot . . .' Excavations at Cadbury Castle 1966-70*. London: Thames & Hudson.

Aldhouse-Green, S. ed. 2000. *Paviland Cave and the 'Red Lady'*. Bristol: Western Academic and Specialist Press.

Aldhouse-Green, S. 2000. 'Climate, ceremony, pilgrimage and Paviland: the 'Red Lady' in his palaeoecological and technoetic context', in Aldhouse-Green, S. ed., 227-46.

Allason-Jones, Lindsay & McKay, Bruce 1985. *Coventina's Well*. Chesters: Chesters Museum/Trustees of the Clayton Collection.

Allen, Derek 1980. *The Coins of the Ancient Celts*. Edinburgh: Edinburgh University Press.

Almagro-Gorbea, Martín 1995. 'From Hillforts to *Oppida* in "Celtic" Iberia', in Barry Cunliffe & Simon Keay eds. *Social Complexity and the Development of Towns in Iberia. From the Copper Age to the Second Century AD*. Oxford: Oxford University Press (for the British Academy), 175-207.

Alvarez-Sanchis, Jesús 2000. 'The Iron Age in Western Spain (800 BC - AD 50): an overview', *Oxford Journal of Archaeology* 19 (1), 65-89.

Anati, Emanuel 1965. *Camonica Valley*. London: Jonathan Cape.

Arnold, Bettina 1995. '"Honorary Males" or Women of Substance? Gender, status and power in Iron-Age Europe', *Cambridge Archaeological Journal* 3:2, 153-68.

Babbitt, Frank Cole, trans. 1936. *Plutarch's* Moralia. Cambridge Massachusetts: William Heinemann, 127-9.

Barber, John, Halstead, Paul, James, Heather & Lee, Frances 1989. 'An unusual Iron Age burial at Hornish Point, South Uist', *Antiquity* 63, 773-8.

Barker, Francis 1933. *The Culture of Violence. Essays in Tragedy and History*. Manchester: Manchester University Press.

Bäckman, Louise 1981. *Kort Berättelse Om Lapparnas Bjoerna-Fänge samt Deras der wid brubade widskeppelser af Pehr Fjellström, Stockholm 1755*. Umeå: Norrläbdska Skrifter, Nr. 5.

Balsdon, J.P.V.D. 1979. *Romans and Aliens*. Chapel Hill: University of North Carolina Press.

Bauchhenss, Gerhard & Nölke, Peter 1981. *Die Iupitersäulen in den germanischen Provinzen*. Köln/Bonn: Rheinland Verlag.

Beattie, J.H.M. 1980. 'On understanding sacrifice', in Bourdillon & Fortes eds., 29-44.

Beckwith, Roger, T. & Selman, Martin J, eds. 1995. *Sacrifice in the Bible*. Carlisle: Paternoster Press.

Bell, Gavin 1994. *In search of Tusitala. Travels in the Pacific after Robert Louis Stevenson*. London: Picador/Macmillan.

Bennike, Pia 1999. 'The Early Neolithic Danish bog finds: a strange group of people!', in Coles, Coles & Jørgensen eds., 27-32.

Bennike, Pia & Ebbesen, Kalus 1986. 'The Bog find From Sigersdal. Human Sacrifice in the Early Neolithic', *Journal of Danish Archaeology* 5, 85-115.

Benoit, Fernand 1969. *L'Art Primitif Méditerranéen de la Vallée du Rhône*. Aix-en-Provence: Publications des Annales de la Faculté des Lettres.

Benoit, Fernand 1981. *Entremont*. Paris: Ophrys.

Berlin, B. & Kay, P. 1969. *Basic Color Terms: their universality and evolution*. Berkeley, CA: University of California Press.

Bhreathnach, Edel & Newman, Conor 1997. *Tara*. Dublin: Stationery Office.

Billington, Sandra & Green, Miranda 1996 eds. *The Concept of the Goddess*. London: Routledge.

Birkhan, H. 1999. *Kelten-Celts: Images of their Culture*. Vienna: Österreichen Akademie Der Wissenschaften.

Blacker, Carmen 1996. 'The Mistress of the Animals in Japan: Yamanokami', in Billington & Green eds., 178-185.

Bloch, M. & Parry, J. 1982. 'Introduction: death and the regeneration of life', in M. Bloch & J. Parry eds., *Death and the Regeneration of Life*. Cambridge: Cambridge University Press, 1-44.

Blundell, Sue & Williamson, Margaret 1998. *The Sacred and the Feminine in Ancient Greece*. London: Routledge.

Bonenfant, Pierre-Paul & Guillaumet, Jean-Paul 1998. *La Statuaire Anthropomorphe du Premier Age du Fer*. Besançon: Presses Universitaire Franc-Comtoise.

Bonnamour, Louis 2000. *Archéologie de la Saône. 150 ans de recherches*. Chalon-sur-Saône: Co-édition Editions Errance.

Boon, George Counsel 1982. 'A coin with the head of the Cernunnos', *Seaby Coin and Medal Bulletin* No. 769, 276-82.

Borca, Frederico 2000. 'Towns and marshes in the ancient world', in Hope & Marshall eds., 74-84.

Boulestin, Bruno & Séguier, Jean-Marc 2000. 'Le Culte du Crâne', in Guichard & Perrin eds., 38.

Bourdillon, M.F.C. 1980. 'Introduction', in Bourdillon & Fortes eds., 1-27.

Bourdillon, M.F.C. & Fortes, M. eds. 1980. *Sacrifice*. London: Academic Press (for the Royal Anthropological Institute of Great Britain and Ireland).

Bradley, Ian 1995. *The Power of Sacrifice*. London: Darton, Longman & Todd.

Bradley, Keith. 1989. *Slavery and Rebellion in the Roman World 140 BC - 70 BC*. Bloomington & Indianapolis: Indiana University Press.

Bradley, Richard 1990. *The Passage of Arms*. Cambridge: Cambridge University Press.

Bradley, Richard 2000. *An Archaeology of Natural Places*. London: Routledge.

Brewster, T.C.M. 1976. 'Garton Slack', *Current Archaeology* 5, no. 51, 104-16.

Bridgeford, Sue 1997. 'Mightier than the pen? An edgewise look at Irish Bronze Age swords', in Carman ed. 95-115.

Bridgewater, Daisy 2000. 'Carnival amid the snow and winter misery', *The Times* 31.3.2000

Briggs, Stephen 1995. 'Did they fall or were they pushed? Some unresolved questions about bog-bodies', in Turner & Scaife eds., 168-82.

Brindley, A.L. & Lanting, J.N. 1995. 'Irish Bog Bodies: the Radiocarbon Dates', in Turner & Scaife eds., 133-6.

Brookes, Alison 1997. *An investigation of aspects of funerary practice in Iron Age Britain*. Newport: University of Wales unpublished MA dissertation.

Brown, Shelby 1991. *Late Carthaginian Child Sacrifice and Sacrificial Monuments in their Mediterranean Context*. Sheffield: JSOT/Sheffield Academic Press.

Browne, David, Silverman, Helaine & García, Rubén 1993. 'A cache of Nasca Trophy Heads from Cerro Carapo, Peru', *Latin American Antiquity* 4 (3), 274-94.

Brunaux, Jean-Louis 1988. *The Celtic Gauls. Gods, Rites & Sanctuaries*. Paris: Errance.

Brunaux, Jean-Louis 1996. *Les Religions Gaulois. Rituels Celtiques de la Gaule Indépendente*. Paris: Errance.

Brunaux, Jean-Louis *et al.* 1985. *Gournay I: Les Fouilles sur le sanctuaire et l'oppidum (1975-1984)*. Paris: Errance.

Brunaux, Jean-Louis ed. 1991. *Les sanctuaires celtiques et leurs rapport avex de monde Méditerranéen*. Paris: Dossiers de Protohistoire/Errance.

Brunaux, Jean-Louis 2000. 'Être Prêtre en Gaule', in Guichard & Perrin eds., 26-9.

Brunt, Peter A. 1971. *Italian Manpower*. Oxford: Clarendon Press.

Burkert, W. 1983. *Homo Necans. The Anthropology of Ancient Greek Sacrificial Ritual and Myth* (trans. P. Bing). Berkeley/Los Angeles: University of California Press.

Burkert, W. 1985. *Greek Religion*. Oxford: Oxford University Press/Clarendon Press.

Cadoux, J.-L. 1984. 'L'ossuaire gaulois de Ribemont-sur-Ancre. Premières observations, premières questions', *Gallia* 42, 53-78.

Cadoux, J.-L. 1991. 'Organisation spatiales et chronologie du sanctuaires de Ribemont-sur-Ancre (Somme)', in Brunaux ed., 156-63.

Carman, John ed. 1997. *Material Harm. Archaeological Studies of War and Violence*. Glasgow: Cruithne Press.

Carr, G. & Knüsel, C. 1997. 'The ritual framework of excarnation by exposure as the mortuary practice of the early and middle Iron Ages of central southern Britain', in Adam Gwilt & Colin Haselgrove eds., *Reconstructing Iron Age Societies. New approaches to the British Iron Age*. Oxford: Oxbow Monograph no. 71, 167-73.

Cary, Ernest 1914. *Dio's Roman History I*. London: Heinemann (Loeb Edition).

Cary, Ernest 1969. *Dio's Roman History III*. London: Heinemann (Loeb Edition).

Chadwick, Nora 1966. *The Druids*. Cardiff: University of Wales Press.

Charter, David 2000. 'They used to be cannibals at Eton', *The Times* 15.4.00, 19.

Chaudhri, Anna 1996. 'The Caucasian hunting-divinity, male and female: traces of the hunting-goddess in Ossetic folklore', in Billington & Green eds., 166-77.

Clarke, Simon 1999. 'Contact, Architectural Symbolism and the Negotiation of Cultural Identity in the Military Zone', in Patricia Baker *et al.* eds., *TRAC 98: Proceedings of the Sixth Annual Theoretical Roman Archaeology Conference, Leicester 1998*. Oxford: Oxbow, 36-45.

Clarke, Simon 2000. 'In Search of a Different Roman Period: The Finds Assemblage at the Newstead Military Complex', in Garrick Fincham *et al.* eds., *TRAC 99: Proceedings of the Ninth Annual Theoretical Roman Archaeology Conference, Durham 1999*. Oxford: Oxbow, 22-9.

Cleal, R.M.J., Walker, K.F. & Montague, R. 1995. *Stonehenge in its landscape. Twentieth-century excavations*. London: English Heritage Archaeological Report No. 10.

Clottes, Jean & Lewis-Williams, David 1998. *The Shamans of Prehistory. Trance and Magic in the Painted Caves*. New York: Abrams.

Coles, Bryony & Coles, John 1989. *People of the Wetlands. Bogs, Bodies and Lake-Dwellers*. London: Thames & Hudson.

Coles, Bryony, Coles, John & Jørgensen, Mogens Schou eds. 1999. *Bog Bodies, Sacred Sites and Wetland Archaeology*. Exeter: Wetland Archaeology Research Project (*WARP*).

Coles, John 1990. *Images of the Past*. Uddevalla: Hällristningsmuseet, Vitlycke.

Collis, John 2000. 'Survey and Settlement in Central France: Celts, Arverni and Julius Caesar', Newport: University of Wales College, Newport SCARAB Research Seminar 3.5.00.

Connah, G. 1987. *African Civilizations: Precolonial cities and states in Tropical Africa. An Archaeological Perspective*. Cambridge: Cambridge University Press.

Cornwell, T. 1997. 'Eat, drink, man, woman?', *The Times Higher Education Supplement* 23.5.97, 17.

Creighton, John 2000. *Coins and Power in Late Iron Age Britain*. Cambridge: Cambridge University Press.

Croom, Alexandra 2000. *Roman Clothing and Fashion*. Stroud: Tempus.

Crummy, Philip 1997. 'Colchester. The Stanway Burials', *Current Archaeology* 153, 2, no. 9, 337-41.

Cunliffe, Barry 1983. *Danebury. Anatomy of an Iron Age Hillfort*. London: Batsford.

Cunliffe, Barry 1984. *Danebury. An Iron Age Hillfort in Hampshire*. York: CBA Research Report 52.

Cunliffe, Barry 1991. *Iron Age Communities in Britain*. London: Routledge (2nd Edition).

Cunliffe, Barry 1992. 'Pits, preconceptions and propitiation in the British Iron Age', *Oxford Journal of Archaeology* 11 (1), 69-83.

Cunliffe, Barry 1993a. *Danebury*. London: Batsford/English Heritage.

Cunliffe, Barry 1993b. *Fertility, Propitiation and the Gods in the British Iron Age*. Amsterdam: Vijftiende Kroon-Voordracht Gehouden voor de Stichting Nederlands Museum voor Anthropologie en Praehistorie te Amsterdam. Op. 26, November 1993.

Curchin, Leonard 1991. *Roman Spain. Conquest and Assimilation*. London: Routledge.

Curle, J. 1911. *A Roman Frontier Post and its People*. Glasgow: Glasgow University Press.

Davidson, Hilda Ellis 1993. *The Lost Beliefs of Northern Europe*. London: Routledge.

Day, John 1989. *Molech. A god of human sacrifice in the Old Testament*. Cambridge: Cambridge University Press.

De Gracía, Ángel Almazán 1998. *El Cister de Huerta Medinaceli Valle del Jalón*. Salamanca: Grálicas Varona/Sotabur.

De Sélincourt, Aubrey 1965 (trans.). *The War with Hannibal. Books XXI-XXX of Livy's The History of Rome from its Foundation*. Harmondsworth: Penguin.

De Sélincourt, Aubrey 1965 (trans.). *Herodotus. Histories*. Harmondsworth: Penguin.

De Vaux, Roland 1964. *Studies in Old Testament Sacrifice*. Cardiff: University of Wales Press.

Detienne, M. & Vernant, J.-P. *The Cuisine of Sacrifice among the Greeks*. Chicago: University of Chicago Press.

Detienne, Marcel 1989. 'Culinary Practice and the spirit of sacrifice', in Detienne & Vernant, 1-20.

Devoto, Giacomo 1940. *Tabulinae Iguvinae*. Romae: Typis Regiae Officinae Polygraphicae.

Diamond, J.M. 2000. 'Talk of Cannibalism', *Nature* No. 407, September 2000, 25-6.

Diemberger, H. 1993. 'Blood, sperm, soul and the mountain. Gender relations, kinship and cosmovision among the Khumbo (N.E. Nepal)', in Teresa Del Valle ed., *Gendered Anthropology*. London: Routledge, 88-127.

Dunning, C. 1991. 'La Tène', in S. Moscati *et al.* eds., *The Celts*. London: Thames & Hudson, 366-8.

Durand, J.-L. 1989. 'Greek Animals: a Typology of Edible Bodies', in Detienne & Vernant, 87-118.

Durand, J.-L. 1989. 'Ritual as Instrumentality', in Detienne & Vernant, 119-28.

Duff, Ernest 1949 (trans.). *Silius Italicus Punica*. London: Heinemann (Loeb Edition).

Duff, J.D. 1977 (trans.). *Lucan. The Civil* War. London: Heinemann (Loeb Edition).

Duval, Paul-Mari 1976. *Les Dieux de la Gaule*. Paris: Petite Bibliothèque Payot.

Edwards, H.J. 1986 (trans.). *Caesar. The Gallic War.* London: Heinemann (Loeb Edition).

Evans-Pritchard, E.E. 1956. *Nuer Religion.* Oxford: Clarendon Press.

Fantham, G. *et al.* 1994. *Women in the Classical World. Image and Text.* New York/Oxford: Oxford University Press.

Fernández, A. 1992. *Diccionario ritual de voces nahuas: Definiciones de palabras que expresan el pensamiento mítico y religioso de los Nahuas prehispánicos.* México DF: Panaramo Editorial.

Field, N. & Parker Pearson, M. in press. *Fiskerton: an Iron Age Timber Causeway with Iron Age and Roman Votive Offerings.* Oxford: Oxbow.

Finlay, N.J. *et al.* 1997. 'Warp Speed in Denmark: A Review of *Bog Bodies, Sacred Sites and Wetland Archaeology*, September 13-16 1996, Silkeborg, Denmark', *PAST* 25, 6-8.

Finlay, Nyree ed. 1999. *Disability and Archaeology.* Cambridge: Archaeological Review from Cambridge 15:2.

Fischer, Christian 1999. 'The Tollund Man and the Elling Woman and other bog bodies from Central Jutland', in Coles, Coles & Jørgensen eds., 93-7.

Fitzpatrick, Andrew 1984. 'The deposition of La Tène Iron Age metalwork in watery contexts in southern England', in Barry Cunliffe & David Miles eds., *Aspects of the Iron Age in Central Southern England.* Oxford: Oxford University Committee for Archaeology Monograph No. 2, 178-90.

Fitzpatrick, Andrew 1997. *Archaeological Excavations on the Route of the A27 Westhampnett Bypass, West Sussex 1992.* Vol. 2. Salisbury: Wessex Archaeology.

Fitzpatrick, Andrew 2000. 'Les Druides en Grande-Bretagne', in Guichard & Perrin eds., 47-9.

Fokkens, Harry 2001. 'Cows, wars and wisdom: martiality and the constitution of man'. Presentation at conference entitled *Warfare, Violence and Slavery in Prehistory and Protohistory.* Sheffield: The Prehistoric Society and University of Sheffield Archaeology Society.

Foley, Hélène 1985. *Ritual Irony: Poetry and Sacrifice in Euripides.* Ithaca/London: Cornell University Press.

Foster, B.O. 1926 (trans.). *Livy (Books VIII-X).* London: Heinemann (Loeb Edition).

Foulston, Lynn 1998. 'Succour or scourge: goddesses of the village of Khurdapur-Orissa'. Newport: University of Wales College, Newport SCARAB Research Seminar 4.3.98.

Foulston, Lynn 1999. *At the Feet of the Goddess. A Comparative Study of Local Goddess Worship in Khurdapur, a Village Settlement in Orissa and Cholavandan, a Small Town in Tamilnadu.* Newport: University of Wales unpublished PhD dissertation.

Fox, Cyril 1946. *A Find of the Early Iron Age from Llyn Cerrig Bach, Anglesey.* Cardiff: National Museum of Wales.

Frazer, J.G. 1922. *The Golden Bough.* London: Macmillan.

Frey, Otto-Hermann 1991. '"Celtic Princes" in the Sixth Century BC', in S. Moscati *et al.* eds., *The Celts.* London: Thames & Hudson, 75-92.

Fulford, Michael & Creighton, John 1998. 'A Late Iron Age Mirror Burial from Latchmere, near Silchester, Hampshire', *Proceedings of the Prehistoric Society* 64, 331-42.

Garland, A.N. 1995. 'Worsley Man, England' in Turner & Scaife eds. 104-7.

Garland, Robert 1995. *The Eye of the Beholder. Deformity and Disability in the Graeco-Roman World.* Ithaca, New York: Cornell University Press.

Gibson, T. 1986. *Sacrifice and Sharing in the Philippine Highlands: Religion and Society among the Buid of Mindora.* London: Athlone Press (LSE Monographs in Social Anthropology 53).

Giles, Melanie 2001. 'Transformational implements and the control of substances in the middle-later Iron Age landscapes of East Yorkshire'. Presentation at conference entitled *Warfare, Violence and Slavery in Prehistory and Protohistory*. Sheffield: The Prehistoric Society & University of Sheffield Archaeology Society.

Girard, René 1977. *Violence and the Sacred*. Baltimore: John Hopkins University Press.

Glob, P.V. 1969. *The Bog People*. London: Faber & Faber.

Goodchild, R.G. 1938. 'A priest's sceptre from the Romano-Celtic temple at Farley Heath, Surrey', *Antiquaries Journal* 18, 391ff.

Grant, Annie 1989. 'Animals and Ritual in early Britain: the visible and the invisible', in J.D. Vigne ed. *L'Animal dans les pratiques religieuses: les manifestations materielles*. Paris: Anthropozoologica Troisième Numéro Special, 79-86.

Gray, Madeleine 2000. *Images of Piety. The iconography of traditional religion in late medieval Wales*. Oxford: British Archaeological Reports/Archaeopress (BS) no. 316.

Green, A.R.W. 1975. *The Role of Human Sacrifice in the Ancient Near East*. Missoula, Montana: Scholars Press.

Green, Miranda 1976. *A Corpus of Religious Material from the Civilian Areas of Roman Britain*. Oxford: British Archaeological Reports No. 24.

Green, Miranda 1978. *A Corpus of Small Cult-Objects from the Military Areas of Roman Britain*. Oxford: British Archaeological Reports (BS) No. 52.

Green, Miranda 1982. 'Tanarus, Taranis and the Chester altar', *Journal of the Chester Archaeological Society* 65, 37-44.

Green, Miranda 1986. *The Gods of the Celts*. Gloucester: Alan Sutton.

Green, Miranda 1991. *The Sun Gods of Ancient Europe*. London: Batsford.

Green, Miranda 1992a. *Animals in Celtic Life and Myth*. London: Routledge.

Green, Miranda 1992b. *Dictionary of Celtic Myth and Legend*. London: Thames & Hudson.

Green, Miranda 1993. 'The Sun Gods of Ancient Europe', in Madanjeet Singh ed. *The Sun in Myth and Art*. London: Thames & Hudson/UNESCO, 295-310.

Green, Miranda 1995. *Celtic Goddesses. Warriors, Virgins & Mothers*. London: British Museum Press.

Green, Miranda 1996. 'Concepts of sacrifice in later prehistoric Britain', in Karlene Jones-Bley & Martin Huld eds. *The Indo-Europeanization of Northern Europe*. Washington DC: Journal of Indo-European Studies Monograph No. 17, 191-203.

Green, Miranda 1997. *Exploring the World of the Druids*. London: Thames & Hudson.

Green, Miranda 1998a. 'Humans as Ritual Victims in the later prehistory of western Europe', *Oxford Journal of Archaeology* 17 (2), 169-89.

Green, Miranda 1998b. 'Vessels of Death: Sacred Cauldrons in Archaeology and Myth', *Antiquaries Journal* 78, 63-84.

Green, Miranda Aldhouse 1999. *Pilgrims in Stone. Stone images from the Gallo-Roman healing sanctuary of Fontes Sequanae*. Oxford: British Archaeological Reports (International Series) 754.

Green, Miranda Aldhouse 2000a. *Seeing the wood for the trees. The symbolism of trees and wood in ancient Gaul and Britain*. Aberystwyth: Centre for Advanced Welsh and Celtic Studies, University of Wales, Aberystwyth Research Paper No. 17.

Green, Miranda Aldhouse 2000b. 'Symbolism, Metaphor and Cosmology: Aspects of Ritual and Religion in Iron Age "Celtic" Europe'. Lecture delivered at the *Curso de Arqueologia: Numancia y el Mundo Celtibérico*. Soria: Fundación de Soria, 26.7.00.

Green, Miranda 2001a. 'Cosmovision and Metaphor: Monsters and Shamans in Gallo-British Cult-Expression', *European Journal of Archaeology* 4 (2), in press.

Green, Miranda 2001b. 'Welsh and Irish Cauldrons in Later Prehistoric Material Culture and Medieval Myth', in Jonathan Wooding ed., *Cymru ac Iwerddon: Ireland and Wales in the Middle Ages. Proceedings of an Inaugural Conference of the Centre for the Study of Religion in Celtic Societies*, 4-6 July, 2000, forthcoming.

Guichard, Vincent & Perrin, Franck eds. 2000. *Les Druides*. Paris: Errance/L'Archéologue Hors Série No. 2.

Haldimann, M.A. & Moinat, P. 1999. 'Des hommes et des sacrifices: aux origines celtiques de Genève', *Archéologie Suisse* 22 (4), 170-81.

Hamilton, Malcolm B. 1995. *The Sociology of Religion*. London: Routledge.

Hartley, B.R. 1957. 'The Wandlebury Iron Age Hill-Fort, Excavations of 1955-6', *Proceedings of the Cambridge Antiquarian Society* 50, 1-27.

Haselgrove, Colin & Millett, Martin 1997. 'Verlamion reconstructed', in Adam Gwilt & Colin Haselgrove eds., *Reconstructing Iron Age Societies*. Oxford: Oxbow Monograph No. 71, 282-96.

Hassall, M.W.C. & Tomlin, R.S.O. 1994. 'Roman Britain in 1993. II. Inscriptions', *Britannia* 25, 293-5.

Hénault, M. 1930. 'Le Puits 717', *Pro Nerva. Etude d'Archéologie Nervienne* VI, 5-9.

Heseltine, M. 1969. (trans.) *Translation of Petronius 368-87*. Cambridge Massachusetts: Harvard University (Loeb Edition).

Hill, Erica 2000. 'The embodied sacrifice', *Cambridge Archaeological Journal* 10:2, 317-26.

Hill, J.D. 1995a. *Ritual and Rubbish in the Iron Age of Wessex*. Oxford: British Archaeological Reports (BS), No. 242.

Hill, J.D. 1995b. 'How should we understand Iron Age societies and hillforts? A contextual study from southern Britain', in J.D. Hill & C.G. Cumberpatch eds., *Different Iron Ages. Studies on the Iron Age in Temperate Europe*. Oxford: British Archaeological Reports (IS), No. 602, 45-66.

Hogg, Gary 1966. *Cannibalism and Human Sacrifice*. New York: Citadel Press.

Holden, T.G. 1995. 'The Last Meals of the Lindow Bog Men', in Turner & Scaife eds., 76-82.

Hole, Christina 1950. *English Custom and Usage*. London: Batsford.

Holst-Warhaft, Gail 1992. *Dangerous Voices. Women's Laments and Greek Literature*. London: Routledge.

Hooper, Bari 1984. 'Anatomical Considerations', in Cunliffe 1984, 463-74.

Hope, Valerie & Marshall, Eireann eds. 2000. *Death and Disease in the Ancient City*. London: Routledge.

Hughes, Dennis 1991. *Human Sacrifice in Ancient Greece*. London: Routledge.

Hughes, Ted 1999. *Alcestis: Euripides in a new version*. London: Faber & Faber.

Hvass, Lone 1998. *Dronning Gunhild — et moselig fra jernalderen*. Vejle: Sesam.

Isserlin, R.M.J. 1997. 'Thinking the Unthinkable: Human Sacrifice in Roman Britain', *Proceedings of the Sixth Annual Theoretical Roman Archaeology Conference*. Oxford: Oxbow, 91-100.

Jackson, Ralph & Ambrose, Timothy 1976. 'A Roman Timber Bridge at Aldwincle, Northants.', *Britannia* 7, 31-72.

James, Simon & Rigby, Valerie 1997. *Britain and the Celtic Iron Age*. London: British Museum Press.

Jaussen, A. 1908. *Coutumes des Arabes au pays de Moab*. Paris.

Jenson, Philip P. 1995. 'The Levitical Sacrificial System', in Beckwith & Selman eds., 25-40.

Jones, D.R. 1991. 'Sacrifice and Holiness', in S.W. Sykes ed., *Sacrifice and Redemption: Durham Essays in Theology*. Cambridge: Cambridge University Press, 9-21.

Jones, G. 1968. *A History of the Vikings*. Oxford: Oxford University Press.

Jones, G. & Jones, T. 1976. *The Mabinogion*. London: Dent.

Jones, H.L. 1923 (trans.). *The Geography of Strabo*. London: Heinemann (Loeb Edition).

Jones, R. 2000. 'Gun-gugaliya rrawai: place, ochre and death — a perspective from Aboriginal Australia', in Aldhouse-Green, S. ed., 247-64.

Jones, W.H.S. 1963 (trans.). *Pliny Natural History* (Loeb Edition. Cambridge Mass.: Harvard University Press.

Jones, W.H.S. 1965 (trans.). *Pausanias. Description of Greece*. London: Heinemann (Loeb Edition).

Kamdar, Seema 1993. 'Shuffling off this mortal coil', *Times of India*, 30.10.93.

Kaul, Flemming 1991. *Gundestrupkedlen*. København: Nationamuseet Nyt Nordisk Forlag Arnold Busck.

Keys, David 1992. pers. comm. (from the Archaeological Correspondent for *The Independent* 9.10.92).

King, Helen 1995. 'Half-Human Creatures', in John Cherry ed., *Mythical Beasts*. London: British Museum Press, 138-67.

Kinsella, Thomas 1969. *The Táin*. Oxford: Oxford University Press.

Klostermeier, Klaus 1998. *A Short Introduction to Hinduism*. Oxford: One World Publications.

Küchler, Susanne 1997. 'Sacrificial Economy and its Objects. Rethinking Colonial Collecting in Oceania', *Journal of Material Culture* 2 (1), 39-60.

Lambot, Bernard 1998. 'Les Morts d'Acy Romance (Ardennes) à La Tène Finale. Pratiques funéraires, aspects religieuses et hiérarchie sociale', *Etudes et Documents Fouillés* 4. *Les Celtes. Rites Funéraires en Gaule du Nord entre le VIe et le Ier siècle avant Jesus-Christ*. Namur: Ministère de la Région Walionne, 75-87.

Lambot, Bernard 2000. 'Victimes, Sacrificateurs et Dieux', in Guichard & Perrin eds., 30-6.

Lambrechts, Pierre 1954. *L'exaltation de la tête dans la pensée et dans l'art des Celtes*. Brugge: Dissertationes Archaeologicae Gandenses 2.

Lange, Carmen 1997. 'Violence and the Face', in Carman ed., 167-73.

Langhorne, J. & W. 1884. *Plutarch's Lives*. London: George Routledge.

Lehmann, R.P.M. 1989. 'Death and Vengeance in the Ulster Cycle', *Zeitschrift für Celtische Philologie* 43, 1-10.

Lejars, Thierry 1994. *Gournay III. Les Fourreaux d'épée: Le Sanctuaire de Gournay-sur-Aronde et l'armament des Celtes de la Tène moyenne*. Paris: Errance.

Lejars, Thierry & Perrin, Franck 2000. 'Des Tombes de Druides', in Guichard & Perrin eds., 37-40.

Lethbridge, T.C. 1936. 'Further Excavations in the Early Iron Age and Romano-British Cemetery at Guilden Morden', *Cambridge Antiquarian Communications* 36, 109-20.

Lewis, I.M. 1996. *Religion in Context. Cults and Charisma*. Cambridge: Cambridge University Press.

Lewis, M.J.T. 1966. *Temples in Roman Britain*. Cambridge: Cambridge University Press.

Lewis, Mostyn 1970. *Stained Glass in North Wales up to 1850*. Altrincham: John Sheratt & Son.

Liebeschütz, J.H.W.G. 1979. *Continuity and Change in Roman Religion*. Oxford: Clarendon Press.

Longton, P.A. 1957. 'The Human Remains', in Hartley 1957, 27.

Lorrio, Alberto 1997. *Los Celtibéricos*. Madrid/Alicante: Universidad Complutense/Universidad de Alicante.

Luff, Rosemary 1996. 'The "bare bones" of identifying ritual behaviour in the archaeological record', in Sue Anderson & Katherine Boyle eds. *Ritual Treatment of Human and Animal Remains. Proceedings of the First Meeting of the Osteoarchaeological Research Group*. Oxford: Oxbow, 1-10.

Lynch, Frances 1991. *Prehistoric Anglesey*. Llangefni: Anglesey Antiquarian Society.

Lynn, Chris 1992. 'The Iron Age Mound in Navan Fort: A Physical Realization of Celtic Religious Beliefs?', *Emania* 10, 33-57.

Macdonald, J.L. 1979. 'Religion', in G. Clarke, *The Roman Cemetery at Lankhills*. Oxford: Winchester Studies 3. Pre-Roman and Roman Winchester, 403-33.

Macdonald, Philip 1996. 'Llyn Cerrig Bach. An Iron Age Votive Assemblage', in Stephen Aldhouse-Green ed. *Art, Ritual and Death in Prehistory*. Cardiff: National Museum of Wales, 32-3.

Maier, F. 1990. 'Le petit arbre cultuel de Manching', in Brunaux ed., 240-9.

Maloney, C. with Moulins, D. 1990. 'The Upper Walbrook Valley', *The Archaeology of Roman London 1*. London: Council for British Archaeology Research Report No. 69.

Marcus, Joyce & Flannery, Kent V. 1994. 'Ancient Zapotec Ritual and Religion : an application of the direct historical approach', in Colin Renfrew & Ezra B.W. Zubrow eds. *The Ancient Mind. Elements of Cognitive Archaeology*. Cambridge: Cambridge University Press (New Directions in Archaeology Series), 55-74.

Maringer, J. 1942-3. 'Menschnopfer im Bestattungsbrauch Alteuropas. Eine Untersuchung über die Doppel- und Mehrbestattungen im vor- und frühgeschichtlichen Europa, besonders Mitteleuropa', *Anthropos* 37-8, 1-112.

Marsh, G. & West, B. 1981. 'Skullduggery in Roman London', *Transactions of the London and Middlesex Archaeological Society* 23, 86-102.

Martínez, Alfredo Jimeno 1999. 'Religión y Ritual Funerario Celtibéricos', *Revista de Soria* No. 25, 5-18.

Matthews, C.L. 1981. 'A Romano-British Inhumation Cemetery at Dunstable', *Bedfordshire Archaeology Journal* 15, *passim*.

Matthews, Keith 1999. 'Death into Life: population statistics from cemetery data', in Alan Leslie ed. *Theoretical Archaeology and Architecture*. Glasgow: Cruithne Press, 141-61.

Mattingly, H. 1948 (trans.). *Tacitus on Britain and Germany*. Harmondsworth: Penguin.

Mays, Simon 1993. 'Infanticide in Roman Britain', *Antiquity* 67, 883-8.

Mays, Simon & Steele, James 1996. 'A mutilated human skull from Roman Saint Albans, Herts, England', *Antiquity* 70, 155-61.

Megaw, J. Vincent 1970. *Art of the European Iron Age*. Bath: Adams & Dart.

Megaw, J.V.S. & Simpson, D.D.A. 1979. *Introduction to British Prehistory*. Leicester: Leicester University Press.

Meniel, Patrice 1987. *Chasse et élevage chez les Gaulois*. Paris: Errance.

Meniel, Patrice 1989. 'Les animaux dans les pratiques religieuses des Gaulois', in J.-D. Vigne ed., *L'animal dans les pratiques religieuses: les manifestations materielles*. Paris: Anthropozoologica Troisième Numéro Special, 87-97.

Meniel, Patrice 1992. *Les Sacrifices d'Animaux chez les Gaulois*. Paris: Errance.

Merrifield, Ralph 1987. *The Archaeology of Ritual and Magic*. London: Batsford.

Miles, Henrietta 1970. 'The Cosgrove Roman Villa', *Wolverton Historical Journal*, 9.

Millar, Fergus 1964. *A Study of Cassius Dio*. Oxford: Clarendon Press.

Molleson, Theya 1999. 'Archaeological Evidence for Attitudes to Disability in the Past', in Finlay ed., 69-77.

Murray, A.T. 1963 (trans.). *Homer. The Iliad*. London: Heinemann (Loeb Edition).

Mytum, Harold 1999. 'Castell Henllys', *Current Archaeology* 161, February 1999, 164-72.

Nayling, Nigel & Caseldine, Astrid 1997. *Excavations at Caldicot, Gwent. Bronze Age Palaeochannels in the Lower Nedern Valley*. York: CBA Research Report No. 108.

Niblett, Rosalind 1992. 'A Catuvellaunian Chieftain's burial', *Antiquity* 66, 917-29.

Niblett, Rosalind 1999. *The Excavation of a Ceremonial site at Folly Lane, Verulamium*. London: Britannia Monograph Series No. 14/Society for the Promotion of Roman Studies.

Ó Catháin, Séamus 1992. 'Hearth-Prayers and the Traditions of Brigit', *Journal of the Royal Society of Antiquaries of Ireland* 122, 12-34.

O'Connor, D. 1993. *Ancient Nubia. Egypt's Rival in Africa*. Philadelphia: University Museum of Archaeology & Anthropology, University of Pennsylvania.

Ó Duilearga, Séamus ed. 1981. *Seanchas Stiofáin Ó Ealaoire*. Baile Átha Claith: Comhairle Bhéaloideas Éireann.

Ó Flóinn, R. 1995. 'Recent Research into Irish Bog Bodies', in Turner & Scaife eds., 137-45.

Oldfather, C.H. 1939 (trans.). *Diodorus of Sicily*. London: Heinemann (Loeb Edition).

Olmsted, Garrett S. 1979. *The Gundestrup Cauldron*. Brussels: Latomus.

Page, R.I. 1990. *Norse Myths*. London: British Museum Press.

Parfitt, Keith 1995. *Iron Age Burials at Mill Hill, Deal*. London: British Museum Press.

Parker Pearson, Michael 1999. *The Archaeology of Death and Burial*. Stroud: Sutton.

Parker Pearson, Michael 2000. 'Great Sites: Llyn Cerrig Bach', *British Archaeology* no. 53, 8-11.

Penn, W.S. 1960. 'Springhead: Temples III & IV', *Archaeologia Cantiana* 74, 113ff.

Perrin, Bernadotte 1971a trans. *Plutarch's Lives: Agesilaus & Pompey, Pelopidas & Marcellus*. London: William Heinemann.

Perrin, Bernadotte 1971b trans. *Plutarch's Lives: Demosthenes and Cicero, Alexander and Caesar*. London: Heinemann (Loeb Edition).

Perrin, Franck 2000. 'Le Gui', in Guichard & Perrin eds., 21-2.

Pertlwieser, M. 1998. 'Opfer für den Donnergott', *Oöstereicher Museumsjournal* 1, 3-4.

Philpott, R. 1991. *Burial Practices in Roman Britain: a survey of grave treatment and furnishing AD 43-410*. Oxford: British Archaeological Reports (British Series), No. 219.

Poe, Edgar Allan 1844. *The Premature Burial*. Short story, published in *Sixty-Seven Tales*. London: Leopard, 432-41.

Poulteney, James Wilson 1959. *The Bronze Tables of Iguvium*. Baltimore: American Philological Association.

Pryor, Francis 1991. *Flag Fen, Prehistoric Fenland Centre*. London: Batsford.

Radice, B. 1963 (trans.). *The Letters of the Younger Pliny*. Harmondsworth: Penguin.

Raftery, Barry 1981. 'Iron Age Burials in Ireland', in D. Ó' Corráin ed., *Irish Antiquity. Essays and Studies presented to Professor J. Ó'Kelly*. Cork: Tower Books, 173-204.

Raftery, Barry 1994. *Pagan Celtic Ireland. The Enigma of the Irish Iron Age*. London: Thames & Hudson.

Randsborg, K. 1995. *Hjortspring: Warfare and Sacrifice in Early Europe*. Åarhus: Åarhus University Press.

Rapin, André 1988. 'Boucliers et Lances', in Jean-Louis Brunaux & André Rapin, *Gournay II. Boucliers et Lances, Depôt et Trophées*. Paris: Revue Archéologique de Picardie/Errance, 7-142.

Rhoades, James 1957 (trans.). *The Poems of Virgil*. London: Oxford University Press.

Rives, J. 1995. 'Human Sacrifice among Pagans and Christians', *Journal of Roman Studies* 85, 65-85.

Rives, J.B. 1999 (trans.). *Tacitus. Germania*. Oxford: Clarendon Press.

Robertson-Mackay, Reay 1987. 'The Neolithic Causewayed Enclosure at Staines, Surrey: Excavations 1961-63', *Proceedings of the Prehistoric Society* 53, 23-127.

Rogerson, J.W. 1980. 'Sacrifice in the Old Testament: Problems of Method and Approach', in Bourdillon & Fortes eds., 45-59.

Roper, Simon 2001. *The development of the use of the human form from the Iron Age period through to the Roman period until the third century AD in Britain and Gaul*. Newport: University of Wales M.Phil. dissertation.

Ross, Anne 1968. 'Shafts, Pits, Wells — Sanctuaries of the Belgic Britons?', in John Coles & Derek Simpson eds. *Studies in Ancient Europe*. Leicester: Leicester University Press, 255-85.

Sakellarakis, Yannis & Sapouna-Sakellaraki, Efi 1997. *Archanes. Minoan Crete in a New Light. Vol. I* Athens: Ammos Publications.

Savory, Hubert N. 1976. *Guide Catalogue of the Early Iron Age Collections*. Cardiff: National Museum of Wales.

Scholfield, A.F. 1959 (trans.). *Aelian. On the Characteristics of Animals*. London: Heinemann (Loeb Edition).

Scott, Eleanor 1991. 'Animal and Infant Burials in Romano-British Villas: A Revitalization Movement', in Paul Garwood, David Jennings, Robin Skeates & Judith Toms eds. *Sacred and Profane. Proceedings of a Conference on Archaeology, Ritual and Religion*. Oxford: Oxford University Committee for Archaeology Monograph No. 21, 115-21.

Scott-Kilvert, Ian 1960 (trans.). *Plutarch. The Rise and Fall of Athens: Nine Greek Lives*. Harmondsworth: Penguin.

Scott-Kilvert, Ian 1965 (trans.). *Plutarch. Makers of Rome*. Harmondsworth: Penguin.

Selman, Martin T. 1995. 'Sacrifice in the Ancient Near East', in Beckwith & Selman eds., 88-104.

Sharples, Niall 1991. *Maiden Castle. Excavations and Field Survey 1885-6*. London: English Heritage Archaeological Report No. 19.

Shinnie, Peter 1967. *Meroe. A Civilization of the Sudan*. London: Thames & Hudson.

Sillar, W. 1992. 'The social life of the Andean dead', *Archaeological Review from Cambridge* 11, 107-23.

Simón, Francisco Marco 1999. 'Sacrificos humanos en la Céltica antigua: entre el estereotypico literario y la evidencia interna', *Archiv für Religionsgeschichte* 1 Band, Heft 1. Stuttgart und Leipzig, 1-17.

Smith, Alexander 2000. *The differential use of constructed sacred space in southern Britain from the late Iron Age to the fourth century AD*. Newport: University of Wales (unpublished PhD thesis).

Smyth, Herbert Weir 1963 (trans.). *Aeschylus*. London: Heinemann (Loeb Edition).

Sopeña Genzor, Gabriel 2000. 'Apuntes sobre ritos funerales en Celtiberia', in Zapatero, Gonzalo Ruiz & Martínez, Alfredo Jimeno eds., *Numancia y el Mundo Celtibérico 'Paisaje Social y Simbólico en la Europa Céltica'*. Soria: Fundación Duques de Soria. Curso de Arqueologia, July 2000.

Staal, Frits 1983. *Agni: The Vedic Ritual of the Fire Altar*. Berkeley: University of California Press.

Stampholidis, Nicolas Chr. 1996. *Reprisals. Contribution to the study of customs of the Geometric-Archaic period. Eleutherna, Sector III, 3*. Rethymnon: University of Crete.

Stead, Ian 1988. 'Chalk figurines of the Parisi', *Antiquaries Journal* 68, 9-21.

Stead, Ian 1991. *Iron Age Burials from East Yorkshire*. London: English Heritage.

Stead, Ian *et al.* 1986. *Lindow Man. The Body in the Bog*. London: British Museum Publications.

Stead, Ian & Rigby, Valerie 1989. *Verulamium: The King Harry Lane Site*. London: English Heritage Archaeological Report No. 12.

Taylor, Tim 1992. 'The Eastern Origins of the Gundestrup Cauldron', *Scientific American* No. 266 (3), March 1992, 66-71.

Taylor, Tim 2001a. 'Ambushed by a Grotesque (or how and why we downplay the extent and nature of ancient slavery)', in *Warfare, Violence and Slavery in Prehistory and Protohistory*. Conference, University of Sheffield, 2-3.2.01.

Taylor, Tim 2001b. 'Believing the ancients: quantitative and qualitative dimensions of slavery and the slave trade in later prehistoric Eurasia', *World Archaeology* 33:1, in press.

Taylor, Tim 2001c. 'The edible dead', *British Archaeology* 59, 8-12.

Thomas, Julian 1996. *Time, Culture and Identity: an interpretative archaeology*. London: Routledge.

Thurston, E. 1907. *Ethnographic Notes in Southern India*. Madras: Superintendent, Government Press.

Tierney, J.J. 1959-60. 'The Celtic Ethnography of Posidonius', *Proceedings of the Royal Irish Academy* 60, 189-275.

Tierney, P. 1989. *The Highest Altars: the Story of Human Sacrifice*. New York: Viking.

Tilley, Christopher 1999. *Metaphor and Material Culture*. Oxford: Blackwell.

Trevarthen, David 2000. 'Illuminating the Monuments: Observation & Speculation on the Structure and Function of the Cairns at Balnuaran of Clava', *Cambridge Archaeological Journal* 10:2, 295-315.

Turner II, Christy G. & Turner, Jacqueline A. 1999. *Man Corn. Cannibalism and Violence in the Prehistoric American Southwest*. Salt Lake City: The University of Utah Press.

Turner, R.C. 1995. 'The Lindow Bog Bodies: Discoveries and Excavations at Lindow Moss 1983-8', in Turner & Scaife eds., 10-18.

Turner, R.C. 1996. 'Lindow Man — The Body in the Bog', in Stephen Aldhouse-Green ed., *Art, Ritual and Death in Prehistory*. Cardiff: National Museum of Wales, 34-5.

Turner, R.C. 1999. 'Dating the Lindow Moss and other British bog bodies', in Coles, Coles & Jørgensen eds., 227-33.

Turner, R.C. & Scaife, R.G. eds. 1995. *Bog Bodies. New Discoveries and New Perspectives*. London: British Museum Press.

Van der Sanden, W.A.B. 1995. 'Bog-Bodies on the Continent: Developments since 1965, with Special Reference to the Netherlands', in Turner & Scaife eds., 146-65.

Van der Sanden, Wijnand 1996. *Through Nature to Eternity. The bog bodies of northwest Europe*. Amsterdam: Batavian Lion International.

Van Driel, Carol 1999. 'And did those Feet in Ancient Time . . . Feet and shoes as a material projection of the self', *TRAC 98. Proceedings of the Eighth Annual Theoretical Archaeology Conference*. Oxford: Oxbow, 131-40.

Van Straten, F.T. 1995. *Hierà Kalá. Images of Animal Sacrifice in Archaic and Classical Greece*. Leiden: E.J. Brill.

Vellacott, Philip 1961 (trans.). *Aeschylus. Prometheus Bound, The Suppliants, Seven against Thebes, The Persians*. Harmondsworth: Penguin.

Vellacott, Philip 1974 (trans.). *Euripides. Alcestis/Hippolytus/Iphigeneia in Tauris*. Harmondsworth: Penguin.

Vernant, J.-P. 1989. 'At Man's Table: Hesiod's Foundation Myth of Sacrifice', in Detienne & Vernant, 21-86.

Vitebsky, Piers 1995. *The Shaman*. London: Macmillan.

Viziak, E.H. ed. 1969. *Milton. Complete Poetry and Selected Prose*. Glasgow: Nonesuch Library, Glasgow University Press.

Walker, Lucy 1984. 'The deposition of the human remains', in Cunliffe 1984, 442-63.

Way, Arthur S. 1959 (trans.). *Euripides Vol. I*. London: Heinemann (Loeb Edition).

Wenham, Gordon J. 1995. 'The Theology of Old Testament Sacrifice', in Beckwith & Selman eds., 75-87.

West, B. 1996. 'Ritual or Fluvial? A further comment on the Thames skulls', *Antiquity* 70, 190-1.

Wheeler, R.E.M. & T.V. 1932. *Report on the excavation of the Prehistoric, Roman and post-Roman Site in Lydney Park, Gloucestershire*. Oxford: Society of Antiquaries of London.

White, Roger & Barker, Philip 1998. *Wroxeter. Life and Death of a Roman City*. Stroud: Tempus.

Whitehead, H. 1921. *The Village Gods of South India*. New Delhi: Cosmo (1983 reprint of original edition).

Wiedemann, T. 1992. *Greek and Roman Slavery*. London: Routledge (3rd reprint).

Wightman, Edith M. 1970. *Roman Trier and the Treveri*. London: Hart-Davis.

Wightman, Edith M. 1985. *Gallia Belgica*. London: Batsford.

Willis, Roy ed. 1991. *Signifying Animals*. London: Routledge.

Wiseman, Anne & Wiseman, Peter 1980 (trans.). *Julius Caesar. The Battle for Gaul*. London: Chatto & Windus.

Wood, Juliette 1992. 'Celtic Goddesses: myth and mythology', in C. Larrington eds., *The Feminist Companion to Mythology*. London: Pandora Press/Harper-Collins, 118-36.

Yerkes, Royden K. 1953. *Sacrifice in Greek and Roman Religions and Early Judaism*. London: Adam & Charles Black.

Zwicker, Johannes 1934. *Fontes Historiae Religionis Celticae*. Berlin: Walter de Gruyter.

Abbreviations:

C.I.L.   *Corpus Inscriptionum Latinarum* 1863-1986 (Berlin).

R.I.B.   *The Roman Inscriptions of Britain. Vol. I. Inscriptions on Stone*. R.G. Collingwood & R.P. Wright, 1965 (Oxford University Press).

Index

Sallust 57

Saluvii 97

Samnitae 85

San José Mogote 90, 196

Saône, river 104

Saturn 75-6, 153-4, 174, 192

Saturnalia 176

scalping 106-9 (*see also* defleshing, heads, skulls)

scapegoat 30, 42, 48-9, 66, 116, 127, 144-5, 168-9, 193

Scythia(ns) 95, 163-4, 171-2

seasons 20, 67, 69, 85, 176

seer (*see* prophecy, shaman)

selago 115

selection *passim*, but especially 139-60

self-sacrifice (*see* auto-sacrifice)

semen 81

Semnones 143, 176

Senones 96

sexuality 81, 156

Sigersdal Mose 125

Shakespeare 29, 57

shaman 41, 73, 101, 120, 189, 194, 196-7

sheep 22, 26, 42-3, 49, 74-7, 116, 131, 151, 154, 165, 184

Sheol 74

Shiva 61

Silchester 189

Silius Italicus 46

Silures 166

skinning (*see* defleshing, scalping)

skulls 44-5, 47, 51-2, 55-6, 59-60, 87, 95-110, 120-1, 131, 146, 151, 155-7, 173, 184, 195-6 (*see also* head)

sky 47, 66-7, 172-4

slaves 26-30, 35, 90, 121, 132, 139-40, 143-5, 147-9, 163-4, 192, 196

smithing 66, 87, 160, 185, 201

snake, ram-horned 114

Soissons 42, 165

Sophocles 194

Soranos 159

South Cadbury 135, 146, 166

Sparta 81

sphageion 81

spoons 185-6

springs 29, 117

Springhead 34, 155, 166

Stanway 185

Stanwick 104

Star Villa 167

status 65, 85, 124, 126, 129, 132, 134, 139-46, 148-9, 163-5, 186, 203

Strabo 13, 27, 31, 45, 58, 68, 83-6, 88, 95-7, 115, 143, 169, 172, 181, 187, 191, 193-4

strangulation (*see* garrotting)

Stratford, London 45-6

Styx, river 29

substitution 26, 28-30, 39, 47-9, 66, 68, 74, 121, 139-40, 143-4, 152-3, 156, 160, 163, 169, 191-2

Suebi 116, 176

Suetonius 190

Suetonius Paulinus 84, 190

suffocation 113-35

suicide 164-5

Sulis Minerva 181

sun 20, 41, 65-7, 69, 73, 126, 130-1, 174, 176

surrogacy (*see* substitution)

suttee 163, 165

Sutton Walls

Sybil/Sybilline Books 32-3, 128, 173

Syracuse 49, 76, 153, 169

Tacitus 13, 19, 84-5, 113, 115-17, 120, 143-4, 176, 185, 190-3

Táin Bó Cuailnge 110

Tamora 29

Tanit 153

Tara 135

Taranis 68-70, 171-2, 174

Taranucnus 70

Tarasque of Noves 100, 102

Tartigny 185-6, 188

Tatian 174

Taurians 193

Teiresias 160, 194

Telagu 49

Tell Halâf 75

Ten Commandments 115

Tenedos 48-9

Tertullian 76, 89, 153, 174, 192

Teucer 174

Teutates 85, 113, 171

Thames, river 14, 59, 105

Tharros 75

Themistocles 140-2

Thracians 114

threshold (*see* liminality)

thunder 91, 172, 174 (*see also* Taranis)

thusia 67

Tiber, river 28

Tiberius 58